The Malt Whisky File

John Lamond
and
Robin Tucek

CANONGATE

This book is dedicated to
the memory of
Gordon Brown

The Malt Whisky File

The connoisseur's guide to single malt
whiskies and their distilleries

Tasting notes by
John Lamond

Background and history by
Robin Tucek

Published by Canongate Books Limited
14 High Street
Edinburgh
EH1 1TE
Scotland
Reprinted 1996 and 1997

British Library Cataloguing-in-Publication Data.
A catalogue record for this book is available from the British Library.
ISBN 086241 525X

Printed in Spain by Litografía Danona S. Coop., 20180 Oiartzun

CONTENTS

INTRODUCTION

I was weaned on Scotch Whisky. Of course, that was in 1953, when alcohol was not forbidden to pregnant mothers. Neither was it in 1957 when my sister was born on the 2nd January after my mother had enjoyed a very traditional Scottish Hogmanay. However, my sister, despite strenuous family efforts, does not enjoy whisky!

This, the first edition of *The Malt Whisky File*, is the result of many years work, tasting and researching malt whiskies. Most of the whiskies tasted are readily available through the whisky specialists, if not through the typical High Street off licence. We have also included some tasting notes which, for most people, are merely of academic interest – either because that particular bottling at that particular age/strength has been superseded by the distiller's/bottler's latest offering or because it is from an extremely limited bottling. Where possible both the modern and older bottlings have been included.

I have endeavoured in my tasting to be as objective as possible, but naturally any tasting note is going to contain an element of subjectivity. Each distiller produces whisky to the highest possible quality. The fact that a Speyside tastes very different to an Islay is a matter of geographical, not qualitative, fact.

I am frequently asked, "What is your favourite malt?", or "What is the best malt?" There is no single answer to either question. Taste is very much a personal sense and mine is not necessarily yours. In any case, I do not have any one favourite, I enjoy (almost) all whiskies, depending on the mood. As to which is best – the whisky which you enjoy is the best.

Scotch Whisky has within it a distillation of the colours, flavour and atmosphere of Scotland. Scotland's soft air, water, agriculture and traditional craftsmanship combine to produce the world's premier spirit. *The Malt Whisky File* is a homage to the craftsmen of the industry – be they blenders, mashmen or coopers, they are nature's magicians.

Slainte,

JOHN LAMOND
MASTER OF MALT

The *Classic Malts Collection* embraces a fascinating combination of scents and tastes. Consisting of *Cragganmore, Dalwhinnie, Oban, Talisker, Glenkinchie* and *Lagavulin*, the range allows the consumer to explore the full diversity of flavours and characters of six of Scotland's best-loved malt whiskies.

Scotland's regions of malt whisky production can be defined as follows: The Lowlands, The Highlands, The Western Highlands, Speyside, Islay, Campbeltown and the Islands. The proud distilleries scattered across this land, each in their own unique environment, give the malts their individual personalities and outstanding qualities. The Classic Malts collection offers six of the finest malts from these diverse and different regions.

Glenkinchie

The area around the *Glenkinchie* distillery typifies the Lowlands. The countryside is gentler than the highlands and this, combined with less rain, results in a lighter, drier tasting malt. *Glenkinchie* matures at 10 years due to the relatively warm climate, reaching its balance in a comparatively short time for Scottish malts. It is the mildest in the Collection with a smooth, grassy, sweet flavour and a light, rather dry taste.

Cragganmore

The distinguished single malt whisky produced at *Cragganmore* is an excellent example of the Speyside regional style. The valley of the River Spey has plentiful supplies of soft water which run over peat and give the firm-bodied, smoky character to *Cragganmore*. It has the most complex aroma of any malt - dry, with a firm, herbal palate. As a 12-year-old with a long smoky finish, it is the perfect after-dinner malt.

Dalwhinnie

Dalwhinnie, as Scotland's highest distillery, represents the Highlands region. This single malt is remarkably soft owing to the effects of drastic seasonal temperature changes and the snow-melt waters which are a key ingredient. The 15-year-old malt takes longer to mature than some of the other *Classic Malts* due to the high humidity, and is also influenced by the landscape resulting in its heathery finish and fruity aroma. *Dalwhinnie's* subtle balance of lightness and sweetness makes it an ideal alternative to liqueurs, yet with an altogether different style.

Oban

Owing to the geographical position of the harbour town of *Oban*, the malt whisky of the same name has all the pungency of the Islay malts balanced with the smoothness of Highland malts. It is a superior 14-year-old Highland malt with a delicate peat aroma and fruity, smoky undertones to intensify the palate. An excellent all-round whisky.

Talisker

From the small village of Carbost on the western side of the Isle of Skye comes the inimitable *Talisker*. One of the best-loved of all Scotland's island malts, this 10-year-old whisky has a full flavour that almost defies description owing to its unique seaweedy, peppery nuances and lingering peaty taste. It is robust and powerful with an above-average strength of 45.8%.

Lagavulin

The Isle of Islay has its own malt classification - seaweed, peat, smoke and earth are all elements of the assertive Islay character. *Lagavulin* is arguably the most pungent, an intensely dry 16-year-old malt with firm, robust body and powerful aroma. One to be sipped and savoured into the small hours.

Each of the elements in the *Classic Malts* are constantly affected by their surroundings during the long maturation periods. They breathe the scent in the air and are perfectly matured by either the chill of winter or warmth of summer. These great variations in character result in a range of malts for any occasion, giving a wealth of experimentation and discovery. If ever there was a selection of malt whiskies designed to suit all moods, it is the *Classic Malts*, six highly distinctive whiskies that offer variety and choice every time you pour a dram.

Loyal *Classic Malts* consumers can now learn more about their favourite malt whiskies through the exclusive new *Friends of the Classic Malts of Scotland Society*, formed in 1995. The aim of the society is to provide the increasing number of *Classic Malts* devotees with the opportunity to share information and explore the six-strong range in greater depth. After joining, members will automatically receive a dedicated four-page colour journal, *The Spirit of the Classics*, packed with lively and informative articles by true malt enthusiasts. To join the *Friends of the Classic Malts of Scotland Society*, simply turn to the back of the book and fill in the coupon.

THE ART OF NOSING

It seems somewhat perverse that those who most appreciate the finest spirit in the world spend a great deal of their time not drinking it. They do not even go so far as serious-minded wine connoisseurs who swill it round their mouths before ejecting it. No, the master blender will use nothing other than his nose – and his experience – to assess and evaluate malt whisky. He noses rather than sips to preserve his ability to "taste" after the first sample. The reasoning behind this is simple: unlike wine or other less alcoholic substances, a distilled spirit will anaesthetise the taste buds, the very taste mechanisms which need to be used time and time again.

Aromatics

Our sense of aromatics (or "volatiles" as they are sometimes called) is derived from an organ known as the olfactory epithelium, located at the back of the nasal passage, which is directly linked to the brain. This is helps to explain why we cannot taste so well when we have a cold.

Using the nose to detect aromatic ingredients provides a more immediate route to this area than via the back of the throat. The palate can only detect four taste elements: salt, sweet, sour and bitter. All other flavour characters are created when the palate warms the contents of your mouth and causes aromas to rise through your nasal passages to the olfactory epithelium. The palate should merely confirm the aromas detected by the nose, although there will be slight differences and the strength of individual flavours may vary.

Our sense of smell is one of the most under-used of the human senses, being relegated in most cases by sight and taste to a subordinate role and only called into use for rather crude analysis of whether something smells "good" or "bad". In fact, it is one of the most subtle of the senses, capable of detecting even faint changes in style or balance, and having a large "vocabulary" of its own. The tasting vocabulary used throughout this book has evolved over the years and, we hope, is easily comprehended by the reader.

The Master Blender

A master blender has an "educated" nose and can detect more than 150 separate flavours or characters in a whisky. Some of these will tell him that the product has been adversely affected in some way during maturation; others will indicate the type or style of wood in which it has matured. But although your senses are not as highly tuned as the blender's, each whisky has a sufficient number of different characteristics to enable you to distinguish one from another.

THE ART OF NOSING

The Nosing
In general, the nosing of malt whiskies is carried out in a small, tulip-shaped or similar glass which, being bulbous at the base and reducing to a relatively narrow rim, releases the aromatics and concentrates them at the rim, where the nose can pick up aromas. The sample is always diluted, or cut, with water; this releases the esters and aldehydes and thus makes the aroma more pronounced, the amount of water to be added depends on the alcoholic strength of the spirit which is being nosed. As a rough guide, malt whisky in the strength band 40% to 43% alcohol by volume (abv) should be cut with one third water, preferably a soft water - Scottish spring water - or clean tap water. Avoid waters with high mineral contents.

Higher Strength Whiskies
Other, higher strength whiskies should be cut with a greater quantity of water to reduce the sample to approximately the same strength. A high strength whisky of, for example 60% abv, should be diluted with twice its volume of water for sampling. There is a very good reason for this. The olfactory senses are adversely affected by the high alcohol level, even to the extent of feeling pain. Dilution removes the likelihood of this pain being inflicted. The quantity used for sampling should be fairly small, to allow plenty of room for the aromatics to collect in the glass. There is enough spirit for an adequate assessment in a 25ml measure of whisky diluted with water.

You will find that different elements in the sample become dominant at different periods of the nosing. You may become confused by concentrating too hard and, very often, your first opinion will be the correct one. As you become more expert, you will discover a greater range of aromas in the glass. For example, one person may detect a hint of rubber in a whisky, while that same characteristic may come over to another as something else - liquorice, for example. The difficulty with either tasting or nosing is in the descriptions used by individuals to describe sensation or flavour. Attempts have been made to categorise these flavours and John Lamond produced a *Malt Whisky Wheel* for *Aberlour*. This helped identify the principal flavour characteristics, and their taste relationships, using taste bands rather like spokes on a bicycle wheel.

While it is possible to create a common language to describe the aromas, the sense of smell is very subjective. Malt whisky is a gregarious spirit, so that the next time you are with friends discussing flavour, let your nose lead your opinions. You can still have as much fun trying to describe the aromas in your own words as you will get from finally drinking the whiskies. This is the fascination of single malts.

FILE NOTES

The notes in this book have been compiled in alphabetical order according to the names of brands of malt whisky, not by distillery or bottler. Where the whisky is from an independent bottling source, this has been noted in the tasting notes.

There are three types of Scotch whisky: **Malt** whisky, **Grain** whisky and **Blended** whisky. **Malt** whisky is produced only from 100% malted barley. **Grain** whisky is produced from a variety of cereals which may, or may not, include a proportion of malted barley. **Blended** whisky is a combination of **Malt** whisky and **Grain** whisky, mixed together in the same bottle.

Single Malts
Most of the whiskies covered in this book are **Single Malt** whiskies. These are the products of individual malt whisky distilleries. For example, *Aberlour, Edradour, Laphroaig* or *Macallan*. However, the actual distillery name does not have to be identified on the label for a whisky to be called a single malt. Single malt may come from different casks of various ages, but they must all be from the same distillery. Not all distillery owners bottle their single malts under the name of the distillery. For example, the single malt from Macduff distillery is bottled as *Glen Deveron* by its owners.

Vatted Malts
Vatted malts are whiskies from more than one malt distillery which have been blended together, according to the specifications of the blender, to produce a fine, consistent product with a personality of its own. This whisky may well be given an individual name, such as *Sheep Dip* or *Poit Dhubh*. A **vatted malt** may not contain any **grain whisky,** otherwise it is **blended whisky.** Some **vatted malts** have been included in a section at the end of this book, as have some **single malts** bottled under "brand names" of independent bottlers.

Pure Malt
All Scotch malt whiskies, whether single or vatted, are **pure malt.** They are produced only from malted barley. If a whisky contains just one millilitre of **grain** whisky, then it is a **blended** whisky.

Grain Whisky
Grain whisky is produced from a mash of various cereal grains usually, but not exclusively, made from wheat, maize and barley. Both **malted barley** (barley which has started to germinate and then been dried to arrest its germination) and **unmalted barley** (barley which remains dormant) are used in the production of **grain whisky.**

FILE NOTES

Scotch Whisky

All **Scotch** (and **Irish**) whisk(e)y is produced by first grinding the particular cereal grain(s) to a coarse flour and then steeping this in hot water in a **mash tun**. The resultant liquid, called **wort**, is then cooled to between 22° and 24°C and run into a **wash back**. Yeast is then added. Once the yeast has been fermented out, a strong ale called **pot ale** remains, which is about 9% alcohol by volume. This pot ale is then distilled by heating it in **copper stills**, either in a continuous still, called a **Coffey** still, for **Grain** whisky, or twice in the case of **Malt** whisky using a pair of **Pot** stills. Three stills are used for **Irish** whiskey and the Scottish malts Auchentoshan, Benrinnes and Rosebank, these all being **triple distilled.** Pot stills are usually onion-shaped, with tall, tapering swan necks designed to help the alcohols condense, after which they are collected, cooled and put into casks.

A whisky, however produced, may only be legally described as **Scotch** whisky if it has matured in oak cask in Scotland for a minimum of three years. It must also have been bottled at a minimum strength of 40% alcohol by volume. There is no legal requirement for Scotch whisky to be bottled in Scotland. The same legal restrictions also apply to **Irish** whiskey (note the addition of an "e") in Ireland.

Whisky casks are made of oak, from the genus Quercus. The species Q. cerris, (French oak), Q. falcata (Spanish oak), or Q. alba (American white oak), are used. Oak is a natural substance and therefore variations in density, quality and porosity are inherent. To further complicate and confuse the issue, the wood is split by hand and the casks are constructed by hand. Thus each cask is unique in that it is larger or smaller than its neighbours, its staves vary in thickness and no two pores are the same size. Its influence on the maturing spirit which it holds is therefore going to be different from that of any of its neighbours.

That is why the recipe for each blended whisky is different. A blender cannot state categorically that the blend for his "Hamish's Choice" Blended Whisky is, for example:

    23 casks of Glenardle, 10-year-old
    2 casks of Harport, 18-year-old
    15 casks of Royal Lochmaben, 7-year-old
    13 casks of Leith grain, 5-year-old etc.

because the proportions of each constituent whisky will vary with each blend. When you enjoy a bottle from a single cask bottling, you are drinking a very finite resource, you are consuming our heritage.

Continued on page 12

Scotland's malt distilleries

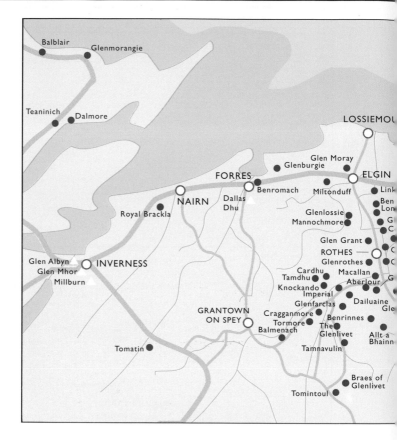

A **hogshead** will yield roughly 300 bottles (bottled at 40% abv strength) after 10 to 12 years, a **butt** 500, a **barrel** 200. The variations in the oak cask mean that the distiller cannot deliberately exactly repeat this magic of creation.

Generally the whisky drunk pre-1900 was young, only the landed gentry being able to afford to mature their spirit. The ageing cask could be new or previously have held wine, or rum, or butter, or herring, or anything which a cask could hold. Until the 1850s, whisky was sold by the distiller in cask and the publican or whisky merchant bottled it as required. From 1916, the government insisted whisky be aged in cask for a minimum of three years. The industry was then obliged to find supplies of casks in which to age their product. At this time, all Sherry imported into the United Kingdom was shipped in cask, to be bottled in the UK by the British merchants. Once emptied, the casks were surplus to the importers' requirements.

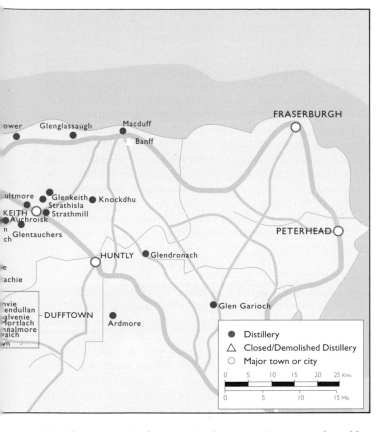

Ever keen to save a few pennies, the canny Scots were thus able to pick them up very cheaply. Likewise, because of the strength of the coopers' union in the USA at the time the laws governing Bourbon production were being created by Congress, it was written into American law that a Bourbon barrel could only be used once. When empty, they were worth only their value as firewood. Once again the thrifty Scots stepped in and established another economic source of cask. The situation has now changed in that, since 1983, the Spanish government has decreed that all Sherry must be bottled in Jerez and Sherry butts are now reusable by the Jerezanos. New Sherry casks are now a considerable cost to the whisky distiller.

With casks being used as many as four or five times over, the most usual type of cask used for filling Scotch and Irish whisky is what is known as a **Refill** cask. The casks are carefully checked by coopers between each fill to ensure that there will be no leakage of precious spirit. **First fill** Sherry casks are nowadays very rarely used to fill new grain whisky, second, third and fourth refill casks being the usual choice for such whiskies.

One element which has developed in importance in the past 20-25 years is the distiller's awareness of the origins of the cask. So much so that some now have them made to order by Spanish or French coopers and loan them to a Sherry bodega. *Glenmorangie*, preferring Bourbon casks has even gone to the length of buying an oak forest in the Ozark mountains in Missouri to ensure continuity of supply of a particular quality of oak. The cask has moved a very long way from being a vehicle for transporting whisky or a container of a handy size for sale, and companies are now experimenting with whiskies aged in oak casks that have previously held Port, Brandy and Rum. Sometimes whiskies are filled in one type of cask, e.g. Bourbon, and then "finished" for their last few months or so of maturation in another, e.g. Sherry.

The respect of age
Much is made of the age of a whisky, and great respect and often considerable prices are given to whiskies of more senior years. The age of a whisky, if given on a bottle, must be that of the youngest whisky contained in that particular bottling. If all of the whisky used except for one centilitre is 21 years old and that centilitre is 11 years old then the whisky may only carry an age statement that is not more than 11 years, although it could be described as being of a younger age e.g. 10 years. The date of distillation of a particular cask, as well as the date of bottling may be given on a label, but the age of the whisky itself, unless given in days, may only be given as not more than the number of complete years that the whisky has remained in cask. For example. if a whisky was distilled in May 1960 and bottled in April 1973, then the whisky is 12 years old, although it could be sold as an 11- or 10-year-old or less, or even not be given an age statement.

Whisky is usually about 70% alcohol by volume when distilled, slightly higher in the case of triple distilled whisky. The remainder of volume is water from steam condensed with the distillation. It is a clear, colourless spirit, with few subtleties of flavour, and the actual volume of alcohol will vary slightly from batch to batch. With the exception of a few selected casks, it is now industry practice to reduce all casks by the addition of water to a standard 11 degrees over proof, 63.4% by volume. While in cask, a whisky loses about 2% a year in evaporation. This is known as the **Angel's Share**. A whisky matures and changes in cask, the spirit leeching out tannins and other flavours from the oak cask, and absorbing notes from the air passing through the porous wood while it lies slumbering in the warehouse. Just as the type of cask can make quite a difference to the whisky, so can the location at which it lies. A cask of Islay malt, maturing in a warehouse next to the Atlantic Ocean, for example, will give a very different whisky to a similar cask maturing in warehouse at Broxburn or Leith. Most whisky is reduced further in volume in the bottling hall, being reduced to 40% by volume for the standard European strength and 43% by volume for the general Export strength. A few selected casks may be bottled at a higher strength. **Cask Strength** whisky is whisky that is bottled straight from cask without the further addition of any water.

The longer a whisky remains in cask, the more flavour it will acquire and the less spirit will remain. A 21-year-old whisky, for example, will therefore usually have more complex flavours than a 12-year-old whisky, although the degree of change is greatly dependent on the quality and type of cask used for filling. It will certainly be more expensive. Some whiskies are known to mature more quickly than others, Lowland whiskies generally being the quickest maturing, while others age particularly well, as is the case with many of the Speyside malts. However, although greater age means a more expensive whisky, it does not necessarily mean a better one. It is all a matter of personal taste. Some will not care much for a very woody, tannic 25-year-old malt, preferring a soft, honeyed 18-year-old and yet others may choose a sherried 12-year-old. As with most things in life, it is a matter of personal preference.

The following are some of the independent bottlers:

Gordon & MacPhail
Established as licensed grocers in Elgin, Moray, in 1895, Gordon & Macphail has just celebrated its centenary. Scotland's leading independent bottler, and largely responsible for the availability of so many bottled single malts, Gordon & Macphail were shipping single malt whiskies round the world when many of today's best-selling single malt whiskies were were unheard of away from the distillery.

William Cadenhead
Established in Aberdeen in 1842 and now based in Campbeltown, William Cadenhead are Scotland's oldest established firm of independent bottlers. The business is owned by J & A Mitchell of Springbank. The company has for several years now run a malt whisky shop at the bottom of Edinburgh's Royal Mile. In 1995, Cadenhead opened a second shop in Covent Garden, London.

FILE NOTES

Signatory
A relatively young company, The Signatory Vintage Malt Whisky Company, to give it its full name, was established in Leith in 1988.

The Adelphi Distillery Ltd
Established in 1993 by the great grandson of the former owner of the Adelphi Distillery, Glasgow, which closed in 1902.

The Scotch Malt Whisky Society
The Edinburgh based Society bottles cask strength whiskies for members. Each cask is bottled under a numerical code, so as not to identify the source distillery on the label.

The Vintage Malt Company
Another young company, based in Bearsden, Glasgow, they specialise in vatted and single malts under their own brand names.

The Master of Malt
Based in Tunbridge Wells, Kent, The Master of Malt offers a good selection of malt whiskies bottled under its own label.

Blackadder International
Based in Larkhall, Scotland, Blackadder International offers rare premium malts under the *Blackadder* and *Limited Editions* labels.

Judging and understanding the differences
Each of our tasting notes contains its own numerical rating system. This system, developed by John Lamond and Robin Tucek, is designed to give you an approximate idea of **Sweetness**, **Peatiness** and **Availability** for each whisky. It is intended as a helpful guide only and is not meant to be used as a qualitative or quantitative rating system for malt whiskies. In our opinion, malt whisky is too much of a personal preference to justify any attempt to give rating scores to individual whiskies. After all, one man's *Macallan* in another woman's *Laphroaig*. Some will choose *Bowmore* and others *The Balvenie*. We would not wish to position any malt before any other – all are to be respected and enjoyed for their relative qualities, all are made to similar quality levels and *all* are aged in oak casks. Only *you* can decide the whiskies which are your favourites.

The Malt Whisky File Tasting Codes
The scales run from 0 to 10, with 0 being the driest and least peated end of the scale, 10 the sweetest and most pungent. The ratings are a statement of fact; a guide to help you find those malt whiskies which are most akin to your own taste. If, for example, you like a malt with a **Sweetness** factor of 7 and a **Peatiness** factor of 4, then those other malts which have a similar rating should be of interest to your palate.

FILE NOTES

Most bottlings from the independents are of limited availability. We have given such bottlings a maximum **Availability** rating of **4**. If the vintage listed is finished, then they normally follow up with the next vintage which will usually, making allowances for individual cask influences, be very similar to its predecessor. The **Availability** factor **0** means that this whisky is no longer available, **1 to 3** mean that these whiskies are difficult to obtain; **4 to 6** are available from the more specialist shop, **7 to 10** are increasingly more widely available. The **Availability** rating is based on the UK market, including Duty Free.

Following the success of the independent companies in marketing single cask and cask strength whiskies, several of the major brand owners have now followed suit, making some very interesting whiskies available. These whiskies are often bottled with little or minimum filtration and it is increasingly frowned on to add caramel colouring to them. Such limited edition bottlings are an important and growing market but, because of the extra production costs involved, these whiskies are very much a specialist interest. Because each single cask of whisky can be such an individual product, they cannot possibly have the same consistency of style and taste as the more widely available malt whisky brands, each of which is bottled after blending together several carefully selected casks from the owner's warehouses of maturing whiskies.

The popularity of single malt whisky today owes much to the efforts of the specialist bottler in making such whiskies available when, with one or two notable exceptions, the brand owners showed little interest in producing malt whisky for anything other than blending. With the growth in interest and availability of single malt whisky, certain brand owners have let it be known that they do not like the independents bottling casks filled at their distilleries as single malts. This is a pity, as distilleries' own bottlings are always clearly identified for what they are, while the independents recognisably make their own name a clear endorsement of quality as part of their own label design. Some independent bottlings can be quite superb, with each cask bottled having its own differing and interesting personality. However, the better and rarer of these bottlings usually carry a price premium. With today's consumer increasingly wanting to know exactly what it is he is drinking, it is clearly neither realistic not fair to the consumer to expect such whiskies to be bottled without their origin being disclosed. Some distillery owners keep all of their cask fillings for their own use and this would seem to be the sensible approach for those distillers not happy about other companies bottling their own distillery's product.

FILE NOTES

Vocabulary

We feel that, as any tasting note is necessarily a very personal and subjective thing, some of our descriptions may need explanation, in particular for readers outwith Scotland. **Tablet** is a Scottish confection, similar to a firm fudge, very sweet and sugary. We have "created" some words which pedants might object to – for this we apologise. Some of these are: **toffeeyed**, meaning having the character of toffee; **cerealy**, having the aromas of the grain from which the malt is produced; **mashy**, retaining the aromas of malt and sugars from the mash tun. We hope that our manipulation of the language does not upset too many of you and that our reasons for this are understood!

Labels

In some cases, the labels depicted above the tasting notes are not the vintage tasted. This is usually because of the bottler "following" on with the next vintage — which has not yet been tasted. The current vintage should be very similar to the previous vintage when the whisky is bottled at a similar age. It is only where there are much greater older, or younger, age differences that these nuances become more noticeable.

Water

Although water from a kitchen tap is safe to drink in many parts of the world, it can often be far from ideal as an accompaniment to malt whisky. In some areas, the water is naturally quite chalky or has a high mineral content. In others, for reasons of public health, various additives are put into water supplies. In Britain, for example, varying amounts of chlorine are added to drinking water and this can affect the nose of a whisky.

Water filters can be an answer, but even they cannot refresh the water. In a perfect world, the water which we would add would come from the distillery's own water supply. As an alternative, clear, pure soft spring water with a low mineral content, such as one of the bottled Scottish waters, is eminently suitable.

Choose a still water rather than a sparkling one and avoid the more strongly flavoured waters. These may be excellent as a drink in their own right, but they adversely affect the delightful aromas of malt whiskies. Finally, don't be put off adding water. The belief that nothing but more malt whisky should be added to malt whisky is a misconception. Try it for yourself; one glass with one third water and one without. Your enjoyment will be enhanced.

FILE NOTES

Whiskies by post

The following offer a mail order whisky service, as do many of the specialists listed on page 222:

The Malt Whisky Association, Largs, Ayrshire, KA30 8BR
(membership fee charged)

The Whisky Connoisseur, Thistle Mill, Biggar, ML12 6LP
(membership fee charged)

The Scotch Malt Whisky Society, The Vaults, 87 Giles St, Leith, EH6 6BZ
(membership fee charged)

Gordon & Macphail, 58-60 South St, Elgin, Moray, IV30 1JY
(no membership fee)

William Cadenhead, 172 Canongate, Royal Mile, Edinburgh, EH8 8DF
(no membership fee)

Blackadder International, Logie Green, Glenview, Larkhall, ML9 1DA
(no membership fee)

Loch Fyne Whiskies, Inverary, Argyll, PA32 8UD
(no membership fee)

Abbreviations

Certain companies are mentioned throughout the text in abbreviated form. These include:

IDV — International Distillers and Vintners, part of Grand Metropolitan

DCL — The Distillers Company Limited, now United Distillers (UD), a part of Guinness plc

SMD — Scottish Malt Distillers. The malt distilling operational arm of DCL. This has now been merged with SGD, Scottish Grain Distillers, to form SMGD, Scottish Malt and Grain Distillers, also part of Guinness plc

IDG — The Irish Distillers Group

Visitors

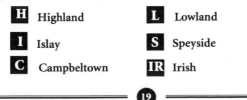 indicates that the distillery welcomes visitors

Key to Symbols

The following symbols are used at the head of each entry to denote the geographical area of production.

H	Highland	**L**	Lowland
I	Islay	**S**	Speyside
C	Campbeltown	**IR**	Irish

HINTS ON PRONUNCIATION

Unless you are an expert Gaelic speaker, you may have difficulty in pronouncing some of the names of the malts in this book or of the areas in which they are produced. The following list contains those names that may cause a problem, with their phonetic alternatives in italics, thus:

Aberlour	*Aber-lower*
Allt-a'Bhainne	*Olt-a vane*
Auchentoshan	*Ochentoshen*
Auchroisk	*Othrusk*
Balmenach	*Bal-MAY-nach*
Bruichladdich	*Brew-ich-laddie*
Bunnahabhain	*Boon-a-havun*
Caol Ila	*Kaal-eela*
Cardhu	*Kar-doo*
Clynelish	*Klyn-leesh*
Craigellachie	*Krai-GELLachy*
Dailuaine	*Dall-YEWan*
Dallas Dhu	*Dallas Doo*
Drumguish	*Drum-oo-ish*
Edradour	*Edra-dower*
Glen Garioch	*Glen Gee-ree*
Glenglassaugh	*Glen Glass-och*
Glen Mhor	*Glen Voar*
Glenmorangie	*Glen-MORanjee*
Glentauchers	*Glen-tockers*
Glenury-Royal	*Glen-you-ree*
Islay	*Eye-la*
Knockdhu	*Nock-doo*
Laphroaig	*La-froyg*
Ledaig	*Led-chig*
Old Pulteney	*Pult-nay*
Pittyvaich	*Pit-ee-vay-ich*
St Magdalene	*Magdaleen*
Strathisla	*Strath-eye-la*
Tamdhu	*Tam-DOO*
Tamnavulin	*Tamna-VOO-lin*
Teaninich	*Tee-an-inich*
Tomintoul	*Tomin-towel*
Tullibardine	*Tully-bard-eye-n*

and finally...

Slainte (Cheers!)	*Schlan-jer*

HIGHLAND
SINGLE MALT
SCOTCH WHISKY

ABERFELDY

distillery was established in 1898 on the *road* to *Perth* and south *side* of the *RIVER TAY*. Fresh *spring water* is taken from the nearby *PITILIE burn* and used to produce this *UNIQUE single MALT SCOTCH WHISKY* with its *distinctive* PEATY nose.

AGED **15** YEARS

Distilled & Bottled in *SCOTLAND*
ABERFELDY DISTILLERY
Aberfeldy, Perthshire, Scotland

43% vol 70 cl

ABERFELDY, PERTHSHIRE EST. 1896

Built between 1896-8 by Perth-based blenders, John Dewar & Sons Ltd. Run by SMD since 1930, Dewar's having joined DCL in 1925. The distillery building is most impressive. The still house and tun-room were rebuilt in 1972/3 using the original stonework. Four stills. Now part of United Distillers plc, Aberfeldy remains at the heart of the world famous Dewar's blend.

LOCATION   Immediately to the east of the village of the same name; next to the former railway line and the main A827 road and overlooking the River Tay.

NOTES   Previously about a dozen distilleries had been opened in the Aberfeldy neighbourhood by men who had been smugglers in earlier times. The distillery lies in a beautiful setting, with close by woodland housing a rare colony of red squirrels, hence the label above. Tommy Dewar set off on a two year world tour in 1892. He returned with 32 new agents in 26 different countries.

WATER   The Pitilie Burn.

Age 15 years   **Strength** 43% abv

Sweetness 7   Peatiness 7   Availability 6

Colour Straw/amber with gold highlights **Nose** Quite full and ripe with rich oaky vanilla, a creamy lanolin oiliness with a slight nuttiness **Flavour** Full, smooth, round and medium-sweet with layers of oak at the back **Finish** Full, round and rich, smooth and almost luscious **Notes** United Distillers bottling

Age 13 years **Strength** 43% abv

Sweetness 5 Peatiness 7 Availability 2

Colour Very pale straw with lemon tinges **Nose** Fresh, medium-bodied with a fruity character and an earthy smokiness **Flavour** Fresh, medium-dry and smooth with an orangey fruitiness **Finish** Fresh, rich and quite long **Notes** Master of Malt bottling, cask nos. 7786-7

Distillation 1974 **Strength** 40% abv

Sweetness 6 Peatiness 7 Availability 4

Colour Straw/amber, gold highlights with a hint of green **Nose** Quite full, earthy, medium-sweet, quite peaty for the region with hints of hazelnuts **Flavour** Medium-dry, quite full and rich with a slight oily smoothness **Finish** Rich, slightly spicy with a touch of bitter chocolate and a smokiness on the tail **Notes** Gordon & MacPhail bottling

Distillation 1970 **Strength** 40% abv

Sweetness 6 Peatiness 6 Availability 4

Colour Straw/golden with yellow highlights **Nose** Fresh, crisp, slightly peaty, surprisingly so for a malt from such a southerly distillery **Flavour** Big, round, dry, slightly woody and malty **Finish** Reasonably long and clean **Notes** Gordon & MacPhail bottling

ABERLOUR, BANFFSHIRE EST. 1826

Founded in 1826 by James Gordon & Peter Weir. Rebuilt in 1879 after a fire. This is the date which appears on the label. Re-equipped with four stills in 1973. The Aberlour Glenlivet Distillery Company is a subsidiary of Campbell Distillers, itself a part of Pernod-Ricard.

LOCATION Aberlour is situated about a quarter of a mile below the Linn of Ruthrie, a 30 foot cascade on Ben Rinnes which falls into the pool which gives rise to the Lour Burn. The distillery is about 300 yards from the Lour's confluence with the River Spey.

NOTES Aberlour is a delightful village by the Lour at the foot of Ben Rinnes, from the summit of which, ten counties (from Caithness in the north, to Perthshire in the south) are visible. The early Christian missionary, St. Dunstan (or St. Drostan as he was known in Scotland) used the waters of the Lour for baptisms.

WATER A spring on Ben Rinnes.

Age 5 years **Strength** 40% abv

Sweetness 7   Peatiness 4   Availability 2

Colour Very pale, yellowy green with pale yellow highlights **Nose** Green fruit with a hint of sweetness, slightly mashy and with a green hedgerow aroma **Flavour** Lightish, spirity, quite round and nutty with a touch of sweetness **Finish** Spicy, almondy and quite good length. **Notes** Campbell Distillers bottling purchased in Italy

Age 10 years **Strength** 40% abv

Sweetness 7 Peatiness 4 Availability 10

Colour Deep amber/golden **Nose** Full, rich, sweet and slightly toffee-like **Flavour** Quite full-bodied and sweet with a well-balanced richness **Finish** Good, full and long **Notes** Campbell Distillers bottling

Age 19 years **Distillation** 1970 **Strength** 43% abv

Sweetness 7 Peatiness 5 Availability 1

Colour Pale to mid-amber with yellow/gold highlights **Nose** Quite full-bodied, medium-sweet, rich, soft and almost honeyed with a slight oily note **Flavour** Full, medium-sweet, a touch of Sherry-nuttiness, smooth and spicy **Finish** Rich, nutty, fresh and delicately smoky **Notes** Master of Malt bottling

Age 21years **Distillation** 1970 **Strength** 43% abv

Sweetness 7 Peatiness 6 Availability 5

Colour Deep, bright amber with rich old gold highlights **Nose** Quite fresh, lanolin, oily character, ripe, almost walnut character with a touch of hedgerow greenness at the back, full-bodied and delicately peated **Flavour** Medium-dry, full, fresh, walnuts, creamily smooth with a touch of spice and a hint of citrus **Finish** Long, clean and creamy with a gentle smokiness on the tail **Notes** Campbell Distillers bottling

ABERLOUR 100

Age No age statement **Strength** 57.1% abv

Sweetness 8 Peatiness 3 Availability 3

Colour Quite deep amber with old gold/bronze highlights **Nose** Quite full-bodied, almost stickily sweet, rich and honeyed with a slight green apple character **Flavour** Sweet, soft and round, with good body, a slight green edge and a touch of spice **Finish** Long, slightly chewey, sweet and lingering **Notes** Campbell Distillers bottling

ABERLOUR ANTIQUE

Age No age statement **Strength** 43% abv

Sweetness 8 Peatiness 3 Availability 3

Colour Quite deep amber with bronze highlights **Nose** Full-bodied, medium-sweet with a slightly green apple perfumed hedgerow character, rich and softly oaky **Flavour** Rich, sweet, quite full-bodied and with a touch of spice **Finish** Long, sweet and lingering **Notes** Campbell Distillers bottling

ALLT-A-BHAINNE

THE CASTLE COLLECTION

Distilled 10/79
Bottled 2/93

Number 1

Cask No.
026329

ALLT-Á-BHAINNE
Aged 13 Years
Bottled In Scotland For
The Whisky Castle
Tomintoul

70cl.   43% vol.

NEAR DUFFTOWN, BANFFSHIRE EST. 1975

A modern building of contemporary architecture, built in 1975 by Chivas Brothers Ltd, a subsidiary of the Seagram Company of Canada. As a reminder of the traditional distillery, four small pagoda roofs are set on the main roof.

LOCATION Sited on the southern slopes of Ben Rinnes to the north of the B9009, some 8 miles south-west of Dufftown.

NOTES Allt-a' Bhainne is the Gaelic for Burn of Milk.

WATER A spring on Ben Rinnes.

Age 13 years **Distillation** 1979 **Strength** 43% abv
Sweetness 9 Peatiness 4 Availability 1

Colour Pale straw with lemon highlights **Nose** Quite soft and sweet with a rich, ripe fruitiness - dried apricots, lightly smoky with a floral note at the back **Flavour** Soft, quite sweet, smooth and round with a fruity character and gently peated **Finish** Long, smooth, soft and almost stickily sweet **Notes** Cask no 026329, distilled 10/79 and bottled 2/93 for The Whisky Castle of Tomintoul

Distillation 1980 **Strength** 60.5% abv
Sweetness 8 Peatiness 6 Availability 4

Colour Deep amber with old gold highlights **Nose** Full, rich, unctuous, almost rancid, over-ripe character, toffee, vanilla, tablet and coffee **Flavour** Medium-sweet, ripe, rich, toffee, tablet with a tang of smokiness **Finish** Smoky and rich **Notes** Cadenhead bottling - cask no 100027

KNOCK, BANFFSHIRE EST. 1893

Knockdhu, as the distillery is known, was the first to be built by the DCL, being licensed to John Haig & Co. Closed in 1983. Sold late 1988 to the Knockdhu Distillery Company Ltd, a subsidiary of Inver House Distillers plc and re-opened in 1989. Two stills.

LOCATION   West of the B9022, seven miles north of Huntly.

NOTES   Built of local grey granite by Gordon & Macbey, architects of Elgin. The water supply, owned by the company, is piped from Knock Hill and is also supplied to the villagers of Knock. The distillery was occupied by a unit of the Indian Army from 1940 to 1945. As Inver House want to avoid confusion with, or suggestion of another malt, the single malt from Knockdhu is now marketed under the Gaelic name "An Cnoc".

WATER   A spring on the southern slopes of Knock Hill.

Age 12 years   **Strength** 43% abv

Sweetness 6   Peatiness 7   Availability 4

Colour Straw/amber with gold highlights **Nose** Fresh, medium-bodied, malty and   medium-sweet with a touch of greenness **Flavour** Sweet, round, quite full-bodied and lightly peated **Finish** Long, smooth and sweet with a green smokiness **Notes** Inver House bottling as *An Cnoc*

Distillation 1974   **Strength** 40% abv

Sweetness 9   Peatiness 3   Availability 4

Colour Pale straw/gold with yellow highlights **Nose** Fatty, slightly sweet, quite full-bodied **Flavour** Sweet, malty and slightly peppery **Finish** Quite long and slightly oily **Notes** Gordon & MacPhail bottling as *Knockdhu*

CONNOISSEURS CHOICE

Connoisseurs Choice, a range of single malts from various districts of Scotland

The island of Islay traditionally produced heavy peated and smokey whiskies.

SINGLE ISLAY
MALT SCOTCH WHISKY
DISTILLED AT
ARDBEG
Distillery
Trade Mark of Proprietors: Ardbeg Distillery Ltd..

DISTILLED **1974** DISTILLED

Specially selected, produced and bottled by and under the responsibility of
70cl GORDON & MACPHAIL 40%vol
REGD. BOTTLER ELGIN · SCOTLAND
PRODUCT OF SCOTLAND

NEAR PORT ELLEN, ISLAY, ARGYLL EST. 1794

The original distillery was run by a notorious band of smugglers, before excisemen overran the place, destroying the buildings. John McDougall established the present distillery in 1815. Owned since 1979 by Hiram Walker, itself now part of Allied Lyons, it is operated by Allied Distillers Ltd.

LOCATION   A very romantic, lonely site at the water's edge on the south coast of Islay.

WATER   Supply from Lochs Arinambeast and Uigidale.

Age 10 years   **Strength** 40% abv

Sweetness 1   Peatiness 10   Availability 4

Colour Pale straw with golden reflections **Nose** Big and peaty with an unexpected unusual sweet edge   **Flavour** Full-bodied, peaty and rich with no hint of the sweetness indicated on the nose **Finish** Long and smoky **Notes** This was the company's own bottling

Distillation 1974   **Strength** 40% abv

Sweetness 1   Peatiness 10   Availability 4

Colour Amber with gold highlights **Nose** Big-bodied, dark and pungent with a burnt peaty character and hints of ozone **Flavour** Big, powerful and slightly salty with a burnt mahogany peatiness and quite firm tannins **Finish** Big, long, chewy and pungent with a salty touch on the tail **Notes** Gordon & MacPhail bottling

KENNETHMONT, ABERDEENSHIRE EST. 1898

Built by Wm. Teacher with two stills and doubled in size twice - four stills in 1955 and eight stills in 1974. The distillery was built as part of a major expansion programme for the company's popular blended whiskies. Now operated by Allied Distillers Ltd, a part of Allied Domecq.

LOCATION Situated alongside the Aberdeen to Inverness railway line, below the 1,425 ft Knockandy Hill. Close by is Leith Hall.

NOTES Wm. Teacher use the make in blending "Teacher's Highland Cream". The stills are still coal fired and the steam engine, boiler front and other relics of the original distillery are preserved. One of the largest malt whisky distilleries in Scotland, Ardmore also houses extensive research laboratories.

WATER A spring on Knockandy Hill.

Distillation 1977   Strength 40% abv
Sweetness 6   Peatiness 6   Availability 4

Colour Pale amber with pale gold highlights **Nose** Quite full and smoky with a slight green touch, medium-dry with a touch of richness **Flavour** Medium-bodied, quite smoky and medium-dry with good richness **Finish** Sweet with a good underpinning of smokiness a touch of spice and quite chewy **Notes** Gordon & MacPhail bottling

Age 18 years   Strength 46% abv
Sweetness 8   Peatiness 6   Availability 4

Colour Full amber with golden highlights **Nose** Light, slightly sweet and oaky **Flavour** Malty, richly sweet and full **Finish** Creamy and oaky **Notes** Wm. Cadenhead bottling

DALMUIR, DUMBARTONSHIRE EST. CIRCA 1800

The name Auchentoshan is believed to derive from the Gaelic words "achad oisnin" possibly meaning "corner of the field". Not much is known of the distillery's early years, but a Mr Thorne has been recorded as owning it in 1825. It is now one of three distilleries owned by Morrison Bowmore Distillers, itself owned by Suntory of Japan. Although not the only distillery to experience war damage (see Banff) it had the misfortune to suffer heavily when Clydebank's shipyards were the target of enemy bombing, an event which caused extensive damage and great loss of spirit!

LOCATION The distillery is situated close to the Erskine Bridge on the A82, between Duntocher and the River Clyde.

NOTES Although geographically situated south of the Highland Line, the source of Auchentoshan's water supply is north of the line. Thus the distillery is a Lowland one, but its water supply is Highland. The make is triple distilled and very lightly peated. The first distillation takes an hour, the second five, the third nine hours.

WATER Water: Near Cochna Loch in the Kilpatrick Hills.

AUCHENTOSHAN SELECT
Age No statement   **Strength** 40% abv

Sweetness 2	Peatiness 7	Availability 8

Colour Straw with lemon/gold highlights **Nose** Fresh and dry with a touch of green cereals and quite good body **Flavour** Dry and smooth with a slight richness and a touch of perfume **Finish** Quite perfumed with a touch of richness **Notes** Bottled as *Auchentoshan Select*. Carries no age statement. Morrison Bowmore bottling

Age 10 years **Strength** 40% abv

Sweetness 4 Peatiness 4 Availability 8

Colour Very pale straw with a slight green edge **Nose** Fresh, clean and floral **Flavour** Light, soft, quite sweet and slightly fruity **Finish** Finishes quite well, although light **Notes** Morrison Bowmore bottling

Age 21 years **Strength** 43% abv

Sweetness 2 Peatiness 4 Availability 3

Colour Mid-amber with old gold highlights **Nose** Soft, round, nutty and quite full-bodied with an almost buttery character **Flavour** Dry, soft and smooth with a hint of richness, gentle tannins and medium bodied **Finish** A hint of sweetness at first, nutty, long, quite delicate and complex **Notes** Morrison Bowmore bottling

SPEYSIDE
SINGLE MALT *SCOTCH WHISKY*

AULTMORE

distillery located between *KEITH* and *BUCKIE* began production in
1897. The name, derived from the *Gaelic*, means *"big burn"*.
Ideal supplies of *water* and *peat* from the *Foggie Moss* made this area
a haunt of *illicit distillers* in the past. *Water* from the *Burn* of
AUCHINDERRAN is now used to produce this *smooth, well balanced*
single *MALT* & *SCOTCH WHISKY* with a *mellow* finish.

AGED **12** YEARS

43% vol Distilled & Bottled in *SCOTLAND*. AULTMORE DISTILLERY Keith, Banffshire, *Scotland.* 70 cl

KEITH, BANFFSHIRE EST. 1895

Built by Alexander Edward of Sanquhar, Forres with two stills. The first of the make was produced in early 1897. It became a part of DCL in 1925 and was transferred to SMD's management in 1930. Rebuilt in 1970/71 and doubled to four stills. Now part of United Distillers plc.

LOCATION An isolated building standing on the A96 Keith to Elgin road close to the turning to Buckie.

NOTES Until 1969 a steam engine had been providing power, operating 24 hours a day, seven days a week since 1898. The old engine is still kept for show.

WATER The burn of Auchinderran.

Age 12 years **Strength** 43% abv
Sweetness 5 Peatiness 4 Availability 6

Colour Pale straw with lemon highlights **Nose** Rich, round, medium-bodied, a cooked mash character, appley and spirity **Flavour** Medium-bodied, lightly peated and medium-dry **Finish** Smooth, malty and quite long **Notes** United Distillers bottling

Age 12 years **Strength** 40% abv
Sweetness 5 Peatiness 4 Availability 0

Colour Pale golden **Nose** Fresh, lightly peated and slightly sweet **Flavour** Medium-bodied, slightly fruity **Finish** Light and warming **Notes** DCL bottling. (Pre-Guinness /United Distillers)

EDDERTON, ROSS-SHIRE EST. 1790

The present distillery was built in 1872 when the then owner, Andrew Ross, decided to extend the business, the new buildings being higher up the slope of the hill. The older buildings were converted into a bonded warehouse. Extended from two to three stills in the 1970s by owners Hiram Walker and now operated by Allied Distillers Ltd. The fermenting of ale on the site is said to have taken place as long ago as 1749.

LOCATION Less than a quarter of a mile from the Dornoch Firth, about six miles from Tain on the A9.

NOTES Distilling in the area predates Balblair by a considerable number of years, there being many suitable sources of water and peat in abundance. Indeed, the Edderton area is known as "the Parish of the Peats" and once abounded in smuggling bothies. One of the malts associated with Ballantine's blended Scotch Whisky.

WATER The Allt Dearg, a burn four miles from the distillery.

Age 5 years **Strength** 40% abv

Sweetness	6	Peatiness	4	Availability	1

Colour Very pale straw **Nose** Peaty, aromatic, quite light and spirity **Flavour** Slightly sweet, faintly peaty, spirity and quite light **Finish** Shortish and light **Notes** Sold on German market

Age 10 years **Strength** 40% abv

Sweetness	8	Peatiness	3	Availability	4

Colour Mid-amber with gold highlights **Nose** Quite full-bodied, dark and sweet and lightly nutty with a toffee/aniseed character **Flavour** Sweet, nutty, quite round and smooth with quite good body and lightly peated **Finish** Clean and quite sweet **Notes** Gordon & MacPhail bottling

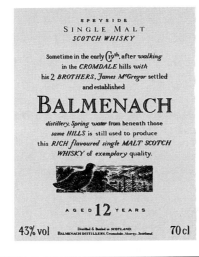

SPEYSIDE
SINGLE MALT
SCOTCH WHISKY

Sometime in the early (19th), after *walking*
in the *CROMDALE* hills *with*
his 2 BROTHERS, *James McGregor* settled
and established

BALMENACH

distillery. Spring water from beneath those
same *HILLS* is still used to produce
this *RICH flavoured single MALT SCOTCH
WHISKY* of *exemplary* quality.

AGED 12 YEARS

43% vol — Distilled & Bottled in SCOTLAND. BALMENACH DISTILLERY, Cromdale, Moray, Scotland. — 70 cl

BALMENACH, CROMDALE, MORAY EST. 1824

The distillery was established in 1824 by James McGregor. At the time, it was at the centre of an area which was full of smugglers' bothies and illicit distilling was a way of life. Bought by SMD in 1930 and extended from four stills to six stills in 1962. A Saladin Box malting system was installed in 1964 and used until the mid-1980's. It is now part of United Distillers plc, but was closed and mothballed at the end of May, 1993.

LOCATION The distillery lies in a bowl in the hills off the A95 main road heading towards Bridge of Avon from Grantown-on-Spey. The distillery stands about a mile from the former Cromdale station on the Spey Valley railway line.

NOTES A branch line was built to the distillery in the late 1880s and the steam engine which worked the line is preserved on the Strathspey railway at Aviemore. Local lore tells that farmer James McGregor was visited by an excise officer just after the 1823 Excise Act had been passed. He was shown round the farm and experienced typical hospitality with a bottle of fine whisky. The officer then pointed out an outbuilding and asked what it was used for. "That's just the peat shed," came the reply. The officer said nothing, and continued to enjoy his whisky. After a few more drams, the officer made to leave. "If I were you, Mr McGregor," he said, "I'd take out a licence for that peat shed." McGregor took the hint and took out the necessary licence. In 1690 the Jacobites were defeated by William of Orange in a battle on the hills above the village of Cromdale.

WATER The Cromdale Burn.

Age 12 years **Strength** 43% abv

Sweetness 7 Peatiness 5 Availability 6

Colour Quite deep amber with bronze highlights **Nose** Quite full-bodied, heather floral characters, medium-sweet, rich and sherried with a light honeyed nuttiness **Flavour** Full-bodied, sherried and nutty with a touch of oily vanilla **Finish** Long, nutty and medium-sweet with a touch of tannin **Notes** United Distillers bottling

Distillation 1981 **Strength** 62.6% abv

Sweetness 6 Peatiness 5 Availability 4

Colour Very pale, watery straw with pale lemon highlights **Nose** Very mashy, youthful character, lightly spirity with a sweetness at the back **Flavour** Medium-sweet, rich and unctuous with gentle tannins, a hint of austerity at the front of the palate and lightly peated **Finish** Quite short, but smooth with a light chewiness **Notes** Wm Cadenhead bottling

Distillation 1972 **Strength** 40% abv

Sweetness 6 Peatiness 7 Availability 4

Colour Mid-amber with light bronze highlights **Nose** Medium-sweet, quite full-bodied, dark, rich, brazil nutty and smoky, oaky with a good unctuous richness **Flavour** Medium-dry, nutty, of good body with a soft richness and smoky oak **Finish** Long and slightly chewy with a slight perfumed smokiness **Notes** Gordon & MacPhail bottling

Distillation 1971 **Strength** 40% abv

Sweetness 5 Peatiness 7 Availability 4

Colour Amber/straw with yellow/gold highlights **Nose** Quite smoky & peaty, medium-bodied with a slight green nuttiness **Flavour** Dryish, smoky, quite full and delicately peaty with an edge of sweetness **Finish** Dry with oaky tannin and reasonable length **Notes** Gordon & MacPhail bottling

Distillation 1970 **Strength** 40% abv

Sweetness 5 Peatiness 6 Availability 4

Colour Straw/golden **Nose** Light, but faintly sweet **Flavour** Much bigger than the nose suggests, a little woody and with a pleasant sweet edge **Finish** Full and distinguished **Notes** Gordon & MacPhail bottling

DUFFTOWN, BANFFSHIRE EST. 1892

Built next to William Grant's Glenfiddich distillery in 1892. The stills came second-hand from Lagavulin and Glen Albyn. Three further stills were added to make eight in all (two in 1965 and one in 1971). Floor malting is still carried out at Balvenie, this supplying about 15% of the distillery's malt requirement. The peat used is hand-cut locally, being dried and seasoned before being used to fire the malt kiln. The stills at Balvenie are heated using the heat waste from Glenfiddich to produce steam heat to boil them.

LOCATION Situated just below Glenfiddich on the lower slopes of the Convals, the hills which dominate Dufftown.

NOTES The Balvenie is an excellent example of just how different single malts can be. Standing next door to its more famous sister, Glenfiddich, it draws its water from the same source and shares the same supply of malt - even the distiller is the same person - and yet the two whiskies are very different in character. In 1992, 100 years after Balvenie was built, the Grants opened another new distillery, Kininvie, next door.

WATER The Robbie Dhu (pronounced "doo") springs.

THE BALVENIE FOUNDER'S RESERVE
Age 10 years   **Strength** 40% abv

Sweetness 8   Peatiness 3   Availability 8

Colour Straw with good golden highlights **Nose** Full and rich with a green edge, medium-sweet with an appley aroma **Flavour** Medium-dry, smooth, oaky and malty **Finish** Of reasonable length, quite rich **Notes** William Grant bottling

THE BALVENIE DOUBLEWOOD
Age 12 years **Strength** 40% abv

Sweetness 7   Peatiness 3   Availability 7

Colour Quite full amber with old gold highlights and a hint of lemon **Nose** Quite full mashy/spirity and ripe with a slightly walnut nutty character and a fresh, almost Riesling-like diesel touch. **Flavour** Medium-sweet, slightly spicy, smooth and round with a dark nuttiness, a chocolatey/malty character and delicately peated **Finish** Fresh, warm, rich, quite tangy, long and with the walnut character of the nose. **Notes** Partly aged in a Bourbon cask, its maturation is finished off in a Sherry cask, hence its name *Balvenie DoubleWood*. William Grant bottling

The maltings floor at Balvenie

THE BALVENIE

THE BALVENIE SINGLE BARREL
Age 15 years **Distillation** 1978 **Strength** 50.4% abv
Sweetness 7 Peatiness 3 Availability 4

Colour Bright, pale mid-amber with yellow-gold highlights
Nose Quite full-bodied, ripe, rich and medium-sweet with an
unctuous oily honeyed vanilla-oak character, delicately peated
with hints of green apples **Flavour** Medium-sweet, quite full-
bodied, smooth and round with a backbone of oaky tannin, an
oily-vanilla texture and a slight green edge to the peatiness
Finish Very long and complex with hints of bitter chocolate,
hazelnuts, toffee, honey and a nice green coffee tang **Notes**
William Grant bottling. Bottle no. 134 from cask no 199. This
cask was filled on 17.01.1978 and bottled on 13.10.1993.
Sold as *The Balvenie Single Barrel*

Age 21 years **Distillation** 1973 **Strength** 52.8% abv
Sweetness 7 Peatiness 2 Availability 4

Colour Mid-amber with gold highlights **Nose** Very soft,
smooth and medium-sweet, malty and delicate with a toffee
apple aroma **Flavour** Soft, sweet, very delicately peated with
quite a fresh green apple character **Finish** Long, smooth and
sweet with a coffee tang **Notes** Wm Cadenhead bottling, distilled February, 1973

BANFF, BANFFSHIRE EST. 1863

Built by James Simpson junior to replace an earlier distillery of the same name built in 1824. Rebuilt after a fire in 1877. Owned by SMD since 1932. Two stills. Closed and dismantled in 1983.

LOCATION Half a mile west of Banff on the B9139.

NOTES One of the first distilleries located to take advantage of the railways. On Saturday, 16th August, 1941, a single German plane machine-gunned and bombed No 12 Warehouse. Exploding casks flew through the air and a local newspaper reported, ". . . thousands of gallons of whisky were lost, either burning or running to waste over the land . . . even farm animals became intoxicated". Cows were not milked because they could not be got to their feet. Banff was known locally as "Inverboyndie distillery".

WATER Springs on Fiskaidly Farm.

Distillation 1974 **Strength** 40 % abv

Sweetness 10 Peatiness 6 Availability 4

Colour Medium-peaty gold **Nose** Quite peaty, slightly oily with a slight hint of ozone **Flavour** Round, mellow and slightly spicy **Finish** Good, long, slightly sugar-sweet, perhaps a little overpoweringly so **Notes** Gordon & MacPhail bottling

Distillation 1976 **Age** 17 years **Strength** 60.5 % abv

Sweetness 6 Peatiness 6 Availability 4

Colour Mid-amber with yellow/gold highlights **Nose** Fresh and clean with a soft green fruitiness, hints of perfume and a cedar note **Flavour** Fresh, smooth, medium-dry and quite round with good body and gentle tannins **Finish** Of reasonable length, it has a light earthy smokiness with a green edge **Notes** Wm Cadenhead bottling

DISTILLED AND BOTTLED IN SCOTLAND

BEN NEVIS

SINGLE HIGHLAND MALT
SCOTCH WHISKY

BEN NEVIS DISTILLERY (FORT WILLIAM) LIMITED
DISTILLED IN 1972

75cl   55.6% vol

LOCHY BRIDGE, FORT WILLIAM EST. 1825

Founded by "Long John" Macdonald in 1825. Owned by various Macdonalds until bought by Seager Evans in the 1920s. Taken over by Ben Nevis Distillery (Fort William) Ltd. who installed a coffey still. Four pot stills. Sold by the Whitbread group to the Japanese company, Nikka, early in 1989.

LOCATION Situated two miles north of Fort William on the A82.

NOTES A cask of Ben Nevis was presented to Queen Victoria on her visit to Fort William on 21 April 1848. The cask was not to be opened until the Prince of Wales reached his majority 15 years later.

WATER Allt a' Mhuilinn (The Mill Burn), which flows from two small lochans, Coire Leis and Coire na' Ciste, situated at over 3,000 ft up Ben Nevis.

Age 21 years   **Strength** 55.6% abv

Sweetness 5   Peatiness 6   Availability 2

Colour Quite deep amber with bronze highlights **Nose** Full-bodied, rich, oaky and medium-sweet with a firm peatiness **Flavour** Full-bodied, dark and nutty with a rich peatiness, medium-sweet with quite gentle oaky tannins **Finish** Long, powerful and delicately smoky with a tangy touch of spice and just an edge of sweetness on the tail **Notes** Ben Nevis bottling

Age 22 years   **Strength** 46% abv

Sweetness 3   Peatiness 6   Availability 4

Colour Deep, peaty amber with good gold highlights **Nose** Spirity, malty, dryish, lightly peated and slightly leafy **Flavour** Dry, lightly peaty, spirity and slightly spicy **Finish** Smooth, clean and enjoyably long **Notes** Wm Cadenhead bottling

Distillation 1967 **Age** 26 years **Strength** 58% abv

Sweetness 4 Peatiness 5 Availability 3

Colour Mid-amber with old gold highlights **Nose** Medium-sweet, quite rich and fresh with a touch of oily oaky vanilla, a green character and medium-bodied **Flavour** Medium-dry, quite full and rich with a slight oily smoothness **Finish** Long and gently smoky with good rich sweetness and a tail of bitter toffee **Notes** Ben Nevis bottling

Distillation 1972 **Strength** 60.5% abv

Sweetness 5 Peatiness 6 Availability 2

Colour Pale amber with gold highlights **Nose** Quite full, earthy, medium-sweet, quite peaty for the region with hints of hazelnuts **Flavour** Medium-sweet, smoky and smooth with a little tannin and a green freshness **Finish** Long and gently smoky with a touch of spice **Notes** Ben Nevis bottling from cask no 619

Distillation 1977 **Age** 15 years **Strength** 60.9% abv

Sweetness 6 Peatiness 5 Availability 2

Colour Straw with yellow/pale gold highlights **Nose** Full-bodied with a dark peatiness and a rich, medium-dry tang of orange peel **Flavour** Soft, medium-sweet, rich and velvety smooth with a gentle peatiness **Finish** Long, fresh, clean and rich with a lightly toffeeyed tail **Notes** Wm Cadenhead bottling

BEN NEVIS DISTILLERY.

BENRIACH

BENRIACH DISTILLERY
EST. 1898
A SINGLE
PURE HIGHLAND MALT
Scotch Whisky
Benriach Distillery, in the heart of the Highlands,
still malts its own barley. The resulting whisky has
a unique and attractive delicacy
PRODUCED AND BOTTLED BY THE
BENRIACH
DISTILLERY CO
ELGIN, MORAYSHIRE, SCOTLAND, IV30 3SJ
Distilled and Bottled in Scotland
AGED 10 YEARS
70 cl ℮ 43% vol

LONGMORN, NR ELGIN, MORAY EST. 1898

Founded in 1898 as the whisky market moved suddenly into recession. It was then closed in 1900 and did not open again until 1965, when it was rebuilt by The Glenlivet Distillers Ltd. Owned by The Seagram Company of Canada since 1977. Four stills.

LOCATION Situated three miles south of Elgin to the east of the A941.

NOTES The floor maltings are still in use. Previously only available from independent bottlers, Seagram introduced their own bottling in 1994. The sister distillery to the much prized Longmorn next door, both distilleries were built within four years of each other in the boom years of the 1890's. Like Longmorn, it is an important constituent of the flagship Seagram blend, Chivas Regal.

WATER Local springs.

Age 10 years **Strength** 43% abv

Sweetness 6	Peatiness 3	Availability 7

Colour Quite pale straw with lemon highlights **Nose** Fresh, green appley bubble-gum character, lightly malty and lightly peated, medium-sweet **Flavour** Medium-dry, soft, quite full-bodied with a chocolatey richness and touches of spice and coffee **Finish** Rich with a tang of coffee, quite long and lingering **Notes** Seagram bottling

Distillation 1969 **Strength** 40% abv

Sweetness 6	Peatiness 3	Availability 4

Colour Pale straw with gold highlights **Nose** Sweet, distinctive fruitiness, fresh and appley **Flavour** Sweet, appley, distinctive, reminiscent of Calvados **Finish** Spicy and good with the apple flavour lingering **Notes** Gordon & MacPhail bottling

CONNOISSEURS CHOICE

Connoisseurs Choice, a range of single malts from various districts of Scotland.

The distilleries situated in the area of the valley of the River Spey produce some of the finest malt whiskies.

SINGLE SPEYSIDE
MALT SCOTCH WHISKY
DISTILLED AT

BENRINNES
DISTILLERY
Proprietors: A. & A. Crawford Ltd

DISTILLED **1969** DISTILLED

SPECIALLY SELECTED, PRODUCED AND BOTTLED BY

70cl **GORDON & MACPHAIL** 40%vol
ELGIN · SCOTLAND
PRODUCT OF SCOTLAND

ABERLOUR, BANFFSHIRE EST. 1835

The original distillery was located at Whitehouse Farm, three quarters of a mile to the south east and was washed away in the great flood of 1829. The present building was founded in 1835 by William Smith & Co. as an extension of the farm steading. Acquired by Dewar's in 1922, and thereby becoming a part of DCL in 1925. Run by SMD since 1930, the licensees were A. & A. Crawford Ltd. Major reconstruction took place between 1955 and 1956. Doubled from three to six stills in 1966. Now part of United Distillers plc.

LOCATION Situated one and a half miles south of the A95 on a loop of an unclassified road which runs between the A95 at Daugh of Kinermony and the B9009 at Succoth in Glen Rinnes.

NOTES A form of triple distillation is practised.

WATER The Scurran and Rowantree Burns.

Age 15 years **Strength** 43% abv

Sweetness 8 Peatiness 4 Availability 4

Colour Amber with old gold highlights **Nose** Medium-bodied, biscuity-yeasty, fresh, vanilla and medium-sweet with a slight floral note **Flavour** Medium-sweet, round, smooth, biscuity and honeyed **Finish** Nice, sweet, round, biscuity and honeyed **Notes** United Distillers bottling

Distillation 1977 **Strength** 43% abv

Sweetness 7   Peatiness 6   Availability 1

Colour Pale straw with pale yellow highlights **Nose** Quite full-bodied and mashy with a soft, slightly unctuous smoky character **Flavour** Good body, medium-dry and smoky with a bubble-gummy character **Finish** Very clean, quite fresh and spicy **Notes** From "The Ultimate Selection" bottled for Van Wees of Holland - cask no 5559 distilled 11.11.77

Age 20 years **Distillation** 1974 **Strength** 43% abv

Sweetness 6   Peatiness 4   Availability 1

Colour Quite full amber with old gold highlights **Nose** Medium-bodied, rich and dark nuttiness with a slight charcoal character **Flavour** Big, chunky, dark and nutty with quite full tannins, round, medium-sweet and quite smooth **Finish** Chewy with tangs of spice and vanilla, quite long **Notes** From "The Ultimate Selection" bottled for Van Wees of Holland - cask no. 2577 distilled 18.3.74

Distillation 1968 **Strength** 40% abv

Sweetness 6   Peatiness 6   Availability 4

Colour Straw/gold with good bright highlights **Nose** Sweet, nutty and slightly fatty in an unctuous way **Flavour** Medium-sweet, smoky, spicy and oaky **Finish** Good, smoky and dry, smooth and creamy **Notes** Gordon & MacPhail bottling

CONNOISSEURS CHOICE

Connoisseurs Choice, a range of single malts from various districts of Scotland

In the Highlands are situated the greatest number of malt whisky distilleries.

SINGLE HIGHLAND
MALT SCOTCH WHISKY
DISTILLED AT
BENROMACH
DISTILLERY
Proprietors: J. & W. Hardie Ltd

DISTILLED **1971** DISTILLED

SPECIALLY SELECTED, PRODUCED AND BOTTLED BY
70cl   **GORDON & MACPHAIL**   40%vol
ELGIN - SCOTLAND
PRODUCT OF SCOTLAND

FORRES, MORAY EST. 1898

Built by the Benromach Distillery Company. Bought by Associated Scottish Distilleries Ltd. in 1937, who sold it to DCL in 1953. It was managed by SMD and licensed to J & W Hardie. The stillhouse was rebuilt in 1966 and the mash house was rebuilt and the tunroom modernised in 1974. Two stills. Bought by Gordon & MacPhail in 1992, who plan to re-open it in late 1995/6.

LOCATION   Sited to the north of Forres on the north side of the railway line.

NOTES   In 1925 the mash tun was wooden. Benromach was designed by Elgin architect Charles Doig and has high pitched gables and narrow mullioned windows in the Scots vernacular style of the 17th century.

WATER   Chapeltown springs near Forres.

Distillation 1968   **Strength** 40% abv
Sweetness 8   Peatiness 4   Availability 3

Colour Deepish amber with slightly grey-green tints **Nose** Full, ripe, sweet and definitely fruity **Flavour** Sweet, mellow, soft & a little spirity **Finish** Spicy and long with a little touch of a floral note **Notes** Gordon & MacPhail bottling

Distillation 1969   **Strength** 40% abv
Sweetness 7   Peatiness 4   Availability 3

Colour Mid-amber with yellow/gold highlights **Nose** Fresh and medium-dry with an oily-oaky aroma, soft and smooth with a touch of green apples **Flavour** Medium-dry, quite rich and soft, sweetness develops in the palate, gently peated **Finish** Quite long and lightly smoky with a touch of spice in the tail **Notes** Gordon & MacPhail bottling

BLADNOCH, WIGTOWN EST. 1817

Founded in 1817 by John & Thomas McClelland. Sold by Dunvilles, the Irish whisky distillers, in 1936 for £3,500, this "representing a considerable loss for the premises and plant". Closed in 1938 and re-opened in 1956. Run by United Distillers plc who closed it in 1993.

LOCATION The southernmost distillery in Scotland. Situated on the river of the same name, just a mile outside Wigtown.

NOTES Close to the distillery is Baldoon Farm, where stands the ruined castle to which Janet Dalrymple, the "Bride of Lammermoor", came to die after her marriage to David Dunbar of Baldoon.

WATER The River Bladnoch.

Age 10 years **Strength** 43% abv

Sweetness 4 Peatiness 4 Availability 6

Colour Straw/amber with yellow highlights and green tinge **Nose** Fresh, quite full, fruity and floral, medium-dry with an attractive grape spirit-like aroma **Flavour** Fresh with good weight, a sweet edge and a touch of spice **Finish** Fresh with nice sweetness and quite light **Notes** United Distillers bottling

Age 10 years **Distillation** 1984 **Strength** 43% abv

Sweetness 2 Peatiness 5 Availability 2

Colour Pale straw with lemon highlights **Nose** Medium-bodied, almost dry with a slight rubber aroma and herby/rosemary/citrus character and a touch of perfume **Flavour** Off-dry, smooth, quite round with a delicate smokiness and a herby and cereal touch **Finish** Fresh, clean and of reasonable length **Notes** Blackadder International bottling

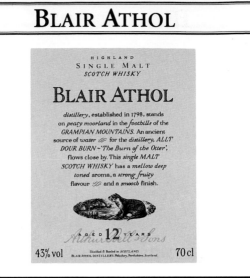

HIGHLAND
SINGLE MALT
SCOTCH WHISKY

BLAIR ATHOL

distillery, established in 1798, stands
on *peaty moorland* in the *foothills* of the
GRAMPIAN MOUNTAINS. An ancient
source of *water* for the *distillery, ALLT'
DOUR BURN ~ 'The Burn of the Otter',*
flows close by. This *single MALT
SCOTCH WHISKY* has a *mellow deep
toned* aroma, a *strong fruity*
flavour and a *smooth* finish.

AGED 12 YEARS

Arthur Bell & Sons

43% vol

Distilled & Bottled in SCOTLAND.
BLAIR ATHOL DISTILLERY, Pitlochry, Perthshire, Scotland

70 cl

PITLOCHRY, PERTHSHIRE EST. 1798

Although originally founded almost 30 years earlier, the present distillery was established in 1826, when revived by John Robertson. It passed into the hands of John Conacher & company in 1827. It closed in 1932 and, although purchased by Arthur Bell & Sons the following year, it did not come into production again until 1949 after rebuilding. Extended from two to four stills in 1973. Now part of United Distillers plc.

LOCATION Not at Blair Atholl, as its name suggests, the distillery is to be found on the southern approach road to Pitlochry, just off the main A9.

NOTES The Conacher family, who owned the distillery for a time in the 1800s, are said to be descended from the chivalrous young Conacher who so admired Catherine Glover, the Fair Maid of Perth. The distillery has a large modern visitor centre. Blair Athol is well worth a visit, having an excellent audio-visual presentation as part of a tour of the distillery. Blair Athol malt (note the difference in spelling from the place) plays an important part in the Bell's blend.

WATER From a spring on the nearby 2,760 ft. high Ben Vrackie.

Age 12 years   **Strength** 43% abv

Sweetness 7 Peatiness 6 Availability 6

Colour Pale, mid-amber with gold highlights **Nose** Quite full with touches of nuttiness and greenness, medium-sweet with a fresh smokiness **Flavour** Medium-sweet and quite full-bodied, spicy and round with a definite smoky tang **Finish** Fresh, quite long and smoky with a sweetness on the tail **Notes** United Distillers bottling

Age 8 years **Strength** 40% abv

Sweetness 5 Peatiness 5 Availability 1

Colour Straw/golden **Nose** Fresh, clean and lightly peated **Flavour** Sweet, almost almondy **Finish** Quite good and distinctive **Notes** Arthur Bell Distillers bottling

Age 23 years **Distillation** 1966 **Strength** 57.1% abv

Sweetness 6 Peatiness 5 Availability 2

Colour Mid-amber with yellow/gold highlights **Nose** Medium-sweet, quite good body and round with nice vanilla-oak and a citrus oil tang **Flavour** Soft, smooth, medium-sweet with a dry oakiness, quite gentle tannins and good body **Finish** Long with a distinctive perfumed sweetness and a gentle smokiness **Notes** Wm Cadenhead bottling distilled October, 1966

The workforce at Blair Athol, 1895

BOWMORE, ISLE OF ISLAY, ARGYLL EST. 1779

In 1776, an Islay merchant, David Simpson, obtained permission from the local laird to build dwellings and "other buildings". The "other buildings" were soon converted into a distillery. Bought by Stanley P. Morrison in 1963, the distillery is now owned by Morrison Bowmore Distillers, who were themselves purchased outright by Suntory of Japan in 1994. The company had been part owned by Suntory for some years previously, having had a long term trading relationship with the Japanese company

LOCATION Bowmore stands, almost fortress-like, on the shores of Loch Indaal.

NOTES Bowmore uses a revolutionary waste heat recovery system to reduce energy costs. The distillery donated a warehouse to the village of Bowmore which has been converted to a swimming pool. The waste heat from the distillery is used to heat the swimming pool. The distillery was built early in the village's history, at the foot of Hill Street, and has proved important to its economic survival. It is said to be the oldest legal distillery on the island.

WATER Laggan River.

BOWMORE LEGEND
Age No age statement **Strength** 40% abv
Sweetness 1 Peatiness 8 Availability 9

Colour Light amber with gold highlights and a touch of green **Nose** Full, pungent, a touch perfumed & a phenol character with a little greenness **Flavour** Dry with an edge of richness, perfumed and quite pungent **Finish** Long, gently smoky and perfumed **Notes** Morrison Bowmore bottling. Sold as *Bowmore Legend*

Age 10 years **Strength** 40% abv

Sweetness 0 Peatiness 8 Availability 10

Colour Mid-amber with gold highlights **Nose** Full, dry, pungent with a touch of burnt heather and perfumed **Flavour** Dry, heather-perfumed, fresh and smoky, quite full-bodied with whiffs of ozone **Finish** Long, characterful and smoky **Notes** Morrison Bowmore bottling

Age 12 years **Strength** 40% abv

Sweetness 0 Peatiness 8 Availability 9

Colour Full, amber, very bright **Nose** Lightish, peaty, burnt heather with a characteristic tang of ozone/iodine and even a whiff of chocolate! **Flavour** Smooth, refined flavour with a pronounced smoky peatiness **Finish** Good, long & dry **Notes** Morrison Bowmore bottling

Age 17 years **Strength** 43% abv

Sweetness 2 Peatiness 8 Availability 6

Colour Quite full, deep amber with old gold highlights **Nose** Rich, medium bodied with a pungency, but delicacy and aromas of violets **Flavour** Round, quite full-bodied, smoky and rich with gentle tannins **Finish** Soft, gently smoky, quite elegant and slightly salty **Notes** Morrison Bowmore bottling

Age 21 years **Strength** 43% abv

Sweetness 2 Peatiness 9 Availability 5

Colour Mid-amber with old gold highlights **Nose** Quite big-bodied, dark & smoky, rounded and quite dry with just a hint of ozone **Flavour** Big, round, burnt heather roots, quite pungent with a delicate floral note at the back **Finish** Long with a hint of sweetness/richness and finely smoky with a touch of bitter chocolate on the tail **Notes** Morrison Bowmore bottling

Age 25 years **Strength** 43% abv

Sweetness 3 Peatiness 7 Availability 3

Colour Quite deep amber with pale bronze highlights **Nose** Quite full-bodied, rich with a slightly green hedgerow freshness, a floral smokiness and burnt vanilla notes **Flavour** Full-bodied, fresh and round, medium-dry but rich, a slightly perfumed dark peaty smokiness and a touch of oaky tannin **Finish** Long, gently chewy, almost floral, quite delicately smoky with a hint of seaweed and bitter chocolate - very complex **Notes** Morrison Bowmore bottling

BLACK BOWMORE
Distillation 1964   **Strength** 50% abv

Sweetness 2   Peatiness 7   Availability 1

Colour Very deep, dark mahogany/teak with deep bronze highlights **Nose** Big-bodied, full, dark, nutty and rich, quite delicately peated, dry with slight notes of burnt mahogany **Flavour** Big, powerful, full-bodied, quite tannic with dark nutty flavours, smooth, although chewy **Finish** Long, full-flavoured, quite chewy with a smoky/nutty character, a good perfumed peatiness and a rich salty tang on the tail **Notes** Morrison Bowmore bottling. Known as **Black Bowmore**, this is from a very rare old sherry cask bottling

BOWMORE MARINER
Age 15 years   **Strength** 43% abv

Sweetness 2   Peatiness 8   Availability 5

Colour Amber with gold/bronze highlights **Nose** Rich, gloriously chocolatey and with good body; a delicate note of burnt heather roots and a peatiness at the back **Flavour** Quite full-bodied, smoky, clean and round with a richness at the back **Finish** Long, fresh and smoky with an appealing green edge **Notes** Morrison Bowmore bottling

Vintage 1979
Single Highland Malt Scotch Whisky
Matured in sherry casks for 15 years
Distilled at the Braes of Glenlivet Distillery
on 06.06.79   *Bottled 3.95*
Butt no. 1608   *Bottle no. 570* *of 570*
*This whisky has been selected, produced and bottled in
Scotland for and under the sole responsibility of
Signatory Vintage Scotch Whisky Co. Ltd.
Edinburgh EH6 Scotland*
70cl   60%vol

NEAR TOMINTOUL, BANFFSHIRE EST. 1973

Built between between 1973-4 by Chivas Bros Ltd, a subsidiary of the Seagram Co Ltd of Canada. Originally three stills, with two more being added in 1975 and a sixth in 1978. Although a very modern distillery, it is nevertheless of a most attractive design, with a decorative, albeit non functional pagoda-style roof.

LOCATION High up above the remote hamlet of Chapeltown off the B9008, it is one of the most isolated distilleries in Scotland.

NOTES With this whisky at last becoming available through independent bottlers, comes the news that its owners have renamed it Breval to avoid confusion with its illustrious sister, The Glenlivet.

WATER The Pitilie Burn.

Age 15 years **Strength** 43% abv

Sweetness 7 Peatiness 5 Availability 2

Colour Quite deep amber with bronze highlights **Nose** Quite full-bodied, round and gently peaty; rich and creamy with a slightly perfumed character **Flavour** Round, smooth, full-bodied, medium-sweet with a not unpleasant, slightly perfumed, green edge **Finish** Long, smooth, medium-dry and slightly nutty **Notes** Signatory bottling distilled on 6 June 1979

Age 8 years **Distillation** 1987 **Strength** 60% abv

Sweetness 7 Peatiness 4 Availability 2

Colour Pale straw with pale, watery lemon highlights **Nose** Medium-dry, of quite good body, a young mashy character with a slight touch of citrus, a hedgerow greenness and a soft maltiness **Flavour** Soft, medium-sweet, quite good body and round with a touch of peat at the back **Finish** Clean, of reasonable length, with good sweetness and firm oak **Notes** Wm Cadenhead bottling, bottled July, 1995

NATURAL CASK STRENGTH
SINGLE MALT SCOTCH WHISKY
AGED **22** YEARS
DISTILLED IN 1972 AT THE
BRORA
DISTILLERY
ESTABLISHED 1819
BRORA SUTHERLAND
58.7%vol 70cl℮
PRODUCE OF SCOTLAND
LIMITED BOTTLING

BRORA, SUTHERLAND EST. 1819

Brora was known as Clynelish until 1969. Established by the Duke of Sutherland, who had cleared his tenant-farmers off the land to make way for sheep. Having moved some of the inland farmers to the coastal strip, the distillery was established to create a market for the farmers' grain. Owned by SMD since 1930. Two stills.

LOCATION Just of the A9 at Brora.

NOTES After the modern distillery had been built in 1967-68, the old "Clynelish" re-opened in April, 1969, housed in the former mash-house, which had been rebuilt. It subsequently ceased distillation in May, 1983 . The old buildings are now used as warehouses and the visitor centre for the "new" Clynelish.

WATER The Clynemilton Burn.

Distillation 1972 **Strength** 40% abv
Sweetness 3 Peatiness 9 Availability 2

Colour Mid-amber with gold highlights **Nose** Full and heavily peated with a sooty character **Flavour** Big, and smooth with smoky characters of burnt oak **Finish** Nutty, chewy and smoky with a hint of sweetness **Notes** Gordon & MacPhail bottling

Age 22 years **Strength** 58.7% abv
Sweetness 4 Peatiness 8 Availability 2

Colour Amber with gold highlights **Nose** Big bodied, quite pungent, a dark, smoky - almost sooty, burnt tang with richness at the back **Flavour** Quite big with a soft peatiness, but a burnt character, medium-sweet, quite rich and with big tannins **Finish** Long, with an almost burnt character, spicy with chewy tannins. **Notes** United Distillers bottling

The

BRUICHLADDICH

ISLAY

Single *Malt*

SCOTCH WHISKY

DISTILLED, MATURED AND BOTTLED BY
BRUICHLADDICH DISTILLERY COMPANY LIMITED
BRUICHLADDICH, ISLE OF ISLAY, SCOTLAND

AGED **10** YEARS

70cl 40%vol

BRUICHLADDICH, ISLAY, ARGYLL EST. 1881

Built by Robert, William & John Gourlay Harvey (of the Dundashill & Yoker Harveys). Became the Bruichladdich Distillery Company (Islay) Ltd. in 1886. Doubled from two to four stills in 1975. Owned in recent years by Invergordon Distillers, who were taken over by Whyte & Mackay in late 1993. A lot of very old machinery and distillation techniques were employed in the distillery, making it an exciting distillery to visit. Sadly it was closed abruptly at the end of January, 1995, its new owners having decided to mothball Bruichladdich and two other distilleries in the newly enlarged Whyte & Mackay group, Tamnavulin and Tullibardine.

LOCATION Sited on the western shore of Loch Indaal on the A847 to Port Charlotte and the picturesque village of Portnahaven.

NOTES The distillery is the most westerly in Scotland and, despite this, it has a lighter, more delicate character than the other Islay Malts. It is thought that this is because it is sheltered from the prevailing winds - and weather - by the Rhinns of Islay, a range of hills which lie between Bruichladdich and the open sea.

WATER A reservoir in the local hills.

Age 10 years **Strength** 40% abv

Sweetness 2 Peatiness 7 Availability 7

Colour Pale golden with slight green tinges **Nose** A delicate peatiness, fairly light and with no great pungency **Flavour** Full and flavoursome, smoky and dry without the heavier notes of other Islays **Finish** Of good length and with a well-defined finish **Notes** Invergordon Distillers bottling

Age 15 years   **Strength** 40% abv

Sweetness 3 **Peatiness** 6 **Availability** 4

Colour Straw with amber/gold highlights **Nose** Rich, delicately peated, but with an underlying sweetness **Flavour** Slightly sweet with hints of nuttiness and very little of Islay's heavier characteristics **Finish** Spicy, warm, long, with sweet oak, but finally dry **Notes** Invergordon Distillers bottling

Age 21 years   **Strength** 43% abv

Sweetness 3 **Peatiness** 6 **Availability** 4

Colour Light amber with yellow/gold highlights **Nose** Quite light, fresh and rich with a faint touch of ozone **Flavour** Medium-bodied, fresh, almost dry, but with an edge of richness - an intriguing mixture of sweetness & dryness **Finish** Tangy, fresh, rich & clean and gently smoky **Notes** Invergordon Distillers bottling

"Westering Home"...

Bunnahabhain

SINGLE ISLAY MALT SCOTCH WHISKY

PRODUCT OF SCOTLAND
THE BUNNAHABHAIN DISTILLERY COMPANY,
BUNNAHABHAIN, ISLE OF ISLAY, SCOTLAND. BOTTLED IN SCOTLAND.

40% vol.   70 cl

NEAR PORT ASKAIG, ISLAY, ARGYLL   EST. 1880

Became part of Highland Distilleries Ltd in 1887 when amalgamated with William Grant and Company of Glenrothes. Extended from two to four stills in 1963.

LOCATION   Situated towards the north east tip of Islay on the bay from which it takes its name.

NOTES   Bunnahabhain means "mouth of the river". Prior to the building of this distillery which is the island's most northerly, the adjacent area was inhospitable and uninhabited. Now a small hamlet has built up around the distillery.

WATER   River Margadale

Age 12 years   **Strength** 40% abv

Sweetness 3   Peatiness 6   Availability 9

Colour Straw with golden highlights **Nose** Distinctive, quite light and flowery **Flavour** Smoother, softer and less pungent than other Islays **Finish** Smooth, round, lovely and long **Notes** Highland Distilleries bottling

Age 25 years   **Distillation** 1964   **Strength** 46% abv

Sweetness 5   Peatiness 6   Availability 0

Colour Straw with yellow highlights **Nose** Medium-sweet, rich, ripe and fruity with a dark tarriness at the back and a floral note **Flavour** Medium-sweet and rich with oaky tannins, quite smooth and creamy **Finish** Rich, full-bodied and quite long with an earthy smokiness on tail **Notes** Master of Malt bottling

COUNTY ANTRIM, N. IRELAND EST. 1608

Bushmills was granted a licence to distil in 1608, making it by far the earliest legal distillery of all. Operated by Irish Distillers which, in 1988, was the target of a hard fought takover battle between British giant Grand Metropolitan and French rival Pernod-Ricard, which the latter won.

LOCATION   Near the Giant's Causeway on the north coast of Ulster.

NOTES   Bushmills is triple distilled, although it is not alone in this respect. Auchentoshan, Rosebank and Benrinnes also use forms of triple distillation. Bushmills is also available in duty-free markets at 43% vol. Irish whisky is unpeated, unlike most Scotch whisky. Irish Distillers own two distilleries, Bushmills and the modern Midleton complex near Cork. Irish blends such as Jameson, Original Bushmills, Black Bush, Powers, Paddy and Tullamore Dew are produced from whiskies distilled at these two distilleries. In 1920, there were 23 distilleries in Ireland and 134 in Scotland.

WATER   Saint Columb's Rill.

Age 10 years   **Strength** 40% abv

Sweetness 6   Peatiness 0   Availability 9

Colour Deep amber with gold reflections **Nose** Fresh, clean, slightly oily, grassy, gooseberries, very lightly cereal **Flavour** Delicately sweet, quite complex, fresh, round, mellow, slightly spicy **Finish** Long, fine and almost vinuous or grapey **Notes** Irish Distillers bottling

Age 16 years   **Distillation** 1977   **Strength** 58.6% abv

Sweetness 4   Peatiness 0   Availability 2

Colour Quite pale amber with lemon highlights **Nose** Very fresh unpeated cleanness, a gooseberry greenness and almost grassy Sauvignon Blanc-like, rich, quite full-bodied with a hint of sweet menthol **Flavour** Medium-dry, fresh, clean, green and quite full-bodied, rich and round with a ripe apple flavour **Finish** Long, zingy and spicy with tangy green apples **Notes** Wm Cadenhead bottling, bottled on St. Patrick's Day, 17.3.94

I S L A Y
SINGLE MALT *SCOTCH WHISKY*

CAOL ILA

distillery, built in 1846 is situated near *Port Askaig* on the *Isle of Islay.*
Steamers used to call twice a week to collect *whisky* from this remote
site in a cove facing the *Isle of Jura.* Water supplies for mashing
come from *Loch nam Ban* although the sea provides *water* for
condensing. Unusual for an *Islay* this *single MALT SCOTCH
WHISKY* has a *fresh aroma* and a *light* yet *well rounded* flavour.

A G E D **15** Y E A R S

43% vol Distilled & Bottled in *SCOTLAND.* CAOL ILA DISTILLERY Port Askaig, Isle of Islay, *Scotland.* 70 cl

PORT ASKAIG, ISLAY, ARGYLL EST. 1846

Built by Hector Henderson on a what seems like a very isolated spot when you are at the distillery, The distillery was taken over in 1863 by Bulloch Lade & Co., who extended and rebuilt it in 1879. It came under DCL's control in 1927 and management has been by SMD since 1930. It was completely rebuilt, apart from the warehouses between April, 1972 and January, 1974, when it was extended from two stills to six.

LOCATION Another distillery which is literally at the end of the road, in this case, the northern end of the A846.

NOTES Caol Ila's stillhouse has arguably the finest view in the Scotch Whisky industry. It overlooks Caol Ila (the Gaelic name for the Sound of Islay) to the Paps of Jura. Hot water from the condensers is pumped through a sea water condenser, cooled and returned for re-use in the stillhouse condensers. Never one of United Distillers' mainstream malts and thus mainly available as a single from independent bottles, it is nevertheless an important and extensively building block for blended whisky.

WATER Loch Nam Ban (Torrabolls Loch)

Age 15 years **Strength** 43% abv

Sweetness 2 Peatiness 9 Availability 5

Colour Straw/pale amber with lemon-yellow highlights **Nose** Full, quite pungent and peaty, smoky, burnt heather roots with a touch of unripe greenness **Flavour** Big, full, smoky and pungent with an edge of sweetness **Finish** Long, rich and smoky with a touch of bitter chocolate and spice **Notes** United Distillers bottling

Age 12 years **Strength** 63% abv

Sweetness 5 Peatiness 9 Availability 2

Colour Amber-peaty with good gold highlights **Nose** Peaty, burnt heather, quite earthy and medicinal **Flavour** Medium-sweet Rich, smoky, spicy, full with burnt heather predominating **Finish** Smooth, smoky, spicy and very long **Notes** Sherry cask bottling from James MacArthur & Company. The richness derives from the sherry casks used for maturation

Age 13 years **Distillation** 1980 **Strength** 62.6% abv

Sweetness 1 Peatiness 9 Availability 4

Colour Pale amber with pale gold highlights **Nose** Medium to full-bodied and almost dry with an earthy peatiness and a hint of ozone **Flavour** Dry, gently tannic, round and smooth with an earthy smokiness and a slight edge of richness **Finish** Long, smoky and tangy **Notes** Gordon & MacPhail bottling

Age 17 years **Strength** 43% abv

Sweetness 1 Peatiness 9 Availability 2

Colour Pale amber with a tinge of lemony gold **Nose** Full-bodied, rich, round and nutty, medium pungency, soft peatiness and quite dry **Flavour** Dry, smoky, pungent and full-bodied **Finish** Long and smoky **Notes** Master of Malt bottling

Age 19 years **Strength** 43% abv

Sweetness 1 Peatiness 9 Availability 2

Colour Very pale straw with lemon highlights **Nose** Full-bodied, pungent and dry with the aroma of burnt heather roots **Flavour** Full, pungent, smoky and dry with just a hint of sweetness on the edge **Finish** Long, characterful and smoky with oaky tannins **Notes** Blackadder International bottling

Distillation 1972 **Strength** 40% abv

Sweetness 2 Peatiness 9 Availability 4

Colour Palish gold with green tinges **Nose** Peaty, almost medicinal with a strange touch of sweetness **Flavour** Heavy, clean, peaty, burnt heather with more than a tang of ozone **Finish** Long, distinguished, peaty **Notes** Gordon & MacPhail bottling

Distillation 1974 **Strength** 40% abv

Sweetness 2 Peatiness 9 Availability 4

Colour Bright gold/amber with gold highlights **Nose** Peaty, malty, earthy, more than a hint of the sea, but with a rich, almost perfumed fruitiness to it **Flavour** Dry, round, quite full-bodied and peaty **Finish** Smoky and dry, but rich **Notes** Gordon & MacPhail bottling

CONNOISSEURS CHOICE

Connoisseurs Choice, a range of single malts from various districts of Scotland.

The distilleries situated in the area of the valley of the River Spey produce some of the finest malt whiskies.

SINGLE SPEYSIDE
MALT SCOTCH WHISKY
DISTILLED AT
CAPERDONICH
DISTILLERY
Proprietors: The Glenlivet & Glen Grant Distilleries Ltd

DISTILLED 1968 DISTILLED

SPECIALLY SELECTED, PRODUCED AND BOTTLED BY
70cl   GORDON & MACPHAIL   40%vol
ELGIN - SCOTLAND
PRODUCT OF SCOTLAND

ROTHES, MORAY EST. 1897

Following the industry slump at the end of the 19th century, Caperdonich was closed in 1902 and did not produce again until 1965 following rebuilding. Extended from two to four stills in 1967. Now owned by the Seagram Company of Canada.

LOCATION Situated at one end of the small town of Rothes, across the road from its sister distillery, Glen Grant.

NOTES The distillery was built to supplement the output of Glen Grant and was known as Glen Grant No. 2. The whisky, using the same water, is lighter and fruitier than Glen Grant. The two distilleries were originally joined by a pipe which carried spirit from Caperdonich to Glen Grant across the town's main street. Rothes supports five distilleries, with Caperdonich being the last to be built. Glen Grant, established in 1840, was the first.

WATER The Caperdonich Well, adjacent to the Glen Grant Burn.

Distillation 1979 **Strength** 40% abv

Sweetness 8 Peatiness 3 Availability 4

Colour Pale straw, almost yellow **Nose** Sweet, ripe, grapey with a hint of cloves and apples **Flavour** Sweet and spirity with a slight flavour of cloves **Finish** Quite good for its youth, but shortish **Notes** Gordon & MacPhail bottling

Age 16 years **Distillation** 1972 **Strength** 40% abv

Sweetness 7 Peatiness 3 Availability 2

Colour Honey-amber with old gold highlights **Nose** Full, fruity, almost raisin-like, nutty and delicately peated with hints of demerara sugar **Flavour** Quite full and oaky with good peatiness, smooth and medium-sweet **Finish** Long, creamy and spicy with oaky tannins **Notes** Master of Malt bottling

KNOCKANDO, MORAY EST. 1824

Built on a farm which was known as Cardow, the distillery was known, until recently, by that name also. The original licensee was John Cumming, who had previously gained a string of convictions as a whisky smuggler. Acquired by John Walker & Son in 1893, becoming part of DCL in 1925. Managed by SMD since 1930. Rebuilt in 1960 and extended from four to six stills. Now part of United Distillers plc.

LOCATION Situated high up above the River Spey on its north bank, on the B9102 between Knockando and Craigellachie.

NOTES A "flagship" of the United Distillers Group, the malt has long played an important role in the success of Johnnie Walker's famous Red and Black Label brands. Cardhu means "black rock". A large reception centre was opened in 1988. John Cumming took a lease on Cardow farm in 1811 and made whisky from the very outset. His wife, Helen, played no small part in the business and would always manage to disguise mashing and fermenting as bread-making when Excise officer came calling. She lived to be 85 and villagers still tell colourful stories of her passed on by their grandparents.

WATER Springs on the Mannoch Hill or the Lyne Burn

Age 12 years **Strength** 40% abv

Sweetness 8 Peatiness 7 Availability 9

Colour Pale mid-amber with a definite green tinge **Nose** Quite full-bodied, rich, medium-sweet and smoky with a green apple character **Flavour** Round and mellow, sweet with a delicate peatiness **Finish** Long, peaty and sweet **Notes** United Distillers bottling

GLASGOW ROAD, WISHAW, LANARKSHIRE EST. 1825

Clydesdale distillery was said to have been built by Lord Belhaven and his first tenant was Patrick Chalmers. Lord Belhaven pulled out in 1848. Clydesdale Distillery Co. Ltd. was founded in 1894 and this was one of the founding members of Scottish Malt Distillers Ltd in 1914.

LOCATION On the south east side of Glasgow Road, Wishaw, where the local Glasgow - Lanark railway crosses the road.

NOTES Production ceased in 1919, although the premises were used by DCL as bonded warehouses until 1988 when the buildings were demolished.

WATER A burn rising in the Cambusnethan peat moss.

Age Unknown - circa1900 **Strength** 45% abv

Sweetness 7 Peatiness 3 Availability 0

Colour Quite dark amber with bronze highlights **Nose** Quite full-bodied, rich and sherried, dark nuttiness (brazil nuts), quite soft vanilla with a dryness at the back **Flavour** Round, quite full, sherried, rich, soft, medium-sweet, nuttiness and a greenness **Finish** Long, rich, a touch of oakiness, creamy and nutty with a nice spicy tang. **Notes** One of two bottles taken from the distillery in 1917 and kept by the Campbell family of Wishaw for use at funerals. This sample was also tasted by one of Scotland's master blenders who was of the opinion that it had been aged in a liqueur cask, a common practice at the turn of the century

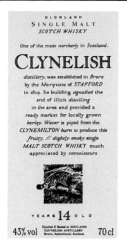

HIGHLAND
SINGLE MALT
SCOTCH WHISKY

One of the most *northerly* in *Scotland,*

CLYNELISH

distillery, was established in *Brora*
by the *Marquess* of *STAFFORD*
in 1819. Its building *signalled* the
end of illicit *distilling*
in the area and provided a
ready market for locally grown
barley. Water is piped from the
CLYNEMILTON burn to produce this
fruity, & slightly smoky single
MALT SCOTCH WHISKY much
appreciated by *connoisseurs*

YEARS **14** OLD

43% vol   Distilled & Bottled in *SCOTLAND,*
CLYNELISH DISTILLERY
Brora, Sutherland, Scotland.   70 cl

BRORA, SUTHERLAND EST. 1967

The original Clynelish distillery was the old, now closed, Brora distillery next door. It was founded by the Marquis of Stafford, later the first Duke of Sutherland. It was intended as a ready market for barley produced by crofters who had been evicted from inland farms and moved down to the coastal plain. Established as a brewery in 1817, it was turned into a distillery two years later. Operated by SMD and now part of United Distillers. Six stills.

LOCATION Just off the A9 north of Brora on the north side of the extensive plain which forms the mouth of Strath Brora.

NOTES Brora was known as Clynelish until 1969. After the modern distillery had been built in 1967-8, the old "Clynelish" re-opened in April 1975, housed in the rebuilt mash house. It subsequently ceased distillation in May 1983. There is no little confusion as Brora is often called "Clynelish". The whisky from the old distillery was only bottled as Clynelish prior to 1967. Between 1967 and 1983, production from the old distillery was stencilled as "Brora" on cask heads, although it was only sold as "Clynelish" for fillings.

WATER The Clynemilton Burn.

Age 15 years   **Strength** 43% abv

Sweetness 6   Peatiness 7   Availability 4

Colour Straw/amber with gold highlights **Nose** Quite full and ripe with rich oaky vanilla, creamy lanolin oiliness and a slight nuttiness **Flavour** Full, smooth, round and medium-sweet with layers of oak at the back **Finish** Full, round, rich, smooth and almost luscious **Notes** United Distillers bottling

Age 12 years   **Strength** 40% abv

Sweetness 4   Peatiness 6   Availability 0

Colour Pale straw with lovely golden edges **Nose** Dry, but with a sweet edge, slightly fruity and softly peated **Flavour** Full-bodied, slightly creamy and spicy **Finish** Long, dry, smoky **Notes** DCL bottling (pre-United Distillers)

Age 12 years   **Strength** 40% abv

Sweetness 6   Peatiness 5   Availability 4

Colour Mid-amber with yellow/gold highlights **Nose** Clean with good body and a richness at the back, gently peated and medium-dry with a light apple touch **Flavour** Good body, medium-sweet, smooth, creamy and gently peated with an apple character at the back **Finish** Quite long with good sweetness and a creamy peatiness **Notes** Gordon & MacPhail bottling

Age 14 years   **Strength** 43% abv

Sweetness 4   Peatiness 6   Availability 6

Colour Pale amber with good green/gold highlights **Nose** Rich, medium-dry, a citrus fruitiness, quite full and round with good smokiness at the back **Flavour** Smoky with a soft sweetness, quite full-bodied and almost luscious - very complex **Finish** Long and elegant with a touch of bitter chocolate **Notes** United Distillers bottling

Age 23 years   **Distillation** 1965   **Strength** 57.1% abv

Sweetness 4   Peatiness 6   Availability 4

Colour Pale amber with a touch of green, good yellow highlights **Nose** Full, fruity, herby, medium-dry with a touch of woodiness and high spiritiness **Flavour** Dry, but with a touch of sweetness, round, full, a slight unctuous oiliness and good fruit character **Finish** Long, nutty, spicy and very full - something of a blockbuster **Notes** Wm. Cadenhead bottling

Age 28 years   **Distillation** 1965   **Strength** 50.7% abv

Sweetness 3   Peatiness 6   Availability 2

Colour Mid-amber with yellow/gold highlights **Nose** Quite full-bodied, fresh, round and medium-sweet with an unctuous sweet-oak character **Flavour** Dry, but with a nice edge of sweetness, rich, round, good dry oaky tannins, nutty and softly unctuous **Finish** Long, elegant and gently smoky with just a touch of sweetness at the front **Notes** Signatory bottling in July, 1993 - butt no 666 filled on 19.2.65

CONNOISSEURS CHOICE

Connoisseurs Choice, a range of single malts from various districts of Scotland.

The distilleries situated in the area of the valley of the River Spey produce some of the finest malt whiskies.

SINGLE SPEYSIDE
MALT SCOTCH WHISKY
DISTILLED AT
COLEBURN
DISTILLERY
Proprietors: J. & G. Stewart Ltd

DISTILLED 1972 DISTILLED

SPECIALLY SELECTED, PRODUCED AND BOTTLED BY
70cl   GORDON & MACPHAIL   40%vol
ELGIN · SCOTLAND
PRODUCT OF SCOTLAND

LONGMORN, ELGIN, MORAY EST. 1897

Built by John Robertson & Son. Became part of DCL in 1925 and managed by SMD from 1930. Two stills.

LOCATION Situated to the east of the A491, four miles south of Elgin. It is "faced on one side by a plantation of Scotch firs and birches, and swept by the cool mountain breezes of Brown Muir" according to Robertson's original announcement in 1896.

NOTES The distillery was built from warm-coloured Moray sandstone and roofed with blue Welsh slates. A problem which faced the architect was the provision of a lavatory to the Excise Office - it took 18 months to resolve! The Excise Officer's house took even longer to be completed. Closed in 1985 and unlikely to re-open.

WATER A spring in the Glen of Rothes.

Distillation 1965 **Strength** 40% abv

Sweetness 8 Peatiness 5 Availability 4

Colour Warm peaty/gold with amber highlights **Nose** Sweet, nutty-almondy oily rich **Flavour** Medium-sweet, delicate, slightly spirity, rich **Finish** Smooth and creamy with good length **Notes** Gordon & MacPhail bottling

Distillation 1972 **Strength** 40% abv

Sweetness 7 Peatiness 6 Availability 4

Colour Straw/amber with yellow/gold highlights **Nose** Medium-bodied, quite heavily peated, fresh and nutty with a touch of greenness **Flavour** Medium-dry, smoky, quite heavy with a richness and an unripe green character **Finish** Smoky with richness at the back and light touches of oaky tannins **Notes** Gordon & MacPhail bottling

CONNOISSEURS CHOICE

Connoisseurs Choice, a range of single malts from various distilries of Scotland.

The distilleries situated in the area of the valley of the River Spey produce some of the finest malt whiskies.

GRAMPIANS

SINGLE SPEYSIDE MALT SCOTCH WHISKY
DISTILLED AT
CONVALMORE
DISTILLERY
Proprietors: W.P. Lowrie & Co. Ltd

DISTILLED **1969** DISTILLED
SPECIALLY SELECTED, PRODUCED AND BOTTLED BY
70cl   **GORDON & MACPHAIL**   40%vol
ELGIN · SCOTLAND
PRODUCT OF SCOTLAND

DUFFTOWN, BANFFSHIRE EST. 1894

Founded 2nd June, 1893 by the Convalmore-Glenlivet Distillery Co. Ltd. Purchased from the liquidator in March 1905 for £6,000 plus stock at 2s 6d (12.5p) per gallon by W P Lowrie & Co Ltd, who were controlled by James Buchanan & Co Ltd from 1906. Fire broke out on 29th October, 1909 and the malt barn, kiln, malt mill, mash house and tun room were destroyed. After the distillery had been rebuilt, it was used for experiments into the continuous distillation of malt. W.P. Lowrie & Co. joined DCL in 1925 and production was carried out by SMD from 1930. Doubled from two to four stills in 1964. Closed in 1985 and the site sold to Wm Grant & Sons in 1990.

LOCATION   Just north of Dufftown on the A941.

NOTES   The distillery accommodated a signals detachment of the 51st (Highland) Division from 1940 to 1942 and then gunners of the 52nd (Lowland) Division until 1944.

WATER   Springs in the Conval Hills

Distillation 1969   **Strength** 40% abv

Sweetness 8   Peatiness 5   Availability 4

Colour Very pale straw, almost watery **Nose** Sweet, with the smell of a field of grain after rain in summer **Flavour** Medium-sweet, nutty, spicy **Finish** Spicy and of reasonable length **Notes** Gordon & MacPhail bottling

Age 31 years   **Distillation** 1962   **Strength** 48.9% abv

Sweetness 6   Peatiness 5   Availability 2

Colour Mid-amber with old gold highlights **Nose** Gently smoky with a slight burnt oak character **Flavour** Quite big-bodied, medium-sweet with an appley malic character **Finish** Quite fresh with a touch of liquorice and good length with a delicate smoky edge **Notes** Wm Cadenhead bottling

BALLINDALLOCH, BANFFSHIRE EST. 1869

Built by John Smith, the lessee of Glenfarclas from 1865 to 1869, manager of Macallan in the early 1850s, Glenlivet from 1858 and Clydesdale in the early 1860s. The distillery never closed for even a fortnight in any year up until the summer of 1901, when reconstruction began. The Cragganmore Distillery Company did not become a wholly-owned subsidiary of DCL until 1965-66. Extended from two to four stills in 1964.

LOCATION Cragganmore occupies a site north of the A95 between Grantown-on-Spey and Ballindalloch, close to the River Spey. It was the first Speyside distillery to be sited to take advantage of railway transport, the former railway line (now the *Speyside Way* footpath) passing the distillery's doors.

NOTES Originally only available at the distillery or through independent bottlers, the make is now widely available as one of United Distillers' Classic Malts portfolio. An interesting feature is that the spirit stills have flat topped, T-shaped lyne pipes instead of the usual swan necks. The stills have cooling worms rather than condensers.

WATER The Craggan Burn - a spring on the Craggan More Hill.

Age 12 years **Strength** 40% abv
Sweetness 6 Peatiness 7 Availability 9

Colour Amber with pale gold highlights **Nose** Clean with quite good body, medium-dry, smokily peaty, slightly creamy with a light green touch **Flavour** Quite full-bodied, round with a hint of spice, smoky and creamy **Finish** Quite long, clean and fresh **Notes** United Distillers bottling, one of the *Classic Malts*

Age 12 years   **Strength** 45.7% abv

Sweetness 7   Peatiness 7   Availability 0

Straw/gold **Nose** Quite dry for a Speyside, nonetheless a richness is present - also quite smoky **Flavour** Round, malty, medium-sweet and classy **Finish** Long and distinguished, slightly smoky **Notes** DCL bottling (pre-Guinness) bottling

Distillation 1976   **Strength** 40% abv

Sweetness 4   Peatiness 7   Availability 4

Colour Quite full amber with bronze highlights **Nose** Quite full and sweet with an oily nutty unctuousness and a slight green edge to the peatiness **Flavour** Big-bodied, medium-dry with firm tannins, a dry smokiness and a light touch of richness **Finish** Long and smooth with a touch of perfume to the smokiness **Notes** Gordon & MacPhail bottling

Age 17 years **Distillation** 1976 **Strength** 53.8% abv

Sweetness 6   Peatiness 7   Availability 2

Colour Pale to mid-amber with yellow/gold highlights **Nose** Quite full-bodied and medium-sweet with a dark nutty peatiness **Flavour** Medium-dry, round and quite smooth with good body, a rich oakiness and a firm smokiness **Finish** Long, clean and gently smoky with richness on the tail **Notes** Gordon & MacPhail bottling; cask nos. 3588-91 distilled 21st July, 1976

CRAIGELLACHIE, BANFFSHIRE EST. 1891

Built by the Craigellachie Distillery Co. Ltd., a partnership formed by a group of blenders and whisky merchants. Rebuilt in 1964-65 and doubled to four stills. Now a part of United Distillers plc.

LOCATION The distillery stands on the spur of a hill, overlooking the village of Craigellachie, the precipitous Rock of Craigellachie, the River Spey and Thomas Telford's elegant single-span iron bridge of 1815.

NOTES Sir Peter Mackie, founder of White Horse, was one of its original owners. The workers in 1923 lived in tied cottages and tended their gardens carefully. The owners of the best-kept gardens received prizes annually from the directors.

WATER A spring on Little Conval hill (552 metres)

Age 14 years **Strength** 43% abv

Sweetness 8 Peatiness 3 Availability 6

Colour Straw with lemon highlights **Nose** Fresh and cerealy with a touch of greenness, a sherbert character, medium-sweet with good body **Flavour** Fresh, round, smooth, sweet and cerealy **Finish** Long and sweet with a touch of spice and a hint of smokiness at the back **Notes** United Distillers bottling

Age 15 years **Strength** 46% abv

Sweetness 7 Peatiness 6 Availability 4

Colour Very pale, almost crystal clear, watery coloured **Nose** Pungent, peaty, burnt heather with a slight orange/citrus tang to the edge **Flavour** Heavy, pungent, peaty , but with an edge of sweetness **Finish** Good, spicy and long - reminiscent of Islay **Notes** Wm Cadenhead bottling

SPEYSIDE

SINGLE MALT *SCOTCH WHISKY*

DAILUAINE

is the GAELIC for "the green vale". The *distillery*, established
in 1852, lies in a hollow by the *CARRON BURN* in *BANFFSHIRE*. This
single Malt Scotch Whisky has a *full bodied fruity* nose and a *smoky* finish.
For more than a *hundred years* all *distillery supplies* were despatched by
rail. The *steam locomotive* "DAILUAINE NO. 1" was in use
from 1939~1967 and is *preserved* on the *STRATHSPEY RAILWAY*.

AGED **16** YEARS

43% vol   Distilled & Bottled in *SCOTLAND*. DAILUAINE DISTILLERY, Carron, Aberlour, Banffshire, Scotland.   70 cl

CARRON, BY ABERLOUR, BANFFSHIRE EST. 1852

Founded by William Mackenzie, a farmer at Carron and Rinnachat, the business was amalgamated with Talisker on Skye and nearby Imperial in 1898 to form Dailuaine-Talisker Distilleries Ltd. Became part of DCL in 1925 and run by SMD since 1930. Rebuilt after a fire in 1917 and again in 1959-60 when it was increased from four to six stills. Now part of United Distillers plc and licensed to SMGD. The old floor maltings were converted to a Saladin Box system, the use of which was discontinued in 1983.

LOCATION Situated in a natural hollow by the Carron Burn with river meadows all round it on an unclassified road between the A95 and B9102 at Archiestown. It is to the south of the River Spey.

NOTES The name "Dailuaine" comes from the Gaelic words "Dail Uaine", meaning "green valley", an apt description of its location. Although electricity reached the Carron area in 1938, it was not introduced to Dailuaine until 1950. For some years from the late 1880s the distillery operated a rail link to the Spey Valley line at Carron Station, a few hundred yards away. The steam locomotive which once worked the line is preserved on the Strathspey Railway which runs from Aviemore to Boat of Garten. The Spey Valley line itself fell to the Beeching axe in 1967, but much of it is now given over to walkers as *The Speyside Way*. Like its near neighbour, Cardhu, Dailuaine is one of the principle malts used in the Johnnie Walker blends.

WATER The Bailliemullich Burn.

Age 16 years **Strength** 43% abv

Sweetness 5 Peatiness 7 Availability 6

Colour Deep, full amber with bronze highlights **Nose** Quite full and sherried, a nutty, rubbery and damp oak character, medium-dry, slightly spirity **Flavour** Full-bodied, nutty, rubbery, medium-dry with a touch of tannin and a hint of richness **Finish** Long, dark and quite smooth with a touch of peat **Notes** United Distillers bottling

Age 23 years **Strength** 46% abv

Sweetness 4 Peatiness 6 Availability 4

Colour Very pale straw with a slight green tinge **Nose** Slightly medicinal, sweet with a gentle smokiness **Flavour** Very sweet, rich, peppery , fruity and spicy **Finish** Fine, smooth and with a nice sweetness **Notes** Wm Cadenhead bottling

Distillation 1971 **Strength** 40% abv

Sweetness 3 Peatiness 6 Availability 4

Colour Straw/amber with lemon/gold highlights **Nose** Quite dry with a rich fruitiness at the back **Flavour** Not quite dry, softly smoky and quite big-bodied with an oaky fullness **Finish** Smooth with good smoky length, but no real pungency **Notes** Gordon & MacPhail bottling

DISTILLERY SELECTION

Dallas Dhu

20 years old
SINGLE MALT SCOTCH WHISKY

Dallas Dhu near Forres produced its first whisky in 1899 and its last in 1983. With the distillery now home to a fascinating museum of malt whisky production, Dallas Dhu is becoming increasingly rare.

For a free malt whisky information pack write to:
Blackadder International
Larkhall ML9 1DA
Scotland

70cl   43%vol

Produce of Scotland

FORRES, MORAY EST. 1899

Originally to be called Dallasmore in 1898, the plans for the new distillery, designed by local Elgin architect Charles Doig, caused much correspondence in the local paper, the *Forres Gazette*. This included some verses from a local councillor. The fillings were eventually advertised as Dallas Dhu in November 1899, when it came on stream. One of several distilleries on the estate of the local laird, Alexander Edward, who in 1900 sold the distillery to the proprietors of Roderick Dhu, a whisky brand popular at the turn of the last century. The stillhouse was burned down on 9 April, 1939 and it did not re-open until 1947. It closed in 1983 and the licence was cancelled in 1992.

LOCATION   Built in a hollow to the east of an unclassified road which forks south of the A940 on the southern outskirts of Forres.

NOTES   The distillery buildings were handed over by Scottish Malt Distillers to the Historic Buildings and Monuments department of the Scottish Office who now run them as a model example of a distillery on the tourist trail. It is still possible to obtain special bottlings from old casks, although supplies of the whisky are now dwindling all the time. Dallas Dhu is a perfectly preserved example of what a small Highland distillery would have been like at the turn of the century. Had its water supply been more plentiful, it is most likely that the distillery would have been one of the ones chosen for expansion in recent years. As it is, its single pair of old stills has been preserved, as have all the old plant and machinery and the fine old distillery buildings.

WATER   The Altyre Burn (known locally as the Scourie Burn).

Age 20 years **Strength** 43% abv

Sweetness 6 Peatiness 4 Availability 2

Colour Medium-pale straw with yellowy-gold highlights **Nose** Quite full-bodied, green, unripe and a character of slightly musty apples **Flavour** Medium-bodied with an oily texture (from the oak), ripe and rich wood **Finish** Slightly spicy, quite long and chewy **Notes** Blackadder International bottling

Age 18 years **Distillation** 1974 **Strength** 60.8% abv

Sweetness 4 Peatiness 3 Availability 2

Colour Mid-amber with gold highlights **Nose** Medium-bodied, nutty and malty, medium-dry with an edge of richness and a touch of lanolin **Flavour** Medium-dry, gently peaty, oaky tannins and a woody character **Finish** Quite dry, almost astringently tannic and spirity **Notes** Signatory bottling

Age 24 years **Strength** 60.6% abv

Sweetness 4 Peatiness 4 Availability 2

Colour Pale amber with pale gold/lemon highlights **Nose** Medium-dry, slightly peppery with oaky vanilla **Flavour** Oaky, quite full, round and medium-dry **Finish** Chewy, spirity and gently oaky **Notes** United Distillers bottling

Distillation 1974 **Strength** 40% abv

Sweetness 6 Peatiness 4 Availability 4

Colour Straw/amber with yellow/gold highlights **Nose** Quite full, gently peated, oaky vanilla and a slight greenness **Flavour** Round, smooth, medium-sweet with a touch of nuttiness **Finish** Almost dry, oaky **Notes** Gordon & MacPhail bottling

Distillation 1971 **Strength** 40% abv

Sweetness 3 Peatiness 6 Availability 4

Colour Amber with old gold highlights **Nose** Quite rich, medium-sweet and appley with a smokiness at back **Flavour** Medium-dry, rich, quite fresh, clean and peaty with an appley richness **Finish** Clean, gently smoky, of medium length with a richness on the tail **Notes** Gordon & MacPhail bottling

Distillation 1969 **Strength** 40% abv

Sweetness 7 Peatiness 4 Availability 4

Colour Peaty/gold with good yellow highlights **Nose** Sweet, oaky and malty **Flavour** Medium-sweet, peppery with good body **Finish** Woody and dry with a good vanilla note on the finish **Notes** Gordon & MacPhail bottling

THE
DALMORE™

SINGLE
HIGHLAND MALT
SCOTCH WHISKY

AGED 12 YEARS

70cl e WHYTE & MACKAY DISTILLERS GLASGOW G2 5RG SCOTLAND 40%vol

ALNESS, ROSS-SHIRE EST. 1839

Alexander Matheson was a partner in the Hong Kong trading firm Jardine Matheson & Co, traders in everything from tea to opium and, of course, whisky. In 1839, the very year of the first Opium War between China and Britain, Matheson purchased Ardross farm, on the shore of Cromarty Firth and opened a distillery. Whisky production at Dalmore was taken over by the Mackenzie family, who were able to buy the distillery and land as a result of the 1886 Crofters Act. Much of the whisky went to supply long standing customers and friends, James Whyte and Charles Mackay, who owned the popular blend of Whyte & Mackay. The two businesses eventually merged in 1960. Whyte & Mackay is now owned by American Brands, who also own Jim Beam bourbon.

LOCATION Situated just off the A9, the distillery is in a beautiful position overlooking the Cromarty Firth to the Black Isle.

NOTES The distillery was well sited by its founders in the middle of a fine barley growing district. Its handsome offices are panelled with carved oak taken from a nearby shooting lodge. During the First World War, it was used by the U.S. Navy as a base for manufacturing deep sea mines and was burned down as the result of a fire. Production resumed again in 1922. Doubled from four to eight stills in 1966. Two of the stills in use today date from 1874.

WATER The River Alness which flows from Loch Morie.

Age 12 years   **Strength** 40% abv

Sweetness 6   Peatiness 6   Availability 8

Colour Full deep amber with good gold highlights **Nose** Slightly sweet, lightly oaky, with a fruitiness that is almost grape-like **Flavour** Full, medium-sweet, quite round and spicy with a slight smokiness **Finish** Lightly malty, smooth and almost dry - quite distinguished **Notes** Whyte & Mackay bottling

Age 30 years   **Distillation** 1963   **Strength** 54.5% abv

Sweetness 6   Peatiness 5   Availability 2

Colour Straw with pale yellow highlights **Nose** Quite full-bodied, round, medium-sweet and smooth with a rich liquorice/aniseed aroma **Flavour** Big-bodied, medium-sweet and round with a tangy touch of spice, pleasantly chewy tannins and gently peated **Finish** Long and gently chewy with a tang of aniseed **Notes** Wm Cadenhead bottling

Age 52 years   **Distillation** 1939   **Strength** 51.5% abv

Sweetness 6   Peatiness 3   Availability 0

Colour Full, rich amber **Nose** Enormous! Soft, gentle and smooth, a dark nuttiness, a slight delicate smokiness, very complex and with a liquorice character at the back **Flavour** Very full, still quite a fresh, green flavour, reminiscent of hedgerows **Finish** Long, powerful and very distinguished **Notes** A cask sample supplied by Whyte & Mackay for a tasting at Christie's in Glasgow

Distillation 1978   **Strength** 60.5% abv

Sweetness 6   Peatiness 5   Availability 2

Colour Quite pale straw with pale lemon highlights **Nose** Medium-bodied, fresh, clean and slightly green with an aroma of fennel, medium-dry with a slight mashy/malty character **Flavour** Medium-bodied, fresh, medium-dry with a ripe ripe greenness, slightly chewy with a delicate peatiness **Finish** Long, fresh and clean with a slight hedgerow character **Notes** Scotch Malt Whisky Society bottling: Cask no.13.14; bottled January, 1994

DALWHINNIE, INVERNESS-SHIRE EST. 1897

Originally called Strathspey distillery, the company went into voluntary liquidation the year after it opened. Its name was changed c.1900, when it was purchased from the liquidator by the Dalwhinnie Distillery Co. The distillery was then sold at auction for £1,250 in 1905 to Cook & Bernheimer of New York and Baltimore, who, in turn, sold it to Macdonald Greenlees of Edinburgh in 1919. Macdonald Greenlees joined DCL in 1926 and SMD took over its management in 1930. Badly damaged by fire in 1934, re-opening in 1938. The distillery is now owned by United Distillers and licensed to James Buchanan & Co Ltd. Two stills.

LOCATION The distillery is situated next to the main railway line at the junction of the A9 (Inverness to the north, Perth to the south) and the A889 to Fort William.

NOTES "Dalwhinnie" derives from the Gaelic word meaning "meeting place". At 326 m (1,073 ft) above sea-level, Dalwhinnie is Scotland's highest distillery. The distillery was located to take advantage of plentiful supplies of local peat, access to the railway line and its close access to the abundant supply of pure Highland water from the Lochan an Doire-uaine. The distillery is Station 0582 of the Meteorological Office and it is the manager's duty to take daily readings of maximum and minimum temperatures, the number of hours of sunshine, wind speed and snow depth. Now readily available as one of United Distillers' Classic Malts, Dalwhinnie was previously better known for its role as one of the main building blocks of the Buchanan blends.

WATER Lochan an Doire-Uaine.

Age 15 years **Strength** 43% abv

Sweetness 7	Peatiness 5	Availability 8

Colour Straw/golden, honey-like **Nose** Quite aromatic, with a light peatiness and medium-sweet **Flavour** Round and sweet with a honey-like richness **Finish** Good, slightly sweet richness and excellent length **Notes** United Distillers bottling

Age 8 years **Strength** 40% abv

Sweetness 6	Peatiness 7	Availability 0

Colour Light straw with golden highlights **Nose** Quite light, spirity and aromatic **Flavour** Round, but light, medium-sweet **Finish** Quite good, if a little spirity **Notes** DCL bottling (pre-Guinness)

Distillation 1970 **Strength** 40% abv

Sweetness 5	Peatiness 6	Availability 4

Colour Quite full amber with old gold highlights **Nose** Medium to full-bodied with a freshly hung wallpaper character, medium-dry and quite darkly smoky with a light nuttiness **Flavour** Big-bodied with a dark nuttiness, quite full tannins and medium-dry **Finish** Long, quite spicy and chewy with good richness **Notes** Gordon & MacPhail bottling

Age 27 years **Distillation** 1966 **Strength** 45.5% abv

Sweetness 5	Peatiness 4	Availability 1

Colour Pale amber with pale gold highlights **Nose** Quite full-bodied, medium-sweet and oaky with an aroma of wet cement, a slight burnt wood character and a touch of mint **Flavour** Quite good body, fairly dominant wood, slightly chewy and medium-dry **Finish** Of reasonable length, with a burnt wood tang and a chewy tail **Notes** Wm Cadenhead bottling, bottled October, 1993

DEANSTON
SINGLE MALT
WHISKY

DISTILLED AND MATURED AT THE
DEANSTON DISTILLERY, ORIGINALLY
BUILT AS A TEXTILE MILL IN 1785 ON
THE PURE SOFT WATERS OF THE
HISTORIC RIVER TEITH, NEAR
CASTLE DOUNE, PERTHSHIRE.
A FINE MELLOW SINGLE HIGHLAND
MALT, WITH A FRAGRANT FRUITY
FLAVOUR, AND A LINGERING SWEET
AFTER TASTE.

OVER **12** YEARS

PRODUCT OF SCOTLAND

DOUNE, PERTHSHIRE EST. 1965

Founded by the Deanston Distillery Co. Ltd. and sold to Invergordon Distillers in 1972. Silent from 1982 until sold to Burn Stewart Distillers in 1990. Four stills.

LOCATION Situated on the south bank of the River Teith within two miles of the centre of Doune village.

NOTES Burn Stewart has decided only to use unpeated barley in the production of Deanston, the company believing there to be sufficient peat for their purposes in the waters of the River Teith. Part of the buildings originally housed a textile mill. This was established in 1748 and was designed by Richard Arkwright of Spinning Jenny fame. Like the distillery, the mill also required good water supplies. The River Teith, as well as supplying all the process water, drives generators which provide all the distillery's electrical power needs - and also export power to the National Grid. The distillery complex includes attractive historic warehouses, many underground, in which are housed 45,000 casks of maturing whisky. The film *Monty Python and the Holy Grail* was shot at nearby Doune Castle.

WATER The River Teith.

Age 12 years **Strength** 40% abv

Sweetness 7 **Peatiness** 2 **Availability** 7

Colour Pale straw with lemon highlights **Nose** Medium weight and cerealy with an aroma of chocolate, medium-sweet and fragrant with a mashy character **Flavour** Medium-sweet, good weight, cerealy and smooth **Finish** Quite long and fresh with a touch of honey on the tail **Notes** Burn Stewart bottling

Age 17 years **Strength** 40% abv

Sweetness 4 Peatiness 6 Availability 6

Colour Amber with old gold highlights **Nose** Round, smooth and medium-bodied with good richness, quite lightly peated, nutty and medium-dry **Flavour** Medium-dry, quite full-bodied, round, nutty with a dark smokiness, rich and tangy **Finish** Long, nutty and tangy **Notes** Burn Stewart bottling

Age 25 years **Strength** 40% abv

Sweetness 4 Peatiness 2 Availability 2

Colour Mid-amber with yellow/gold highlights **Nose** Medium-sweet and rich with a soft buttery vanilla character and very lightly peated **Flavour** Medium-dry, round, quite full-bodied and creamy with gentle tannins **Finish** Long, gentle and buttery **Notes** Burn Stewart bottling

Distillation 1977 **Strength** 55.8% abv

Sweetness 4 Peatiness 3 Availability 2

Colour Straw/very pale amber with lemon/yellow highlights **Nose** Fresh and medium-sweet, round with a slight cereal note, lightly peated **Flavour** Medium-dry and round with a gentle smokiness and light oaky tannins **Finish** Fresh, quite zingy, lightly smoky and a hint of coffee **Notes** Wm Cadenhead bottling

Age 8 years **Strength** 40% abv

Sweetness 7 Peatiness 2 Availability 0

Colour Pale straw, pale yellow highlights **Nose** Sweet, with an oily, almost fatty, texture **Flavour** An almost honeyed fruity sweetness - unusual for a distillery so far south **Finish** Quite good, smooth and round **Notes** Invergordon bottling

KINGUSSIE, INVERNESS-SHIRE EST. 1990

Drumguish comes from the new Speyside distillery, built opposite the former distillery of the same name (1895-1911) on land purchased by owners, the Christie family, in 1956 together with stretches of the Spey and Tromie rivers. In the previous year they had formed the Speyside Distillery & Bonding Co. The driving force behind the company, whisky blender George Christie, gradually built the new distillery, starting in 1962 and finally completing the work in 1987. The first spirit ran from the distillery's two stills on 12 December, 1990.

LOCATION At the confluence of the Tromie and Spey rivers.

NOTES The distillery is said to have a maximum capacity of 200,000 gallons a year, although it is planned to just produce 50,000 to 100,000 a year, all of which is intended for the company's own use. The company produces a blended whisky called *Speyside* and a vatted malt, *Glentromie.* The first of the new single malt takes its name, *Drumguish*, from that of its precise location. George Christie lives in the house previously owned by G. McPherson Grant who, as well as building the original Speyside distillery, also built Tomatin and Newtonmore. Only Tomatin of this original trio still exists.

WATER A spring on the neighbouring Gaick Deer estate.

Age 3 years **Strength** 40% abv

Sweetness 5 Peatiness 7 Availability 3

Colour Pale-mid amber with old gold highlights **Nose** Young, quite mashy, soft and medium-sweet, quite fresh with a slight menthol character, gently peated with a slight earthy touch **Flavour** Medium-dry, minty with good body and a firm, but gentle dark earthy smokiness **Finish** Of good length, almost dry with a good peaty character **Notes** Drumguish Distillery Company bottling

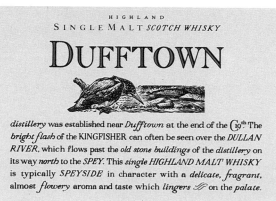

HIGHLAND
SINGLE MALT *SCOTCH WHISKY*

DUFFTOWN

distillery was established near *Dufftown* at the end of the (19th The *bright flash* of the KINGFISHER can often be seen over the *DULLAN RIVER*, which flows past the *old stone buildings* of the *distillery* on its way *north* to the *SPEY*. This *single HIGHLAND MALT WHISKY* is typically *SPEYSIDE* in character with a *delicate, fragrant*, almost *flowery* aroma and taste which *lingers* on the *palate*.

AGED **15** YEARS

43% vol   Distilled & Bottled in *SCOTLAND*. DUFFTOWN DISTILLERY, Dufftown, Keith, Banffshire, *Scotland*   70 cl

DUFFTOWN, BANFFSHIRE EST. 1887

Converted from a former meal mill in 1896 by the Dufftown-Glenlivet Distillery Co. and acquired in 1897 by P. MacKenzie & Co., also owners of Blair Athol distillery, Pitlochry. Purchased by Perth blenders Arthur Bell & Sons in 1933. Originally with two stills extended to four in 1974 and six in 1979. Owned by United Distillers since 1985 and licensed to UMGD from 1992.

LOCATION Situated in the Dullan Glen on the outskirts of Dufftown near the 6th century Mortlach parish church.

NOTES From Dufftown, which has always been a source of good whisky. It is said that Rome was built on seven hills, but Dufftown was built on seven stills. Dufftown was the sixth distillery to be established in Dufftown and the fourth in the 1890's. The original water mill at Dufftown is still in working order. Dufftown, like the malt from its sister distillery, Blair Athol, plays an important role as one of the principal constituents of the Bells blends.

WATER Jock's Well in the Conval Hills.

Age 15 years **Strength** 43% abv

Sweetness 8 Peatiness 3 Availability 5

Colour Pale amber with lemon/gold highlights **Nose** Medium-bodied, medium-sweet, quite rich and fruity with a slight floral note **Flavour** Medium-sweet and fresh, quite rich and delicately peated with a nice sweetness **Finish** Clean and gently smoky with the good sweetness lasting **Notes** United Distillers bottling

Age 10 years **Strength** 40% abv

Sweetness 8 Peatiness 4 Availability 2

Colour Straw/golden **Nose** Light with hints of burnt rubber and a floweriness in the background **Flavour** Medium-sweet, smooth and slightly fruity **Finish** Lasts well, with good richness, but the rubberiness lingers **Notes** Arthur Bell Distillers bottling

Age 12 years **Distillation** 1980 **Strength** 43% abv

Sweetness 7 Peatiness 4 Availability 2

Colour Very pale watery straw with pale lemon highlights **Nose** Quite big-bodied, fresh, young and cerealy, green herby and mashy **Flavour** Medium-dry, quite full-bodied, fresh and spicy with a richness at the back **Finish** Long, slightly vegetal and medium-sweet **Notes** Blackadder International bottling

PITLOCHRY, PERTHSHIRE EST 1825

Founded on land rented from the Duke of Atholl, Edradour appears little changed by the passing of time. The distillery has gone through several interesting changes of ownership, the most notable of which was becoming a subsidiary of William Whitely & Company, which it remained for most of the 20th century. It is now owned by Campbell Distillers, a subsidiary of the French company Pernod Ricard, who have invested substantially in the development of both the distillery and its single malt.

LOCATION   Situated at the roadside at the foot of a steep hill; a collection of ancient farmstead-like buildings, past which tumbles a fast-flowing burn. An idyllic setting.

NOTES   Scotland's smallest distillery whose actual output is only 600 gallons (3,600 bottles) per week. The last remaining of the once numerous Perthshire "farm" distilleries and the last actually distilling by hand. It is run by just three people. The output of single malt is just 2,000 cases a year, the balance being kept as "top dressing" principally for the House of Lords blend. Also previously known as Glenforres, which name is now given to a vatting of several single malts, of which the Edradour is one. An excellent visitor centre.

WATER   A spring on Ben Vrackie

Age 10 years   **Strength** 40% abv

Sweetness 9   Peatiness 3   Availability 7

Colour Richly gold, gloriously viscous **Nose** Sweet, almondy aroma with a slight fruitiness **Flavour** A smooth, malty taste with a hint of dryness **Finish** A buttery aftertaste and creamily smooth **Notes** Campbell Distillers bottling

CONNOISSEURS
CHOICE

Connoisseurs Choice, a
range of single malts from
various districts of
Scotland.

In the Highlands
are situated the greatest
number of malt whisky
distilleries.

SINGLE HIGHLAND
MALT SCOTCH WHISKY
DISTILLED AT
GLEN ALBYN
DISTILLERY
Proprietors: Mackinlay & Birnie Ltd

DISTILLED 1972 DISTILLED

SPECIALLY SELECTED, PRODUCED AND BOTTLED BY

70cl   GORDON & MACPHAIL   40%vol
ELGIN · SCOTLAND
PRODUCT OF SCOTLAND

INVERNESS EST. 1846

Founded by James Sutherland, the then Provost of Inverness on the ruins of the Muirtown Brewery which had catered for the thirst of the men who built the Caledonian Canal. Rebuilt in 1884 after being used as a flour mill following a period of disuse. Acquired in 1972 by DCL from Mackinlay and Birnie Ltd., a company owned by 14 members of the Mackinlay family of the Leith distillers and 11 members of the local Birnie family, John Birnie having been the manager and distiller in 1892. Managed by SMD until its demolition in 1988, distilling having ceased in 1983. When operational it had two stills.

LOCATION   Glen Albyn was situated on the east side of the A9 to the north of Inverness. It faced Glen Mhor distillery across the Great North Road where it crosses the Caledonian Canal.

NOTES   The distillery was closed between 1917 and 1919 and used as a U.S. Naval base for the manufacture of mines. For a long time supplies were delivered by sea. Demolished in 1988, along with Glen Mhor, to make way for a supermarket development. Prior to 1745, Inverness had been the chief malting town in Scotland.

WATER   Loch Ness

Distillation 1972   **Strength** 40% abv

Sweetness 7   Peatiness 5   Availability 4

Colour Amber with yellow highlights and a green tinge **Nose** Quite good body, medium-sweet, ripe and fruity, a slight buttery toffee character with a nice dark smokiness **Flavour** Medium-sweet, rich and cerealy with an almost hop-like flavour, good body and delicately peated **Finish** Clean, quite rich and of good length **Notes** Gordon & MacPhail bottling

Age 12 years **Distillation** 1980 **Strength** 43% abv

Sweetness 7 Peatiness 2 Availability 1

Colour Very pale straw with lemon highlights **Nose** Light, fresh, fruity and medium-dry **Flavour** Medium-sweet, quite full-bodied and round **Finish** Of good length, fresh with a lingering sweetness **Notes** Master of Malt bottling, cask no 294

Distillation 1963 **Strength** 40% abv

Sweetness 7 Peatiness 4 Availability 1

Colour Peaty gold with greenish tinges **Nose** Quite sweet, creamy and fruity with hints of almonds **Flavour** Sweet, nutty and creamy **Finish** Fine, long and delicately sweet **Notes** Gordon & MacPhail bottling

Distillation 1965 **Strength** 40% abv

Sweetness 7 Peatiness 4 Availability 1

Colour Full amber with gold highlights **Nose** Medium-sweet, rich, lanolin and peppery characters with an almost raisiny fruitiness **Flavour** Rich, oaky, of medium weight and quite smooth **Finish** Peppery, oaky and dry **Notes** Gordon & MacPhail bottling

RUTHRIE, ABERLOUR, BANFFSHIRE EST. 1968

Built in 1967-8 by Mackinlay McPherson Ltd, a subsidiary company of Scottish & Newcastle Breweries Ltd. Sold to Invergordon Distillers in 1985 along with its then sister distillery, Isle of Jura. Closed in 1987 and re-opened again in 1989 after being purchased by Campbell Distillers, a subsidiary of the French company Pernod Ricard. Four stills.

LOCATION The distillery nestles at the foot of Ben Rinnes, a short way from the A95.

NOTES Campbell Distillers also owns Aberlour and Edradour distilleries. One of three distilleries designed by Delme Evans, the other two being Jura and Tullibardine.

WATER Springs near Ben Rinnes.

Age 12 years	**Strength** 40% abv	
Sweetness 7	**Peatiness** 4	**Availability** 1

Colour Pale, soft golden **Nose** Full and delightfully leafy **Flavour** Full-bodied, lightly peated, slightly sweet **Finish** Elegant and smooth **Notes** Invergordon bottling

Age 18 years	**Distillation** 1971	**Strength** 40% abv
Sweetness 8	**Peatiness** 4	**Availability** 0

Colour Very deep amber, almost mahogany **Nose** Rich, sherried, very oaky, but clean **Flavour** Woody, nutty and quite sweet **Finish** Smooth, nutty and sherried with quite a lot of oaky tannins **Notes** Bottled in 1989 by private individuals

CONNOISSEURS
CHOICE

Connoisseurs Choice, a
range of single malts from
various districts of
Scotland.

The distilleries situated in
the area of the valley of the
River Spey produce some of
the finest malt whiskies.

SINGLE SPEYSIDE
MALT SCOTCH WHISKY
DISTILLED AT

GLENBURGIE
DISTILLERY
PROPRIETORS: Jas. & Geo. Stodart Ltd

DISTILLED **1968** DISTILLED

SPECIALLY SELECTED, PRODUCED AND BOTTLED BY
75cl **GORDON & MACPHAIL** 40%vol
ELGIN - SCOTLAND
PRODUCT OF SCOTLAND

ALVES, NR FORRES, MORAY EST. 1829

Founded on this site as Kilnflat by William Paul, the grandfather of Dr Listen Paul, a celebrated London surgeon of the latter part of the 19th century. Silent from 1927-35. Controlled by Hiram Walker from 1930, and purchased outright by them in 1936. Now part of Allied Domecq and operated by Allied Distillers Ltd. Two stills.

LOCATION Sited in a valley to the south of the A95 some five miles to the east of Forres.

NOTES The distillery did once have two short-necked "Lomond" stills which produced a heavier malt known as "Glencraig" . Glenburgie is one of the main malts associated with Ballantine's blended whisky. An earlier distillery, possibly founded in 1810, was once on this site.

WATER Local springs

Distillation 1948 **Strength** 40% abv

Sweetness 5 Peatiness 6 Availability 2

Colour Deep amber with bronze highlights **Nose** Very big, dark and powerful, with characters of linseed and soft oak with a slightly green touch, medium-dry, with a slight "burnt" character and a pleasant spiritiness **Flavour** Big, rich and smoky with a not too dominant oakiness, the "burnt" character again and quite big tannins **Finish** Long, quite elegant, slightly chewy and gently smoky **Notes** Botled in 1995 as part of Gordon & MacPhail's *Centenary Reserve* series

Distillation 1960 **Strength** 40% abv

Sweetness 7 Peatiness 5 Availability 4

Colour Pale straw with good yellow highlights **Nose** Woody, slightly sweet and floral **Flavour** Medium-sweet, slightly spicy, oaky, quite heavy **Finish** Oaky of reasonable length **Notes** Gordon & MacPhail bottling

Distillation 1966 **Strength** 61.2% abv

Sweetness 8 Peatiness 3 Availability 4

Colour Amber with gold highlights **Nose** Quite sweet, spirity, fruity and fragrant with a touch of perfume and a slight burnt wood peatiness **Flavour** Fragrant, medium-sweet with soft sweet oak and quite smooth with a slightly unctuous character **Finish** Long, quite sweet and spirity with a slightly floral touch to the tail **Notes** Gordon & MacPhail bottling

GLENCRAIG

Distillation 1970 **Strength** 40% abv

Sweetness 3 Peatiness 1 Availability 2

Colour Mid amber with yellow/gold highlights and a tinge of green **Nose** Light, fresh, fruity, medium-sweet with a greenness **Flavour** Light, clean, medium-dry, very lightly peated with a fresh greenness **Finish** Clean and fresh **Notes** Produced from the Lomond stills and bottled as *Glencraig* by Gordon & MacPhail

GLENCADAM

H

CONNOISSEURS CHOICE

Connoisseurs Choice, a range of single malts from various districts of Scotland.

In the Highlands are situated the greatest number of malt whisky distilleries.

SINGLE HIGHLAND
MALT SCOTCH WHISKY
DISTILLED AT

GLENCADAM
DISTILLERY
Trade Mark of Proprietors: The Glencadam Distillery Co. Ltd

DISTILLED 1974 DISTILLED

Specially selected, produced and bottled by and under the responsibility of

70cl GORDON & MACPHAIL 40%vol
REGD. BOTTLER · ELGIN · SCOTLAND
PRODUCT OF SCOTLAND

BRECHIN, ANGUS EST 1825

Said to have been founded in 1825, the distillery passed through a number of owners until purchased by Hiram Walker in 1954. Now part of Allied Domecq and operated by Allied Distillers Ltd. Two stills.

LOCATION Situated half a mile to the east of the town of Brechin in the cleft of a hill. It is also about half a mile from the River Esk.

NOTES Presently only available through the independent bottlers. Some of the make goes into Stewart's Cream of the Barley blended Scotch Whisky.

WATER Springs in the Unthank Hills.

Distillation 1974 **Strength** 40% abv

Sweetness 7 Peatiness 4 Availability 4

Colour Straw/amber with gold/lemon highlights **Nose** Rich, medium-sweet, woody, spirity with a touch of linseed and greenness **Flavour** Medium-bodied, quite rich, soft oak, quite simple and lightly peated **Finish** Light with a touch of spice **Notes** Gordon & MacPhail bottling

Age 21 years **Strength** 46% abv

Sweetness 8 Peatiness 4 Availability 4

Colour Straw/gold with slight greenish tinges **Nose** Sweet, oily, slight sugar icing **Flavour** Medium-sweet, spirity, smooth **Finish** Quite good, but with a strange cold aftertaste **Notes** Wm Cadenhead bottling

AGED **12** YEARS
DISTILLED, MATURED AND BOTTLED IN SCOTLAND
HIGHLAND
GLEN DEVERON
~ SINGLE MALT ~
SCOTCH WHISKY

MACDUFF DISTILLERY

BANFF, BANFFSHIRE EST. 1962

Built 1962-3 by a consortium which included George Crawford, Morty Dykes and Brodie Hepburn. Acquired by William Lawson in 1972, which in turn became part of the General Beverage Corporation, the Luxembourg company which controls Martini & Rossi's world interests. Extended from two to three stills in 1966 and to four in 1968. Now subsidiary of Bacardi Limited, Hamilton, Bermuda.

LOCATION Situated to the east of Banff on the east bank of the River Deveron, about half a mile from the Moray Firth.

NOTES The malt takes its name from the River Deveron valley rather than the distillery itself, which is known as Macduff. A five-year-old version is sold in Italy. It can be obtained bottled by independents as Macduff.

WATER The Gelly Burn

Age 12 years   **Strength** 40% abv

Sweetness 7	**Peatiness** 3	**Availability** 8

Colour Pale straw with bright golden highlights **Nose** Fresh, leafy, quite full **Flavour** Medium-sweet, very smooth **Finish** Distinguished and lasts very well **Notes** Wm Lawson bottling

MACDUFF
Distilled 1975   **Strength** 40% abv

Sweetness 8	**Peatiness** 3	**Availability** 4

Colour Quite full amber/straw with gold/yellow highlights **Nose** Fresh, green, leafy, quite full and almost grapey **Flavour** Medium-sweet, coffee, very rich, quite full-bodied **Finish** Long, lingering with layers of coffee and bitter chocolate **Notes** Gordon & MacPhail bottling as *Macduff*

FORGUE, NR HUNTLY, ABERDEENSHIRE EST. 1826

Glendronach's founder, James Allardes, was a frequent guest of the 5th Duke of Gordon who was largely responsible for the Excise Act of 1823 which was instrumental in creating the modern malt whisky industry. The distillery has had various owners over the years, including Captain Charles Grant, younger son of William Grant of Glenfiddich fame, who purchased it from the Crown in 1920. It remained in that branch of the Grant family until 1960, when George Grey Grant sold it to Wm Teacher & Sons Ltd. Extended from two to four stills in 1966-7. Now part of Allied Domecq and operated by Allied Distillers Ltd.

LOCATION Situated straddling the Dronach Burn in the valley of Forgue, which supplies the cooling water. The distillery is set amongst tall trees, in which an established colony of rooks is said to bring luck.

NOTES Distilling was undoubtedly carried out in the area in the days before legal distilling came to Glendronach and the noisy rooks would have proved a useful ally to warn of approaching strangers - especially Excise officers. Built in the form of a square and covering four acres, Glendronach is one of the few distilleries where barley is still malted on a malting floor, providing about 15% of the distillery's requirement. It also has coal-fired stills. Glendronach is one of the most important constituents of Teacher's Highland Cream.

WATER "The Source" - a spring about four miles to the east of the distillery.

SHERRY CASK

Age 12 years **Strength** 40% abv

Sweetness 4 Peatiness 4 Availability 0

Colour Quite dark, richly demerara in colour **Nose** Rich, full and sweet with a smoky edge **Flavour** Rich and full with a slight maltiness **Finish** Long with hints of shortbready-sweetness in the aftertaste **Notes** Discontinued

ORIGINAL

Age 12 years **Strength** 40% abv

Sweetness 5 Peatiness 5 Availability 0

Colour Straw with gold highlights **Nose** Slightly sweet, biscuity, quite mellow and buttery **Flavour** Medium-sweet, soft, mellow, round **Finish** Slightly spicy, biscuity, good length **Notes** Caledonian Distillers bottling. Discontinued

TRADITIONAL

Age 12 years **Strength** 40% abv

Sweetness 5 Peatiness 6 Availability 6

Colour Straw with golden highlights **Nose** Quite full, medium-sweet, rich, soft, almost honeyed with a slight oily note **Flavour** Medium-dry, quite rich, full and smooth with a touch of spice, buttery and delicately smoky **Finish** Soft, smooth and long with some smokiness on the tail **Notes** Caledonian Distillers bottling. Traditional is aged in a combination of plain oak and sherry oak casks. It replaced the above two versions

SHERRY CASK

Age 18 years **Strength** 43% abv

Sweetness 6 Peatiness 3 Availability 1

Colour Deep amber with mahogany highlights **Nose** Full, dark oak, nutty, medium-dry with a slight richness **Flavour** Big-bodied, smooth, rich, oaky, nutty and medium-dry **Finish** Long, dark, oaky with a toasted nutty character **Notes** Caledonian Distillers bottling. Very little remains available

Age 20 years **Distillation** 1970 **Strength** 56% abv

Sweetness 6 Peatiness 8 Availability 1

Colour Very deep amber with ruby/bronze highlights **Nose** Full-bodied, medium-dry, dark, burnt and malty with an almost christmas cake richness **Flavour** Quite big-bodied, burnt, medium-sweet and round, rich and powerful with gentle tannins **Finish** Long with a burnt nuttiness and an almost chewy tail **Notes** Signatory bottling; distilled 18.2.1970

SPEYSIDE
SINGLE MALT
SCOTCH WHISKY

GLENDULLAN

distillery, located in a beautiful *wooded*
valley was //// built in 1897 and is one of seven
established in *Dufftown* in the (19th)
The *River Fiddich* flows past the *distillery*;
originally *providing power* to drive
machinery, it is now used //// for cooling.
GLENDULLAN is a firm, mellow *single MALT*
SCOTCH WHISKY with a fruity
bouquet and a smooth *lingering* finish.

AGED **12** YEARS

43% vol

Distilled & Bottled in SCOTLAND
GLENDULLAN DISTILLERY
Dufftown, Keith, Banffshire, Scotland

70 cl

DUFFTOWN, BANFFSHIRE EST. 1897

The last distillery to be built in Dufftown in the 19th century and the distillery which prompted the "Dufftown is built on seven stills" line. The location was chosen not just for its beauty, but also for its practical convenience. It was sited to take advantage of water power and was also able to share neighbouring Mortlach's private railway siding. Two stills. Acquired by DCL in 1926 and managed by SMD, latterly UMGD, from 1930, the licensees are Macdonald Greenlees & Co. Ltd. Rebuilt 1962. An additional distillery with six stills was built on the field between "Old Glendullan" and the employees' homes in 1971-72. The distance between the two units was defined as "a short one when the weather's good and a long one when it isn't". The old distillery was closed in 1985 and is used as UMGD's maintenance workshops. Now part of United Distillers plc.

LOCATION Close by the junction of the A941 and A920

NOTES Glendullan's process water comes from the River Fiddich. Glendullan was a favourite whisky of King Edward VIII and plays an important role in the Old Parr blend.

WATER Springs in the Conval Hills

Age 12 years **Strength** 43% abv

Sweetness **8** Peatiness **4** Availability **4**

Colour Pale straw with a touch of green and lemon/yellow highlights **Nose** Quite full, rich appley, slightly spirity with a hint of cereals and lightly peated **Flavour** Medium-dry, rich, sweet oaky vanilla, a touch of greenness, spirity and malty **Finish** Long, smooth, oaky with a delicately smoky tail **Notes** United Distillers bottling

Age 12 years **Strength** 43% abv

Sweetness 5 Peatiness 3 Availability 0

Colour Pale golden with a slightly greenish edge **Nose** Full and fruity with a distinctly sweet oaky hint **Flavour** Full, round, warm, sweet and spicy with a slight flavour of coffee/toffee **Finish** Long and lingering, sweet and memorable **Notes** DCL (pre-Guinness) bottling

Age 10 years **Distillation** 1983 **Strength** 43% abv

Sweetness 8 Peatiness 3 Availability 1

Colour Very pale watery straw with a pale lemon tinge **Nose** Sweet, fruity, quite full-bodied, a touch mashy, quite fresh and delicately peated **Flavour** Quite sweet, fresh with good body and a nice fruity touch **Finish** Quite fresh, of good length with a firm touch of dry tannin **Notes** Blackadder International bottling

The spirit safe

WHITE HORSE
GLEN ELGIN
SINGLE HIGHLAND MALT
SCOTCH WHISKY

DISTILLED AND BOTTLED IN SCOTLAND BY
WHITE HORSE DISTILLERS, GLASGOW, SCOTLAND

750ml   GLEN ELGIN DISTILLERY, ELGIN, MORAYSHIRE   43% vol

LONGMORN, ELGIN, MORAY EST. 1898

Built between 1898 and 1900 by a partnership of William Simpson, a former manager of Glenfarclas, and James Carle, the local agent for the North of Scotland Bank. Production began on 1 May, 1900. Acquired by SMD in 1930. Extended from two to six stills when rebuilt in 1964. The distiller's licence is held by White Horse Distillers Ltd. Now part of United Distillers plc.

LOCATION Situated on the A941, the main Elgin to Rothes road.

NOTES A very compact distillery, due to a shortage of capital when it was built. The architect, Charles Doig of Elgin, said at the time that Glen Elgin would be the last to be built on Speyside for more than sixty years. He was right! The next was Glen Keith in 1957. Glen Elgin is an important constituent in the White Horse blend.

WATER Springs near Millbuies Loch.

Age 12 years   **Strength** 43% abv
Sweetness 8 Peatiness 4 Availability 1

Colour Pale gold with peaty depths **Nose** Sweet, slightly green with fine, soft oak and hints of honey **Flavour** Soft, pleasantly sweet, smooth and round with honey coming through on the palate **Finish** Smooth, fruity and distinguished **Notes** DCL (pre-Guinness bottling). A more recent version is now available, apparently still 12 years old, but with no age statement on the label

Age 22 years   **Distillation** 1971   **Strength** 50.3% abv
Sweetness 7 Peatiness 8 Availability 2

Colour Bright and clear, but grey/green, almost khaki **Nose** Sweet, round, a strange sooty smokiness with a slight green edge and quite good body **Flavour** Big-bodied, medium-sweet, very smoky with a burnt character **Finish** Long, smoky, slightly austere and tannic **Notes** Wm Cadenhead bottling

First known as Highland Esk when converted from a former flax-spinning mill in 1897 by Septimus Parsonage & Co and James Isles of Dundee, its name was changed to North Esk in 1899 when acquired by J. F. Caille Heddle. Closed during the First World War. Re-opened in 1938, and re-equipped by new owners Associated Scottish Distillers Ltd to produce grain whisky under the name Montrose Distillery. Acquired by DCL in 1954 and operated off and on by SGD until 1964, when it was transferred to SMD and converted back to a malt distillery. A large drum maltings was built in 1968; its capacity was increased in 1973 to enable it to supply a number of SMD distilleries. Renamed Glenesk in 1980.

LOCATION Two miles north of Montrose, half a mile west of the A92 on the south bank of the River Esk.

NOTES Glenesk has also been known as Hillside. The distillery is now closed and unlikely to re-open, however the maltings are in full production for United Distillers. Glenesk was traditionally an important malt to William Sandersons' VAT 69 blend.

WATER The river North Esk.

Age 13 years **Strength** 66.5% abv

Sweetness 5 Peatiness 4 Availability 2

Colour Very pale straw with pale watery-green highlights **Nose** Full, fresh, leafy with a dry smokiness and a green, mashy character **Flavour** Clean, medium-sweet, malty and with a mashy character **Finish** Clean, medium-sweet, good length and a delicate smokiness on the tail **Notes** Wm Cadenhead bottling

MARYPARK, BALLINDALLOCH, BANFFSHIRE EST. 1836

Founded by Robert Hay, a tenant farmer at Rechlerich farm, it is said that the plant used was taken from Dandaleith Distillery, near Craigellachie. It came into the family ownership of the Grant family when Hay died in 1865 and John Grant took over the tenancy. It was let to John Smith until 1870, when he left to run his new Cragganmore distillery. The running of the distillery was then taken over by John Grant himself and it has been run by successive generations of the Grant family ever since. The present John Grant is the fifth generation to be in charge, while his father George Grant sits as Chairman of the company. Extended from two to four stills in 1960 and to six in 1976.

LOCATION   South of the A95, almost midway between Grantown-on-Spey and Craigellachie, lying in quite desolate moorland at the foot of Ben Rinnes.

NOTES   Glenfarclas means "valley of the green grass". The whisky ages very well. "Whisky Tom" Dewar waxed most lyrical of a 30 year old he tasted in 1912, although George Grant considers the 15 year old to be perfection - all a matter of personal taste. Glenfarclas has been the pioneer of cask strength whiskies, the company's "Glenfarclas 105", bottled at 60% by volume, long setting the bench mark for such whiskies and having a loyal following worldwide. Glenfarclas used to be casked in a variety of casks, but all new Glenfarclas spirit is now aged in 100% sherrywood at the distillery. Glenfarclas has an excellent reception centre.

WATER   Springs on Ben Rinnes.

Age 10 years **Strength** 40% abv

Sweetness 9 **Peatiness** 5 **Availability** 9

Colour Straw with good gold highlights **Nose** Slightly rubbery, delicately light and sweet, leafy oak with a slight tang of coffee **Flavour** Sweet, malty, full, rich and round **Finish** Slightly spicy, long and characterful **Notes** J&G Grant bottling

GLENFARCLAS 105

Age No age statement **Strength** 60% abv

Sweetness 7 **Peatiness** 6 **Availability** 7

Colour Deep, peaty amber with gold highlights **Nose** Very spirity, slightly astringent, slightly sweet **Flavour** Spirity, malty, a little oily-oak character, quite austere **Finish** Long, flavoursome and, surprisingly, quite dry **Notes** J&G Grant bottling

Age 15 years **Strength** 46% abv

Sweetness 9 **Peatiness** 4 **Availability** 6

Colour Gold/peaty with very bright rich golden highlights **Nose** Full, rich and sweet, with a luscious, unctuous oily-oak character and delicately peated **Flavour** Sweet, rich and creamy, very intense, full bodied and smooth with hints of burnt peat **Finish** Gloriously sweet, gently smoky - long and distinguished **Notes** J&G Grant bottling

Age 21 years **Strength** 43% abv

Sweetness 9 **Peatiness** 4 **Availability** 3

Colour Quite dark amber with rich gold highlights **Nose** Full, rich, sweet vanilla oak with hints of mint **Flavour** Rich, big, full-bodied, delicately smoky **Finish** Lightly smoky, rich and long-lasting **Notes** J&G Grant bottling

Age 25 years **Strength** 43% abv

Sweetness 9   Peatiness 5   Availability 4

Colour Amber with old gold highlights **Nose** Full, ripe, sweet and round, finely peated with aromas of orange marmalade, honey, coffee and sherry nuttiness **Flavour** Full-flavoured, smooth, sweet with oaky vanilla tannins and coffee and toffee flavours **Finish** Fresh with a smoky nuttiness and long lasting **Notes** J&G Grant bottling

Age 24 years **Distillation** 1969 **Strength** 46.5% abv

Sweetness 8   Peatiness 6   Availability 2

Colour Deep amber with deep bronze/ruby highlights **Nose** Quite full-bodied and rich, a dark nuttiness and medium-sweet with ripe unctuous fruit and a smoky Christmas cake character **Flavour** Smooth, round and sweet with dark smoky tannins, nutty **Finish** Long, gently smoky, quite rich, chewy and nutty **Notes** Signatory bottling - cask no 57 distilled 12.2.69

DUFFTOWN, BANFFSHIRE EST. 1887

When Alfred Barnard published his *Whisky Distilleries of the United Kingdom* in 1887, the home of the world's best selling malt was only just being built. Owned by William Grant & Sons Ltd, it today boasts no less than 28 stills: 10 wash and 18 spirit. No mean achievement for a distillery founded with £120 capital and using second-hand equipment from Cardow distillery; but such has been the success of the family enterprise founded by William Grant of Glenfiddich, the son of a soldier who had served under Wellington.

LOCATION Situated near the junction of the A941 and the B975 to the north of the centre of Dufftown.

NOTES One of only two malt whiskies to be bottled at the distillery (the other being Springbank). The first distillery in Scotland to open a visitor centre, Glenfiddich now attracts 120,000 visitors a year. It welcomed its one millionth visitor, Mr Ronald Pederson from Albany in New York State on 4 August 1987.

WATER The Robbie Dhu springs

GLENFIDDICH SPECIAL RESERVE
Age No age statement **Strength** 40% abv

Sweetness 8 Peatiness 5 Availability 10

Colour Straw/ gold **Nose** Cooked mash, light, soapy, delicately peated **Flavour** Light, sweet, well-balanced and gentle **Finish** Sweet and of medium length **Notes** William Grant bottling

GLENFIDDICH EXCELLENCE
Age 18 years **Strength** 43% abv

Sweetness 8 Peatiness 4 Availability 2

Colour Straw with pale gold highlights **Nose** Fresh, medium-bodied and round, notes of citrus and a grapey character, a slight bubble-gummy sweetness, lanolin character and lightly peated **Flavour** Soft, smooth, medium-sweet and round with an unctuous lanolin oakiness **Finish** Clean, surprisingly dry, but rich, with a fresh, light peatiness **Notes** William Grant bottling

GLENFIDDICH ANCIENT RESERVE
Age 18 years **Strength** 43% abv

Sweetness 8 Peatiness 3 Availability 4

Colour Straw with greeny/gold highlights **Nose** Rich, medium-sweet, grapey, quite soft and with a slight tang of coffee **Flavour** Medium-sweet, spicy, slightly peppery with a slight green leafiness **Finish** Good, smooth and long with hints of coffee **Notes** William Grant bottling

GLENFIDDICH WEDGEWOOD DECANTER
Age 21 years **Strength** 43% abv

Sweetness 9 Peatiness 5 Availability 4

Colour Quite pale straw with good yellow/gold highlights **Nose** Fresh, malty, medium-dry and slightly grapey **Flavour** Soft, warm, grapily fruity, quite big-bodied, spicy and medium-sweet **Finish** Herby, long, sweet and smooth with a soft maltiness at the end **Notes** William Grant bottling

GLENFIDDICH STAG'S HEAD DECANTER

Age 30 years   **Distillation** 1963   **Strength** 51.7% abv

Sweetness 8   Peatiness 4   Availability 1

Colour Mid-amber with good gold highlights **Nose** Rich, quite full-bodied, a fresh oak character, medium-sweet with a citrus note and a dark nuttiness **Flavour** Big-bodied and fresh with a fruity richness, gently peated with a touch of spice and oily smooth oak **Finish** Long, still quite fresh, rich and slightly chewy **Notes** Wm Cadenhead bottling - distilled April, 1963

The workforce at Glenfiddich

GLEN FLAGLER

Vintage 1970
Single Lowland Malt Scotch Whisky
Matured in oak casks for 23 years
Distilled at the Glenflagler Distillery
on 6.10.70   Bottled 5.94
Cask nos. 1260 + 7861   Bottle no.   of 350
This whisky has been selected, produced and bottled in
Scotland for and under the sole responsibility of
5cl   Signatory Vintage Scotch Whisky Co. Ltd. 50.1%vol
        Edinburgh EH6 Scotland

MOFFAT, BY AIRDRIE, LANARKSHIRE   EST. 1965

Founded within the Moffat grain distillery complex by Inver House Distillers, at the time a subsidiary of Publicker Industries Ltd of Philadelphia. The distillery was closed in the mid-1970s and the pot stills dismantled at this time. Inver House was bought from its American parent by its UK directors in 1988. Six stills.

LOCATION   At Moffat Mills on the eastern outskirts of Airdrie

NOTES   The distillery complex was converted from Moffat Mills paper mill. Originally known as Garnheath.

WATER   Lilly Loch.

Age 23 years   **Distillation** 1970   **Strength** 50.1% abv
Sweetness 3   Peatiness 2   Availability 1

Colour Pale to mid-amber with yellow highlights **Nose** Fresh, quite light and delicate, malty, nutty, a dark oaky character and medium-dry **Flavour** Medium-dry, a touch of spice, quite fresh and round with good body and a malic apple touch **Finish** Quite long and round, medium-sweet and fresh **Notes** Signatory bottling - distilled 6 October 1970

OLD MELDRUM, ABERDEENSHIRE EST. 1785

Established by one Thomas Simpson, the first spirit was announced on 1 December 1785 in The Aberdeen Journal, Glen Garioch is one of Scotland's oldest distilleries. In two centuries, ownership has passed through various hands, including SMD who acquired it in 1943. It was closed by SMD in 1968 and sold to Stanley P. Morrison, who extended it from two to three stills in 1973. Now operated by Morrison Bowmore Distillers, who are wholly owned by Japanese company Suntory. As we were going to press it was announced that Glen Garioch was to close in October, 1995.

LOCATION   The distillery is situated in Old Meldrum village on the Banff to Aberdeen road, close by the historic Meldrum House.

NOTES   Garioch is pronounced "Geerie". Waste heat is used to grow tomatoes. The Garioch valley, an 18 mile or so stretch of highly fertile land is known as the granary of Aberdeenshire. Glen Garioch was indeed a canny place to build a distillery. Other dates have been given elsewhere for the opening of this distillery, but The Aberdeen Journal announcement of December, 1785 clearly pre-dates them. Glen Garioch is housed in a very attractive cluster of old buildings with the pagoda heads of the still in use floor maltings adding to the authentic, "lived-in" appeal. These floor maltings supply about half of the distillery's requirements, the rest being bought in from outside maltsters. Pitsligo Moss peat is used for the malt drying, which is finished by gas-firing. Beacause of its location, in 1982 Glen Garioch was the first distillery in Scotland to convert its stills to gas-firing.

WATER   Springs on Percock Hill.

GLEN GARIOCH

Age 8 years **Strength** 43% abv

Sweetness 4 Peatiness 5 Availability 2

Colour Straw/pale amber with lemon/yellow highlights **Nose** Fresh and clean, slightly perfumed, malty and medium-dry **Flavour** Medium-dry. perfumed, fresh and quite rich **Finish** A spirity youthfulness with a lingering flavour of violets **Notes** Morrison Bowmore bottling

Age 10 years **Strength** 40% abv

Sweetness 4 Peatiness 5 Availability 7

Colour Bright gold **Nose** Delicately peated, flowery and smoky **Flavour** Peaty, dry and slightly pungent **Finish** Good, smooth and delicate **Notes** Morrison Bowmore bottling

Age 12 years **Strength** 40% abv

Sweetness 4 Peatiness 5 Availability 8

Colour Mid-amber with gold/green highlights **Nose** Medium-bodied, delicately peated and floral (almost violets), dry with a slight edge of sweetness **Flavour** Medium-dry, slightly spicy, floral and fresh with good body **Finish** Quite long, spicy and tangy with a green edge **Notes** Morrison Bowmore bottling

Distillation 1984 **Strength** 40% abv

Sweetness 4 Peatiness 5 Availability 3

Colour Straw/amber with yellow/gold highlights **Nose** Medium-bodied with a lemon/citrus note, floral peaty and a heathery perfumed character **Flavour** Quite soft and round , a touch perfumed and a gentle smokiness **Finish** Good with a touch of heather and spice **Notes** Morrison Bowmore bottling

Age 15 years **Strength** 43% abv

Sweetness 3 Peatiness 6 Availability 6

Colour Straw/light amber with yellow/gold highlights **Nose** Medium-bodied, malty, round with a smoky peatiness **Flavour** Quite big-bodied and smooth with a rich edge and smoky character **Finish** Long, almost pungent, a gentle heathery smokiness and slightly chewy **Notes** Morrison Bowmore bottling

Age 21 years **Strength** 43% abv

Sweetness 4 Peatiness 5 Availability 5

Colour Pale with yellow/green highlights **Nose** Medium-sweet and quite smoky **Flavour** Full-bodied, rich, medium-dry, and delicately peated **Finish** Smoky, slightly spicy and quite long with touches of oak **Notes** Morrison Bowmore bottling

GLENGLASSAUGH

CONNOISSEURS
CHOICE

*Connoisseurs Choice, a
range of single malts from
various districts of
Scotland*

*In the Highlands
are situated the greatest
number of malt whisky
distilleries*

SINGLE HIGHLAND
MALT SCOTCH WHISKY
DISTILLED AT
GLENGLASSAUGH
Distillery
Proprietors: The Highland Distilleries Ltd.

DISTILLED **1983** DISTILLED

SPECIALLY SELECTED, PRODUCED AND BOTTLED BY
70cl **GORDON & MACPHAIL** 40%vol
ELGIN · SCOTLAND
PRODUCT OF SCOTLAND

NR. PORTSOY, BANFFSHIRE EST. 1875

Founded by the Glenglassaugh Distillery Company. Acquired by the Highland Distilleries Co Ltd in the 1890's. Glenglassaugh was silent from 1907 to 1931 and again from 1936 until it was extensively rebuilt 1959-60. Closed again in 1986, but re-opened. Two stills.

LOCATION Sited on the slope of a steep hillside in the Glassaugh Glen close to the sea approximately two miles west of Portsoy.

NOTES During the period 1907 to 1960, Glenglassaugh only produced for a handful of years in all. When rebuilt, the distillery managed to double its output simply by doubling the size of its stills.

WATER The Glassaugh spring

Distillation 1983 **Strength** 40% abv

Sweetness 5 Peatiness 4 Availability 4

Colour Mid-amber with gold highlights **Nose** Quite full, smoky with an oily-oaky character, medium-dry **Flavour** Medium-dry with good richness in the middle, smooth and round with good body **Finish** Long, medium-dry and rich with a nice spiciness **Notes** Gordon & MacPhail bottling

Age 13 years **Distillation** 1977 **Strength** 59.8% abv

Sweetness 8 Peatiness 4 Availability 4

Colour Straw/pale amber with yellow/gold highlights **Nose** Quite full-bodied, fresh and clean with a touch of cereal and green apple, medium-sweet with a hint of perfume **Flavour** Fresh, green, medium-peated and medium-sweet **Finish** Long and fresh, sweet with a touch of spice and a soft peaty backdrop **Notes** Wm Cadenhead bottling distilled November, 1977

Originally known as Burnfoot, Glengoyne has been owned by Lang Brothers since 1876, that company becoming a part of the Robertson & Baxter group in 1965. Rebuilt in 1966/67 and extended from two to three stills.

LOCATION   About twelve or so miles from the centre of Glasgow and about seven from Loch Lomond, Glengoyne nestles in a truly delightful setting at the foot of Dumgoyne Hill, at the north west end of the Campsie Hills.

NOTES   The distillery is sited on the Highland Line, but, as its water supply comes from north of the Line, it is classified as a Highland malt. The *West Highland Way*, the long distance footpath which runs from Glasgow to Fort William runs past the distillery. Although first licensed in 1833, the distillery is believed to be somewhat older. The make was triple distilled in Victorian times, but is now double distilled. The make is reduced using natural spring water. Not far from the distillery is the hollow tree in which Rob Roy MacGregor, immortalised by Sir Walter Scott - and Hollywood - is reputed to have hidden while fleeing from the English King's men. The malt used to produce Glengoyne is unpeated. This, coupled with the lack of peat in its source water makes Glengoyne the least peated of all Scottish malts. The Excise Officer at Glengoyne at the turn of the century was Arthur Tedder, who later became the Chief Inspector of Excise and was knighted. His son, who had grown up at Glengoyne, was eventually to become Air Chief Marshal of the Royal Air Force. When later he was made a baron, he chose as his title Baron Tedder of Glenguin, the old spelling of Glengoyne. The distillery has an excellent visitor centre which sits at the bottom of the 50 foot waterfall which cascades down the side of Dumgoyne Hill.

WATER   A burn which falls down Dumgoyne Hill and is known locally as "the Distillery Burn".

Age 10 years **Strength** 40% abv

Sweetness 5 Peatiness 0 Availability 10

Colour Pale straw with lemony gold highlights **Nose** Round, fresh and medium-sweet, quite light and rich with a slight floral note and a touch of greenness at the back **Flavour** Round, smooth, creamy, medium-dry, fresh and clean with good body **Finish** Quite long with a smooth, buttery vanilla character and a touch of greenness on the tail **Notes** Lang Brothers bottling

Age 12 years **Strength** 40% abv

Sweetness 5 Peatiness 0 Availability 6

Colour Pale straw with lemony gold highlights **Nose** Medium-bodied, round and fresh, medium-dry with a sweet-oily oak character and hints of buttery toffee **Flavour** Medium-dry, round, smooth and clean, fresh and medium-bodied with a touch of the toffee character **Finish** Long and fresh, buttery, smooth and clean with a touch of oaky vanilla **Notes** Lang Brothers bottling available in export markets

Age 17 years **Strength** 43% abv

Sweetness 6 Peatiness 0 Availability 6

Colour Pale peaty with yellow/golden highlights **Nose** Rich, sweet oak, light fruit and toffee with an almost liquorice-like character **Flavour** Soft, rich and smooth with sweet oaky vanilla **Finish** Spicy, malty and of nice length, quite chewy **Notes** Lang Brothers bottling.

Age 25 years **Distillation** 1968 **Strength** 51.1% abv

Sweetness 8 Peatiness 0 Availability 2

Colour Straw with lemon/yellow highlights **Nose** Fresh, slightly floral, medium-sweet and soft with a hint of citrus **Flavour** Rich and quite full-bodied, sweet and slightly spicy **Finish** Very long and spicy, slightly oily-vanilla and almost stickily sweet and intensely rich **Notes** Lang Brothers bottling.

Age 25 years **Distillation** 1969 **Strength** 47% abv

Sweetness 6 Peatiness 0 Availability 2

Colour Straw/mid-amber with gold/yellow highlights **Nose** Fresh, clean, quite full-bodied and rich with a good unctuous oaky underlay, a hazelnut character, a touch of tarry rope and green apple fruit **Flavour** Quite fresh with a good malty character and a touch of chocolate, firm oaky tannins **Finish** Medium-dry and rich, quite spicy with a note of liquorice on the tail **Notes** Lang Brothers bottling.

GLEN GRANT
DISTILLED & BOTTLED IN SCOTLAND
ESTABLISHED
1840
40% vol.   70 cl e
PRODUCE OF SCOTLAND

THE GLEN GRANT DISTILLERY WAS ESTABLISHED AT
ROTHES IN THE HEART OF THE HIGHLAND SPEYSIDE
REGION IN 1840. THIS PURE, CLEAR MALT WHISKY IS
DISTILLED THERE TO THIS VERY DAY.
PRODUCED & BOTTLED BY GLEN GRANT DISTILLERY COMPANY
EDINBURGH AND ROTHES, SCOTLAND

ROTHES, MORAY EST. 1840

Founded by the brothers James and John Grant who had previously been distillers at nearby Aberlour. Amalgamated with George & J.G. Smith of The Glenlivet in 1953. Owned by the Seagram Company of Canada since 1977. Extended from four to six stills in 1973 and to eight in 1977.

LOCATION At the southern end of Rothes.

NOTES The Glen Grant stills are coal-fired, something of a rarity nowadays, and all have purifiers fitted, which are said to add extra finesse to the style of spirit produced. It is not generally recognised that Glen Grant is the world's second best selling single malt, thanks to its dominant position in Italy, where, as a 5-years-old, it has around 70% of the considerable single malt market. It is also Italy's bestselling whisky. A supply of over-proof Glen Grant is kept in a whisky safe built into the rock at the burnside above the distillery. It is reached through an apple orchard. Taste it cut with water from the burn if you get the chance. Glen Grant was the first distillery to be established in Rothes, and the first industrial building in the north of Scotland to have electric lighting. Although a best seller through its younger ages, Glen Grant also ages well.

WATER The Glen Grant Burn.

Age 5 years **Strength** 40% abv

Sweetness 4 Peatiness 4 Availability 4

Colour Light gold/copper **Nose** Light, somewhat hard and astringent **Flavour** Drier than most Speyside malts, spirity, slightly peppery **Finish** Reasonable length with a strange heathery perfumed tang **Notes** J & J Grant bottling

Age 12 years **Strength** 43% abv

Sweetness 6 Peatiness 4 Availability 6

Colour Straw/gold with amber highlights **Nose** Light, sweet, slightly fruity with an astringent character **Flavour** Light, medium-sweet, spirity and creamy **Finish** Dry, slightly astringent and lingering **Notes** J.& J. Grant bottling

Age 15 years **Strength** 40% abv

Sweetness 6 Peatiness 4 Availability 5

Colour Peaty/gold with good highlights **Nose** Sweet, lightish, nutty and with a slight fruitiness **Flavour** Medium-sweet, nutty, smooth, slightly smoky **Finish** The smokiness comes through on the finish, which is smooth and mellow **Notes** Gordon & MacPhail bottling

Age 18 years **Strength** 46% abv

Sweetness 5 Peatiness 4 Availability 4

Colour Full amber with gold highlights **Nose** Full, quite rich, slightly green and a little austere, soft oaky vanilla with a little smokiness at the back and hints of apricots and apples **Flavour** Medium-dry, quite full, round and rich with a touch of toffee and maltiness **Finish** Long and rich with a nice edge of greenness **Notes** Wm Cadenhead bottling

Age 21 years **Strength** 40% abv

Sweetness 5 Peatiness 4 Availability 4

Colour Amber with good gold highlights **Nose** Fruity, slightly astringent with a note of green wood **Flavour** Medium-sweet, peppery and oaky **Finish** Smooth, well-balanced, dry, of medium length with good oaky vanilla **Notes** Gordon & MacPhail bottling

GLEN KEITH

PRODUCE OF SCOTLAND

GLENKEITH

SINGLE HIGHLAND MALT
SCOTCH WHISKY

Distilled before
1983

A fragrant whisky
from the heart of
the Highlands.
GLEN KEITH
is prized by
experts for its
purity and depth
of flavour.

GLEN KEITH
is matured for
more than ten
years in oak casks.
The whisky is then
bottled under the
supervision of our
Head Distiller.

The pool of the Salmon*

The Glen Keith distillery stands beside the fast-flowing river Isla,
above a deep pool where wild salmon swim and leap. The Gaelic name is
*linne a bhradan. Here, nature is unspoilt; the air and the water pure and
sweet. It is in the very heart of Scotch Whisky country.

70 cl ℮   BOTTLED IN SCOTLAND   43%vol

KEITH, BANFFSHIRE EST. 1957

Originally part of an oat mill of uncertain age, it was converted into a distillery by Chivas Brothers Ltd, a subsidiary of The Seagram Company of Canada, between 1957 and 1960. It was originally designed for triple distillation, but converted to the more normal double distillation in 1970.

LOCATION   By the Linn Pool near the centre of Keith

NOTES   The first distillery to be founded in Scotland since the boom years of the late 19th Century. It was also the first distillery in Scotland to have a gas-fired still and the first to use a micro-processor to control the whole operation.

WATER   The Balloch Hill springs.

Distilled before 1983   **Strength** 43% abv

Sweetness 6 Peatiness 3 Availability 6

Colour Pale amber with lemon highlights **Nose** Medium-bodied and medium-sweet with firm peat and soft rich lanolin, a touch mashy and an unctuous oakiness **Flavour** Medium-sweet, soft oak, rich, creamy and smooth **Finish** Rich and smooth with a slight toffee touch **Notes** Seagram bottling

Age 22 years   **Distilled** 1967   **Strength** 45.6% abv

Sweetness 7 Peatiness 3 Availability 1

Colour Bright straw with gold/green highlights **Nose** Quite full, rich, oily, nutty and oaky with a slight citrus note **Flavour** Rich, medium-sweet, gently peated and with an oily creaminess **Finish** Long and sweet with a touch of vanilla **Notes** Wm Cadenhead bottling

PENCAITLAND, EAST LOTHIAN EST. 1837

East Lothian is one of the heartlands of Scottish farming and Glenkinchie and its staff have been involved in agricultural activities since its inception. The distillery managers also looked after the adjoining farm and one manager, who fed his beasts on the distillery by-products, won the Supreme Championship for his Aberdeen Angus cattle at Smithfield, Edinburgh and Birmingham in the 1940s and 50s. Established by John and George Rate, Glenkinchie was disused between 1853 and 1880, when it was revived by the Glen Kinchie Distillery Co. Owned by SMD since 1914, Glenkinchie was one of the founding distilleries in SMD, and licensed to John Haig & Company. Now a part of United Distillers plc. Two stills.

LOCATION Due south of Pencaitland, the distillery is in a hollow in the hills and, although the chimney can be seen from some distance, the road end could easily be missed as the sign was traditionally overgrown.

NOTES The distillery has a unique museum of distilling which was originated around 1968 by Alistair Munro, a former manager, the work being continued by his successors. This includes an enormous model of a Highland malt distillery which was built to a scale of one-sixth of actual size for the Empire Exhibition in 1924-25. Glenkinchie has also been known as Kinchie and is probably also the same distillery as Milton of which records exist of being operated by John and George Rate from 1825 to 1834. Glenkinchie has long been an important malt to the Haig blend.

WATER Reservoirs in the Lammermuir Hills.

Age 10 years **Strength** 43% abv

Sweetness 2 **Peatiness** 5 **Availability** 9

Colour Pale straw/golden with yellow highlights **Nose** Fresh, dry, pleasantly peated and slightly spirity **Flavour** Dry, malty, quite spicy, full and smooth **Finish** Long, lingering, delicately smoky and quite rich **Notes** United Distillers bottling

The
GLENLIVET
AGED **12** YEARS
*Pure Single Malt
Scotch Whisky*
PRODUCT OF SCOTLAND

"UNHURRIED SINCE 1824"
*An exceptional whisky from
The Glenlivet Distillery, aged in oak casks
for more than twelve unhurried years.
Distilled in Scotland by*
GEORGE & J. G. SMITH
THE GLENLIVET DISTILLERY · AB37 9DD
BOTTLED IN SCOTLAND

70 cl℮   40%vol.

MINMORE, BALLINDALLOCH, BANFFSHIRE EST. 1824

George Smith established his distillery in 1824 at Upper Drummin farm, being the first distiller in the Highlands to take out a licence after the passing of the Excise Act of 1823. In 1858, after the original distillery had been destroyed by fire, a new one was built at Minmore on land obtained from the Duke of Gordon. The Glenlivet was amalgamated with J & J Grant of Glen Grant in 1953 and later with Longmorn-Glenlivet Distilleries Ltd in 1970. The enlarged Glenlivet group of companies was purchased by the Seagram Company of Canada in 1977. Eight stills.

LOCATION   Situated on the slopes of the Braes of Glenlivet, the local hills.

NOTES   The very district of Glenlivet is rich in history. It was here that, in 1594, the king's army under the Earl of Huntly defeated the Covenanters commanded by the Duke of Argyll. The real name of the very English sounding Smiths was Gow. They had been supporters of the Jacobites and Bonnie Prince Charlie, but after his defeat at Culloden in 1746, the family apparently changed their name to avoid the oppression which followed. Although many others have laid claim to the "Glenlivet" appellation, following legal action taken by The Glenlivet's then owners in the 1880's, there is only one distillery which can rightly be called "The Glenlivet". So famous had the name Glenlivet already become by then that the wags of the day christened it "the longest glen in Scotland". Such was the reputation for quality that The Glenlivet had gained, that whiskies that had not even been distilled anywhere near the Livet glen were claiming its provenance on their labels.

WATER   Josie's Well.

Age 12 years   **Strength** 40% abv

Sweetness 8	Peatiness 4	Availability 10

Colour Straw with a definite greenness to its edge **Nose** Leafy, floral, slightly malty, very fragrant **Flavour** Sherry cask on palate with typical honeyed shortbread-sweet flavour **Finish** Good length **Notes** George & J.G. Smith bottling

Age 12 years   **Strength** 40% abv

Sweetness 3	Peatiness 6	Availability 4

Colour Amber with gold highlights and a dark tinge **Nose** Slightly dumb, floral, violet character and medium-dry **Flavour** Quite dry with quite big oaky tannins, a slight touch of richness and quite full-bodied **Finish** Long with quite chewy dry tannins and an earthy peatiness **Notes** Gordon & MacPhail bottling

Age 18 years   **Strength** 43% abv

Sweetness 6	Peatiness 5	Availability 1

Colour Quite deep amber with bronze highlights **Nose** Quite full-bdied, medium-sweet with a dark, soft nuttiness, a good, peaty character with a lightly honeyed, almost Christmas cake richness and a gentle peaty fruitiness **Flavour** Big-bodied, smooth, round, soft, rich and medium-sweet, slightly toffeeyed and gently peated **Finish** Rich with a touch of spice, a light, elegant smoky touch to the tail and surprisingly dry **Notes** Glenlivet Distillers bottling, available only in the USA when tasted in June, 1995

Age 15 years **Strength** 57% abv

Sweetness 8 Peatiness 6 Availability 4

Colour Amber with old gold highlights **Nose** Quite full, sweet, rich and malty **Flavour** Rich, Full-bodied and round with a touch of tannin, malty and quite sweet **Finish** Big-bodied, spicy, gently tannic, warm **Notes** Gordon & MacPhail bottling

Age 21 years **Strength** 40% abv

Sweetness 6 Peatiness 7 Availability 4

Colour Full amber with good gold highlights **Nose** Sweet and fruity (peaches) with touches of oaky vanilla **Flavour** Smooth, medium-sweet, round and full-bodied, gently malty **Finish** Long and toffee-like **Notes** Gordon & MacPhail bottling

Age 21 years **Distillation** 1973 **Strength** 56% abv

Sweetness 7 Peatiness 4 Availability 2

Colour Quite full amber with pale bronze highlights **Nose** Rich, oaky and nutty, of light to medium weight (quite closed) **Flavour** Rich, quite full-bodied with big, nutty tannins and medium-sweet **Finish** Long and chewy with a light smoky touch **Notes** Signatory bottling; Butt 3946 distilled 19 April 1973

Age 15 years **Distillation** 1977 **Strength** 59.5% abv

Sweetness 6 Peatiness 7 Availability 4

Colour Mid-amber with bronze highlights and a tinge of ruby **Nose** Quite full and rich, medium-dry with a burnt oak character **Flavour** Full-bodied, rich and medium-sweet with quite big tannins and a quite full smokiness **Finish** Long, chewy and quite tannic with a smoky tail **Notes** Gordon & MacPhail bottling; cask nos. 11302/11303 distilled 6 June 1977

GLENLIVET DISTILLERY.

GLENLOCHY

Vintage 1963
Single Highland Malt Scotch Whisky
Matured in sherry casks for 30 years
Distilled at the Glenlochy Distillery
on 14.3.63   *Bottled 12.93*
Cask no. 762   *Bottle no.158 of 250*
*This whisky has been selected, produced and bottled in
Scotland for and under the sole responsibility of
Signatory Vintage Scotch Whisky Co. Ltd.
Edinburgh EH6 Scotland*
70cl   52.2%vol

FORT WILLIAM, INVERNESS-SHIRE   EST. 1898

Glenlochy was always very up-to-date. All the fittings in 1898 were "arranged throughout with a view to saving labour". A visitor reported, in 1907, that Glenlochy possessed "every modern facility for enabling it to be worked with a minimum of labour". Joseph Hobbs of Associated Scottish Distillers sold it in 1940. Eight years later, he established the Great Glen cattle ranch, an area of 54 square kilometres where beef cattle fend for themselves, as they do on the U.S. prairies. The ranch is still in operation. Glenlochy was silent from 1917-1924 and again from 1926-37. It was bought by DCL in 1953 when the unit was transferred to SMD. It had two stills.

LOCATION   Situated within Fort William on the north bank of the River Nevis, to the west of the A82.

NOTES   The distillery closed for good in 1983.

WATER   The River Nevis

Age 30 years   **Distillation** 1963   **Strength** 52.2% abv

Sweetness 3   **Peatiness** 6   **Availability** 2

Colour Mid amber with gold highlights **Nose** Light, quite fresh with a cooked apple character and quite dry **Flavour** Quite dry with a smoky oak and coffee character **Finish** Good length and delicately smoky **Notes** Signatory bottling

Distillation 1974   **Strength** 40% abv

Sweetness 7   **Peatiness** 4   **Availability** 2

Colour Palish amber with copper highlights **Nose** Spirity, sweet, woody, fruity **Flavour** Sweet, woody and creamy with a note of spice **Finish** Short with a strange woody aftertaste **Notes** Gordon & MacPhail bottling

THOMSHILL, BY ELGIN, MORAY EST. 1876

Built in 1876 by John Duff, tenant of the Fife Arms, Lhanbryde and previously manager of the Glendronach distillery. A controlling interest was obtained by SMD in 1919 and the distillery was taken over completely by DCL in 1930. Extended from four to six stills in 1962. The make is important to John Haig's blends, the distillery being licensed to that company. Now part of United Distillers plc.

LOCATION Sited at Thomshill on an unclassified road to the west of the A941, two miles south of Elgin.

NOTES A purifier has been installed between the lyne arm and the condenser on each of the three spirit stills. Electricity only replaced steam as late as 1960 as the means of power generation at the distillery. A fire at the distillery in 1929 caused some damage. One of the appliances that fought the blaze was the distillery's own engine. Dating from the 1860s and originally horse drawn, it can still be seen at the distillery. The site now houses two distilleries, the other being the much newer Mannochmore, built in 1971.

WATER The Bardon Burn.

Age 10 years **Strength** 43% abv

Sweetness 6 Peatiness 3 Availability 6

Colour Quite pale straw with lemon yellow highlights **Nose** Fresh, cerealy and green, fragrant with a touch of perfume **Flavour** Fresh with a touch of oaky tannin, quite green and gently smoky, medium-dry with richness in the middle of the palate **Finish** Lasts quite well - clean, fresh and spicy **Notes** United Distillers bottling

GLENLOSSIE

Distillation 1968 **Strength** 40% abv

Sweetness 7 Peatiness 4 Availability 4

Colour Palish gold with good bright highlights **Nose** Sweet, fruity, slightly musty, nutty **Flavour** Sweet, fruity, musty and spicy **Finish** Nice fruitiness, good length and with a nuttiness on the tail **Notes** Gordon & MacPhail bottling

Distillation 1969 **Strength** 40% abv

Sweetness 7 Peatiness 4 Availability 4

Colour Straw/amber with gold highlights **Nose** Medium-bodied, quite rich with a tang of gunpowder and a warm nuttiness **Flavour** Quite rich, medium-bodied, lightly peated with a nice sweet edge and a slightly oily texture **Finish** Of reasonable length, rich with a touch of greenness **Notes** Gordon & MacPhail bottling

INVERNESS EST. 1892

Founded by ex-Provost John Birnie and James Mackinlay of Charles Mackinlay & Co, Glen Mhor began production on 8 December 1894. It became a part of DCL in 1972, John Walker & Co. having long had a large shareholding in the company, from which date it was operated by SMD. Closed in 1983 and subsequently demolished to make way for a shopping complex.

LOCATION The distillery was situated at the north end of the Caledonian Canal where it intersects with the Great North Road (the A9) at the north west of Inverness, across the road from Glen Albyn.

NOTES The name Glen Mhor means "Great Glen". It was the first distillery in Scotland to introduce mechanical maltings. Glen Mhor, like its sister Glen Albyn is alas no more.

WATER Loch Ness

Age 8 years   **Strength** 57% abv

Sweetness 4 Peatiness 4 Availability 2

Colour Straw/amber with good gold highlights **Nose** Lightly peated with an edge of sweetness **Flavour** Medium-sweet, slightly woody and quite full-bodied **Finish** Spicy, creamy, long and almost leafy **Notes** Gordon & MacPhail bottling

Age 14 years   **Distillation** 1978   **Strength** 43% abv

Sweetness 4 Peatiness 6 Availability 0

Colour Straw with lemon highlights **Nose** Medium-bodied and quite rich with an appley sweetness and a slight floral touch **Flavour** Quite dry and smooth with big, full, dark, nutty tannins **Finish** Long with a salty smokiness **Notes** Master of Malt bottling; cask nos. 4041/4042 distilled 21 September 1978

Converted from the Morangie Brewery of McKenzie & Gallie by William Mathieson. Rebuilt in 1887 and again in 1979, when it was extended from two to four stills. Glenmorangie has been owned by Macdonald & Muir, the Leith blenders since 1918.

LOCATION Sited on the Dornoch Firth on the A9 between Tain and Edderton, looking across the Firth towards the hills of Sutherland.

NOTES One of the smallest of all Highland distilleries. All of the make is used by the owners, none being made available as fillings. A noted feature of the distillery is that the stills have very tall necks, at 16 feet 10 inches (5.14metres), the tallest in Scotland.

WATER Springs in the Tarlogie Hills above the distillery

Age 10 years **Strength** 40% abv

Sweetness 4 Peatiness 4 Availability 10

Colour Good light gold/pale straw **Nose** Fresh, medium-bodied, steely with floral notes and a touch of peat **Flavour** Light, fresh, slightly smoky with an oily creaminess **Finish** Sweet with good length **Notes** Macdonald & Muir bottling

Age 18 years **Strength** 43% abv

Sweetness 4 Peatiness 4 Availability 6

Colour Honey-amber with good gold highlights **Nose** Fresh, salty, nutty (almonds), with an edge of sweetness, quite full and round **Flavour** Smooth, medium-dry, fresh, good nut-oily glycerine, quite full-bodied **Finish** Medium-dry, spicy, long and almost creamy **Notes** Macdonald & Muir bottling

THE NATIVE ROSS-SHIRE GLENMORANGIE
Age 10 years **Distillation** 1980 **Strength** 57.6% abv

Sweetness 4 Peatiness 4 Availability 4

Colour Bright pale amber, yellow-gold highlights **Nose** A touch of sweetness, fresh, quite full, dried hay, lanolin and vanilla **Flavour** Quite rich, round, medium-dry oaky-vanilla, quite full, fat and soft **Finish** Fresh, clean, aromatic and quite long **Notes** Macdonald & Muir bottling. Cask no. 4336; distilled 15.5.80; bottled 5.9.90. Branded as "The Native Ross-shire Glenmorangie"

Distillation 1963 (Bottled 1988) **Strength** 43% abv

Sweetness 4 Peatiness 4 Availability 1

Colour Quite pale peaty/straw with gold and green highlights **Nose** Rich, full malty, oaky with sweet appley fruit **Flavour** Sweet, full spicy, quite green with a toffee-like richness **Finish** Long, spicy, caramelly and fine **Notes** Macdonald & Muir bottling. Matured in a bourbon cask, as all Glenmorangie is, for 22 years and "finished off" for the last year in an oloroso sherry cask

PORT FINISH GLENMORANGIE
Age No stated age **Strength** 56.5% abv

Sweetness 4 Peatiness 3 Availability 5

Colour Quite full amber with bronze highlights **Nose** Medium-bodied, quite fresh with a slightly green mint character and richness with notes of vanilla, butterscotch and toffee **Flavour** Medium-dry, rich, spicy, fresh, soft round and with good body **Finish** Rich, smooth, spicy and with a long chocolate-sweet tail with a fresh, green edge **Notes** Macdonald & Muir bottling

GLENMORANGIE
PORT WOOD FINISH

This unusual whisky is the direct result of pioneering work into the role of wood in malt whisky maturation. Initially matured in American oak casks for at least 12 years, Glenmorangie Port Wood Finish has been racked into selected port "pipes" for the last few years of its maturation. The results of this "finishing" are truly exceptional.

Trade Mark

ELGIN, MORAY EST. 1897

Like its sister distillery, Glenmorangie, a former brewery, having been built in 1815. It was closed in 1910 and passed into the ownership of Macdonald & Muir in 1923. It was rebuilt in 1958, when it was converted from two to four stills.

LOCATION Situated in a hollow on the bank of the River Lossie, on the western outskirts of Elgin.

NOTES Close by the distillery is Gallowcrook Hill, which was, as its name implies, the scene of public hangings in days gone by. Some of the make goes into Macdonald & Muir's Highland Queen blend. The old steam engine that formerly powered the distillery is still in place.

WATER River Lossie.

Age 12 years **Strength** 40% abv

Sweetness 7 Peatiness 3 Availability 7

Colour Pale gold **Nose** Clean, fresh, aromatic and slightly peppery **Flavour** Light, creamy, heathery and medium-sweet **Finish** Delicate, of reasonable length and soft **Notes** Macdonald & Muir bottling

Age 15 years **Strength** 43% abv

Sweetness 7 Peatiness 2 Availability 5

Colour Amber with gold highlights **Nose** Fresh, medium-bodied with an appley character, sweet soft bubble-gummy vanilla, good richness and a hint of perfume **Flavour** Round with oaky tannins, quite a rich fruity character and good body **Finish** Smooth, spicy and medium-sweet with a rich chewy tail **Notes** Macdonald & Muir bottling

Age 13 years **Distillation** 1980 **Strength** 43% abv

Sweetness 4 Peatiness 6 Availability 2

Colour Pale straw with pale lemon highlights **Nose** Light to medium-bodied, fresh and medium-sweet, a green, almost floral character and quite lightly peated **Flavour** Good body, fresh and medium-sweet, slightly green with a good background of peatiness **Finish** Fresh, clean and smoky with a richness in the middle **Notes** Blackadder International bottling

Age 27 years **Distillation** 1962 **Strength** 55.1% abv

Sweetness 7 Peatiness 3 Availability 1

Colour Rich, mid-dark amber with good gold highlights **Nose** Quite full-bodied, toffee & chocolate, medium-sweet, lightly peated with warm, oaky vanilla **Flavour** Medium-sweet, quite full-bodied, spicy, nutty, almost austere with oaky tannins **Finish** Smooth, medium-dry and quite firm with a smoky touch; it lingers well **Notes** Wm Cadenhead bottling

MUIR OF ORD, ROSS-SHIRE EST. 1838

Founded as the Ord Distillery Company, which was taken over by James Watson & Co. of Dundee in 1896. Watson's were in turn acquired by John Dewar & Sons of Perth in 1923. Dewar's joined DCL in 1925, and the management of the distillery was taken over by SMD from 1930. The floor maltings were converted to Saladin maltings in 1961. Extensively rebuilt and extended from two to six stills in 1966. A large drum maltings was built on an adjacent site in 1968 and supplies malted barley to many other distilleries in the north of Scotland. Ord is now a part of United Distillers plc and licensed to John Dewar & Sons Ltd.

LOCATION About 15 miles to the north of Inverness on the western side of the A832, immediately to the west of Muir of Ord.

NOTES The New Statistical Account of Scotland recorded in 1840 that "distilling of aquavitae" was the sole manufacture of the district. Ord, which was built on the site of a smugglers' bothy, is the only distillery remaining in the area. There were nine other licensed distilleries operating during the last century. The distillery was lit by paraffin lamps until it gained access to the national electricity grid after World War II, but water power was still used for some operations at late as the early 1960's. A visitor centre was opened in 1992. In the late Fifties and early Sixties, Ord was used for a programme of experiments which studied the differences between batches of spirit produced respectively by heating with coal, oil and steam. A colourful local smugglers' tale tells of Excisemen taking a confiscated cask of whisky upstairs to their room for safe keeping while staying overnight in a local inn, The Bogroy Hotel in nearby Beauly. A hole was drilled through the ceiling under the cask from the bar below and the whisky was "liberated" while the Excisemen slept.

WATER Loch nan Eun and Loch nam Bonnach

Age 12 years   **Strength** 40% abv

Sweetness 6   Peatiness 5   Availability 6

Colour Mid-amber with yellow/green highlights and just a tinge of green **Nose** Quite fresh and lightly peated with a green fruitiness, medium-dry with a hint of creamy richness **Flavour** Medium-dry, quite rich and fresh, full and round with a touch of pepperiness **Finish** Long, fresh and quite rich with a dry tail **Notes** United Distillers bottling

ORD

Age 12 years   **Strength** 40% abv

Sweetness 7   Peatiness 5   Availability 0

Colour Gold/straw with amber tints **Nose** Full-bodied, slightly dry, but with an overlying richness **Flavour** Quite full, big-bodied, round and medium-sweet **Finish** Very smooth, long and smoky **Notes** DCL (pre-Guinness) bottling as "Ord"

Age 27 years   **Distillation** 1962   **Strength** 55.4% abv

Sweetness 7   Peatiness 5   Availability 1

Colour Amber with good gold highlights **Nose** Full, round, medium-sweet and quite mellow with a touch of oily-nuttiness **Flavour** Fresh, clean, soft, a touch oaky, quite round and full **Finish** Dry, smooth, slightly austere and nutty **Notes** Wm Cadenhead bottling

ROTHES, MORAY EST. 1878

Built by Wm Grant & Company. Amalgamated in 1887 with the Islay Distillery Company (owners of Bunnahabhain distillery) to form The Highland Distilleries Ltd. Enlarged in 1963 from four to six stills, and from six to ten in 1980.

LOCATION A short way up the glen formed by the Burn of Rothes which flows from the Mannoch Hills.

NOTES The first spirit ran from the stills in 1897 on the night of the Tay rail bridge disaster. The distillery experienced "one of the most disastrous distillery fires" on 15 May 1922 when No. 1 Bonded Warehouse was destroyed, along with 2,500 casks (800,000 litres of maturing spirit): a stream of burning whisky flowed out of the stricken building and into the burn. Glenrothes is one of the malts at the heart of the Famous Grouse and Cutty Sark blends.

WATER Springs in the hills above the distillery.

Age 15 years **Distillation** 1979 **Strength** 43% abv
Sweetness 7 Peatiness 3 Availability 5

Colour Mid-amber with gold highlights **Nose** Rich, soft and round with an unctuous sweetness, a slight nutty character and a touch of fresh citrus **Flavour** Full-bodied, soft, round and medium-sweet with gentle tannins **Finish** Long, quite fresh, delicately peated, rich and smooth **Notes** Berry Bros & Rudd bottling. The bottle, label and individual carton for this presentation was lauded and received many prizes in the 1994 industry awards.

GLEN ROTHES

Age 8 years **Strength** 40% abv

Sweetness 8 Peatiness 3 Availability 4

Colour Full mid-amber with gold highlights **Nose** Full-bodied, quite spirity, rich, dark, lightly peated and medium-sweet **Flavour** Medium-sweet, very rich and toffee-like, light to medium-peated **Finish** Warm, sweet and of good length **Notes** Gordon & MacPhail bottling

Age 16 years **Strength** 46% abv

Sweetness 8 Peatiness 3 Availability 4

Colour Deep gold, quite peaty in depth **Nose** Fruity, sweet, slightly oaky **Flavour** Full-bodied, richly sweet, possibly a little woody **Finish** Long and complex with a dry tail **Notes** Wm Cadenhead bottling

Age 19 years **Distillation** 1974 **Strength** 43% abv

Sweetness 8 Peatiness 3 Availability 0

Colour Pale straw with yellow/gold highlights **Nose** Soft, medium-sweet, caramel/toffee and malty with quite good body and a shortbread character **Flavour** Sweet, malty, soft with gentle tannins, sweet oaky vanilla and quite big-bodied **Finish** Sweet and rich vanilla with good length **Notes** Master of Malt bottling - cask no. 11810 distilled 9th July 1974

Age 27 years **Distillation** 1966 **Strength** 51.3% abv

Sweetness 7 Peatiness 3 Availability 2

Colour Very dark amber with an almost black heart and bronze/ruby highlights **Nose** Big-bodied, dark nutty oak with spirit at the back, almost a beeswax note, rich and medium-dry **Flavour** Big and dark with quite gentle tannins, full-bodied and smooth **Finish** Long, quite spirity and rich **Notes** Signatory bottling - butt no 13512 distilled 3.11.66

Distillation 1978 **Strength** 40% abv

Sweetness 7 Peatiness 4 Availability 4

Colour Straw/pale amber with yellow highlights **Nose** Light to medium-bodied, sweet, with a honeyed nuttiness, delicately peated and a little spirity **Flavour** Quite full-bodied, medium-sweet and quite smooth with a good smoky character **Finish** Good length, quite fresh, clean and rich **Notes** 1995 Gordon & MacPhail Centenary Reserve bottling

CAMPBELTOWN, ARGYLL EST. 1832

Since it was founded as Scotia in 1832 by Stewart, Galbraith & Co., Glen Scotia has gone through many changes of ownership, the most recent being when Gibson International, who had owned it since the 1980s, went into receivership towards the end of 1994. It has two stills of classic swan-necked design.

LOCATION In the centre of the town, at the junction of High Street with Saddell Street.

NOTES One of only two distilleries remaining in Campbeltown, (the other being Springbank); somewhat fewer than the 19 which existed at the start of the economic recession of the 1920s and early 30s, during which time all were closed. Glen Scotia and Springbank were the only two to re-open. After £1,000,000 had been spent upgrading the distillery between 1979 and 1982, it was closed again until 1989 when it re-opened, only to cease production late in 1994 following Gibson International's receivership. The distillery and all maturing stocks have since been purchased by Glen Catrine Bonded Warehouse Ltd.

WATER The Crosshill Loch and two wells bored 80 feet down into the rocks below the distillery.

Age 8 years   **Strength** 40% abv

Sweetness 8   Peatiness 6   Availability 4

Colour Golden with hints of peaty water **Nose** Slightly peaty, complex, but delicate **Flavour** Lightish, smoky, richly sweet and slightly spirity **Finish** Soft and long **Notes** Gibson International bottling

Age 14 years **Strength** 40% abv

Sweetness 4 Peatiness 3 Availability 3

Colour Straw with yellow/gold highlights **Nose** Clean, medium-bodied with a slight bubble-gummy sweetness, a touch of perfume and a hint of greenness **Flavour** Round, smooth and gentle, quite good body and medium-dry with the bubble-gummy note and a soft peatiness **Finish** Long, clean and slightly tangy with a hint of smokiness **Notes** Glen Catrine bottling

Age 27 years **Distillation** 1966 **Strength** 51.5% abv

Sweetness 4 Peatiness 2 Availability 2

Colour Pale straw with yellow/lemon highlights **Nose** Fresh and medium-dry with a leafy greenness, a delicate nuttiness and a slight oaky unctuousness **Flavour** Medium-dry, fresh and clean with a good richness and an almost chocolatey maltiness **Finish** Clean, quite crisp and lightly tangy with good length and concentration **Notes** Signatory bottling - cask nos. 1271-72 distilled April, 1966

Age 16 years **Distillation** 1977 **Strength** 57.6% abv

Sweetness 5 Peatiness 6 Availability 2

Colour Pale amber with yellow/gold highlights **Nose** Medium-bodied, fresh and off-dry with hints of Orange Pekoe tea and a light, earthy peatiness **Flavour** Quite rich, medium-dry with a touch of spice, gentle tannins, a firm peatiness and a flavour of tea **Finish** Quite tangy, softly smoky and of good length **Notes** Wm Cadenhead bottling

ROTHES, MORAY EST. 1878

Established by James Stuart & Company. Owned by W & A Gilbey since 22 September 1887 and now part of the Grand Metropolitan Group. Rebuilt in 1970 when it was extended from two to four stills.

LOCATION The distillery stands just below the ruins of Castle Rothes, the ancient seat of the Leslie family, the Earls of Rothes.

NOTES James Stuart & Company also once owned Macallan distillery, a short distance away at Craigellachie. Like Knockando, Glen Spey is an important constituent of the J & B blends. The original unit covered an area of 2 acres; the distillery beginning life as an extension to a mill which was was the company's original business as a grain merchant. The maturation warehouse was very innovative for its day, 10,000 square feet covered by two arched corrugated iron spans and supported by decorative iron pillars. Regrettably, on 10 January 1892, there was an exceptionally heavy snowfall and the roof collapsed under the weight of a covering of two feet of snow.

WATER The Doonie Burn.

Age 8 years **Strength** 40% abv

Sweetness 7 Peatiness 3 Availability 0

Colour Pale amber with lemon highlights and a definite green tinge **Nose** Quite light and mashy, gently smoky with a greenness at the back **Flavour** Medium-sweet, fragrant, cerealy, spirity, quite fresh and smooth **Finish** Nice sweetness, spirity and spicy **Notes** W & A Gilbey bottling

MULBEN, BANFFSHIRE EST. 1898

The foundation stone was laid on 29 May 1897, on one of the fields belonging to Tauchers Farm, and the first brew was brewed on 16 June 1898. One of the original owners was James Buchanan, later Lord Woolavington of Black & White fame. Merged with DCL in 1925, the distillery came under SMD's wing in 1930. Rebuilt in 1965-66 when it was increased from two to six stills. Closed in May 1983. Sold to Allied Distillers in 1989 and re-opened. Now part of Allied Domecq and operated by Allied Distillers Ltd.

LOCATION On the A95, four miles west of Keith

NOTES Experiments in the continuous distillation of malt whisky were carried out here around 1910.

WATER Springs in the local hills.

Distillation 1979 **Strength** 40% abv

Sweetness 7 Peatiness 3 Availability 4

Colour Light amber with gold highlights **Nose** Medium weight with good richness, nutty, medium-sweet with an aroma of dried apricots and delicately peated **Flavour** Nutty, oaky, medium-sweet with a touch of spice **Finish** Fresh, smooth, good length with a nice light nuttiness **Notes** Gordon & MacPhail bottling

Age 16 years **Distillation** 1977 **Strength** 63.8% abv

Sweetness 5 Peatiness 6 Availability 4

Colour Straw/pale amber with yellow highlights **Nose** Fresh, round and slightly green, medium-sweet with slight floral and aromatic notes **Flavour** Medium-sweet, round and quite full-bodied with a floral note and quite big tannins, gently smoky **Finish** Long, smooth and delicately smoky **Notes** Wm Cadenhead bottling

The Glenturret Distillery Crieff

The GLENTURRET

ESTABLISHED 1775

Single Highland Malt

SCOTCH WHISKY

AGED **12** YEARS

PRODUCT OF SCOTLAND
BOTTLED IN SCOTLAND

70cl e 40%vol

THE HOSH, CRIEFF, PERTHSHIRE EST. 1775

Glenturret, previously called Hosh, is the second to take that name. It was renamed Glenturret in 1875, some 20 or so years after the nearby original distillery of that name closed. The distillery which, with two stills is one of Scotland's smallest, was silent from 1923-1959. It was revived by James Fairlie who, with the later assistance of his son, Peter, has established Glenturret as one of the world's most sought after single malts and the Glenturret distillery as a tourist attraction that is second to none.

LOCATION On the banks of the River Turret north west of Crieff on a secondary road which leads from the A85 round Crieff to Monzie and Gilmerton.

NOTES Now part of Highland Distillers Co. plc. Although the present buildings were erected in 1775, illicit distilling took place at least as early as 1717. The Drummond Arms Hotel in Crieff was the building in which Prince Charles Edward Stuart (Bonnie Prince Charlie) held his stormy council of war on 3 February 1746. Apart from being possibly the oldest distillery in Scotland (see Littlemill) and certainly the oldest in the Highlands, Glenturret has another impressive claim to fame in the Guinness Book of Records. A legend even in her own lifetime, Towser, the distillery's rodent operative, was credited with catching a world record 28,899 mice. Born at the distillery on 21 April 1963, Towser died on 20 March 1987, not far short of her 24th birthday - a very good age for a cat! As well as the mice, Towser was also more than a match for rats, baby rabbits and even pheasants.

WATER Loch Turret.

Age 8 years   **Strength** 40% abv

Sweetness 6   Peatiness 4   Availability 2

Colour Very pale straw with yellowy green highlights **Nose** Full, fruity, quite spirity, malty and dryish **Flavour** Lightweight, medium-dry, round, smooth and slightly nutty **Finish** Lightly spicy, grapey, of medium length **Notes** Glenturret bottling

Age 10 years   **Strength** 57.1% abv

Sweetness 6   Peatiness 4   Availability 2

Colour Very pale straw with pale yellow/green highlights **Nose** Full-bodied, slightly sweet, floral and slightly meaty **Flavour** Quite full-bodied, round, smooth, creamy, slightly meaty and medium-dry **Finish** Smooth, dry and quite long with soft edges **Notes** Glenturret bottling

Age 12 years   **Strength** 40% abv

Sweetness 7   Peatiness 3   Availability 6

Colour Straw/amber with good greeny gold highlights **Nose** Rich and sherried with oaky vanilla, medium-sweet **Flavour** Rich, medium-sweet, sweet oaky vanilla, full-bodied and smooth **Finish** Long and sherried **Notes** Glenturret bottling

Age 15 years   **Strength** 40% abv

Sweetness 7   Peatiness 3   Availability 4

Colour Golden/copper coloured with good yellow highlights **Nose** Big-bodied, full, spicy and medium-sweet with oaky vanilla and characters of liquorice, citrus and mint **Flavour** Full, rich, sweet and slightly peppery with hints of mint and liquorice - very complex **Finish** Smooth, spicy, long and memorable **Notes** Glenturret bottling

Age 18 years **Strength** 40% abv

Sweetness **7** Peatiness **3** Availability **6**

Colour Straw/amber with yellow/gold highlights **Nose** Rich, medium-bodied and slightly perfumed with characters of honey, toffee and green coffee **Flavour** Round, smooth, medium-sweet with a slight apple and coffee tang **Finish** Smooth, sweet and rich with a slight tang of fennel **Notes** Glenturret bottling

Age 21 years **Strength** 40% abv

Sweetness **7** Peatiness **3** Availability **1**

Colour Light mid-amber with old gold highlights **Nose** Rich and quite full-bodied, a greenness and liquorice/aniseed, medium-sweet **Flavour** Medium-sweet, lightly peated, rich aniseed and creamily smooth with a touch of oaky vanilla **Finish** Fresh, clean and long with a touch of sweetness **Notes** Glenturret bottling

Age 25 years **Strength** 43% abv

Sweetness **6** Peatiness **3** Availability **1**

Colour Straw with yellow/gold highlights **Nose** Quite fresh, medium-bodied and medium-sweet, a slight oaky oiliness and a nice citrus character **Flavour** Quite full-bodied and sweet with touches of vanilla and tannin **Finish** Long and sweet, tannic and quite fresh **Notes** Glenturret bottling

Distillation 1966 **Strength** 40% abv

Sweetness **6** Peatiness **3** Availability **1**

Colour Pale to mid-amber with gold highlights **Nose** Rich and quite full-bodied, medium-sweet oaky vanilla with a tang of orange and delicately peated **Flavour** Medium-dry, quite full-bodied, oaky, spicy with characters of liquorice and vanilla, quite round **Finish** Quite long and complex, with rich liquorice/aniseed and a tail of oaky tannin **Notes** Glenturret bottling

Distillation 1968 **Strength** 40% abv

Sweetness **6** Peatiness **3** Availability **1**

Colour Straw with yellow/lemon highlights **Nose** Medium-sweet, grapey and rich with slight chocolate and nutty characters, caramel toffee and bubble-gummy notes **Flavour** Medium-sweet, quite good body, rich and smooth with a coffee/toffee tang **Finish** Long, tangy with a coffee/toffee note, quite rich and clean **Notes** Glenturret bottling

Distillation 1972 **Strength** 40% abv

Sweetness **7** Peatiness **3** Availability **3**

Colour Pale straw with good greeny-gold highlights **Nose** Rich oaky vanilla, malty, medium-sweet and delicate **Flavour** Rich, soft, round with hints of smokiness and medium-sweet **Finish** Smooth, pleasantly soft and with reasonable length **Notes** Glenturret bottling

Age 14 years **Distillation** 1979 **Strength** 43% abv

Sweetness **6** Peatiness **1** Availability **0**

Colour Very pale straw with bright pale lemon highlights **Nose** Slightly subdued, fresh and green with a slight richness and medium-dry **Flavour** Medium-dry with a green tang, fresh, clean and leafy with an edge of richness at the back, very lightly peated **Finish** Fresh, clean with an almost floral, grassy, gooseberry freshness **Notes** Master of Malt bottling - cask no 1057 distilled 12 October 1979

5,000 DAYS

Age 5,000 days old **Strength** 40% abv

Sweetness **6** Peatiness **3** Availability **3**

Colour Pale amber with yellow highlights **Nose** Good body, fresh with a slight floral note, lightly peated and a hint of tablet **Flavour** Soft, smooth, quite sweet, coffee flavour and lightly smoky **Finish** Medium-sweet, quite soft and of good length **Notes** Glenturret bottling

10,000 DAYS

Age 10,000 days old **Strength** 40% abv

Sweetness **6** Peatiness **4** Availability **3**

Colour Mid-amber with yellow/gold highlights **Nose** Quite full, sweet, rich and fruity with a touch of greenness, an oaky lanolin character and a hint of green coffee **Flavour** Good body, quite zesty, fresh and medium-dry with a slight greenness **Finish** Clean, of good length with a touch of coffee **Notes** Glenturret bottling

CONNOISSEURS CHOICE

Connoisseurs Choice, a range of single malts from various districts of Scotland.

In the Highlands are situated the greatest number of malt whisky distilleries.

SINGLE HIGHLAND
MALT SCOTCH WHISKY
DISTILLED AT
GLENUGIE
DISTILLERY
Trade Mark of Proprietors: Long John Distillers Ltd
DISTILLED 1966 DISTILLED
Specially selected, produced and bottled by and under the responsibility of
70cl GORDON & MACPHAIL 40%vol
REGD. BOTTLER · ELGIN · SCOTLAND
PRODUCT OF SCOTLAND

PETERHEAD, ABERDEENSHIRE EST. 1831

Built by Donald McLeod and Company, Glenugie passed through the hands of a number of different owners. More recently, in 1970, it was owned by a company called Long John International, which was purchased by Whitbread & Co. Ltd in 1975, who were also at the time owners of Laphroaig distillery. Unlike many distilleries which were originally breweries, Glenugie was converted into a brewery for a while before being turned back to distilling. Two stills.

LOCATION About three miles south of Peterhead, Glenugie sits close to the sea, below the A92.

NOTES The distillery buildings, with their cast iron frames, are of an unusual and interesting design. Closed in 1983, the buildings have since been sold for use other than distilling.

WATER Springs in the local hills.

Distillation 1966 **Strength** 40% abv
Sweetness 7 Peatiness 4 Availability 4

Colour Quite full amber with old gold highlights **Nose** Full and rich, quite sweet and delicately peated with a ripe fruitiness **Flavour** Medium-sweet, rich and oaky with a green tang **Finish** Clean and lightly smoky with oaky characters **Notes** Gordon & MacPhail bottling

Vintage 1978
Single Highland Malt Scotch Whisky
Matured in oak casks for 15 years
Distilled at the Glenury Royal Distillery
on 22.11.78   Bottled 23.11.93
Cask no. 9770   Bottle no.   of 290
This whisky has been selected, produced and bottled in
Scotland for and under the sole responsibility of
Signatory Vintage Scotch Whisky Co. Ltd.
Edinburgh EH6 Scotland
70cl   62.3%vol

STONEHAVEN, KINCARDINESHIRE EST. 1825

Built to provide a market for barley in a period of agricultural depression by Barclay, McDonald & Co. It was closed from 1925-37, having been sold for £7,500 to Joseph Hobbs the preceding year. He, in turn, sold it to Associated Scottish Distilleries Ltd in 1938 for £18,500. Glenury acted as the "control office" for all of ASD's distilleries and the site was landscaped and roads were built into the unit. ASD was bought by DCL in 1953 and Glenury was worked from that date by SMD. The licensees were John Gillon & Co. Ltd. Glenury was extensively rebuilt from 1965-66, at which time it was doubled from two to four stills. Glenury was closed in 1985 and its license cancelled in 1992, when the site was sold for residential development.

LOCATION On the north bank of the Cowie Water, on the northern outskirts of Stonehaven.

NOTES The water supply was also that of the town of Stonehaven. Glenury's founder, Captain Robert Barclay, was the local member of Parliament. Through influence he was given permission by King William IV to call his whisky "Royal".

WATER The Cowie Water.

Age 12 years **Strength** 40% abv

Sweetness 2 **Peatiness** 7 **Availability** 4

Colour Mid-amber with gold highlights **Nose** Medium-bodied, quite dry, dark and smoky with a dry burnt character **Flavour** Dry, peaty, quite smooth and fragrant with a slight floral character at the back **Finish** Long, smoky and quite fresh **Notes** Gordon & MacPhail bottling

Age 12 years **Strength** 40% abv

Sweetness 3 Peatiness 6 Availability 0

Colour Gold/copper **Nose** Light, spirity, malty and quite dry **Flavour** Light, medium-dry and slightly smoky **Finish** Smoky, but quite short **Notes** DCL (Pre-Guinness) bottling

Age 14 years **Distillation** 1978 **Strength** 43% abv

Sweetness 6 Peatiness 3 Availability 1

Colour Very pale straw with pale lemon highlights **Nose** Light and fresh, medium-dry with a touch of richness and an appley character **Flavour** Medium-sweet, good body, a slightly green character with good richness **Finish** Lasts well: good, rich and delicate with a dry tail **Notes** Blackadder International bottling

Age 15 years **Distillation** 1978 **Strength** 62.3% abv

Sweetness 7 Peatiness 7 Availability 1

Colour Very pale watery straw with pale yellow highlights **Nose** Medium-dry and fresh with a mashy/cerealy character, a slight citrus tang and a light dark smokiness **Flavour** Rich and medium-sweet with a good under-pinning of peat and dry, oaky tannins **Finish** Long, quite chewy, rich and lingering **Notes** Master of Malt bottling

Age 16 years **Distillation** 1978 **Strength** 62.3% abv

Sweetness 4 Peatiness 2 Availability 2

Colour Very pale with hints of watery-green and lemon-green highlights **Nose** Quite full-bodied, malty and almost dry with an apple hint and fresh lanolin characters **Flavour** Medium-dry, round and smooth with a touch of spice and greenness; gentle tannins and lightly peated **Finish** Long, smooth and quite sweet **Notes** Signatory bottling

Vintage 1975
Single Orkney Island Malt Scotch Whisky
Matured in oak casks for 18 years
Distilled at the Highland Park Distillery
on 31.8.75   Bottled 10.93
Cask no. 4277   Bottle no.   of 260
*This whisky has been selected, produced and bottled in
Scotland for and under the sole responsibility of
Signatory Vintage Scotch Whisky Co. Ltd.*
70cl   *Edinburgh EH6 Scotland*   52.1%vol

KIRKWALL, ORKNEY EST. 1798

Said to have been founded by David Robertson, Highland Park is Scotland's most northerly distillery. It had several different owners, before coming into the hands of James Grant and family in the late 1800s. Enlarged from two to four stills in 1898 and operated by James Grant & Co. until 1935, when the company was purchased by the Highland Distilleries Co. Ltd.

LOCATION Sited on a hillside overlooking Scapa Flow to the south and Kirkwall to the north.

NOTES The distillery is built on the spot where the legendary 18th century smuggler Magnus Eunson's bothy stood. A local minister as well as a distiller, he apparently kept a stock of whisky under his pulpit. Hearing that his church was about to be searched by the Excisemen, he had the kegs removed to the manse where they were shrouded in white cloth. A coffin lid was placed next to the cloth and Eunson and his "mourners" knelt in prayer. The whispered word "smallpox" quickly ended any idea of a search by the Excisemen.

WATER From springs below the level of the distillery. The water has to be pumped uphill!

Age 12 years   **Strength** 40% abv

Sweetness 2   Peatiness 7   Availability 10

Colour Pale straw with pale yellow depths **Nose** Pleasantly peaty, dryish and with a hint of smokiness **Flavour** Well-balanced and almost dry **Finish** Long, distinguished and lightly smoky **Notes** Highland Distillers' bottling

Age 10 years **Distillation** 1983 **Strength** 58.6% abv

Sweetness 2 Peatiness 7 Availability 4

Colour Pale amber with yellow/gold highlights **Nose** Fresh, creamy and delicately smoky with a slightly green apple touch **Flavour** Smooth, gently smoky, fruity and floral, medium-dry with a creamy richness **Finish** Quite big, long and fragrant, almost chewy and gently smoky **Notes** Gordon & MacPhail bottling. Distilled 14 April 1983

Age 19 years **Distillation** 1975 **Strength** 52.1% abv

Sweetness 2 Peatiness 6 Availability 2

Colour Pale amber with beige highlights **Nose** Quite good body, round with a touch of perfume and a cereal character, medium-dry, delicate creamy peatiness **Flavour** Quite dry, round, creamily smooth, delicately peated with oaky tannins and a hint of treacle **Finish** Quite big, delicately smoky, elegant and long **Notes** Signatory bottling

Age 21 years **Distillation** 1972 **Strength** 56.5% abv

Sweetness 4 Peatiness 6 Availability 2

Colour Very deep amber with dark bronze highlights **Nose** Big-bodied, full, dark and nutty (brazil nuts) with a burnt oak character and almost dry **Flavour** Big, dark and medium-sweet with a creamy peatiness, a salty tang and big tannins **Finish** Long, chewy, nutty and medium-sweet **Notes** Wm Cadenhead bottling

Distillation 1970 **Strength** 40% abv

Sweetness 3 Peatiness 7 Availability 4

Colour Quite deep amber with bronze highlights **Nose** Full-bodied, fresh, rich and round with a peaty saltiness, medium-dry with a dark oaky, almost burnt Christmas cake character **Flavour** Big-bodied, smooth with quite gentle tannins, medium-dry and smokily peaty **Finish** Full, rich, salty, long and tangy **Notes** Gordon & MacPhail Centenary Reserve bottled 1995

IMPERIAL

Built in 1897, the year of
Queen Victoria's Diamond
Jubilee, the Imperial
Distillery stands
majestically among the
dark woods of Carron,
in a fold of the hills
which encompass the
glittering Spey.

Specially selected,
produced and bottled by
and under the
responsibility of
Gordon & Macphail,
Elgin, Scotland.
Regd. Bottler.

CARRON, MORAY EST. 1897

Built by Thomas Mackenzie in 1897, ownership was transferred to Dailuaine-Talisker Distilleries the following year. It closed in 1899 and was silent until 1919. Became a part of DCL in 1925 and closed again. Re-opened under the control of SMD when rebuilt in 1955. Doubled to four stills in 1965. Closed again in 1985 and sold to Allied Lyons in May, 1989, when it was re-opened. Now part of Allied Domecq and operated by Allied Distillers Ltd.

LOCATION On an unclassified road between the A95 and B9102, some two miles south west of Aberlour in a hollow on the banks of the Spey and next to the former Carron station.

NOTES The distillery was designed by architect Charles Doig of Elgin of red Aberdeen bricks within a framework of iron beams and frames. One of the malt kilns was surmounted by an enormous imperial crown which flashed and glittered in the sun. The crown, which by then had rusted, was taken down in 1955. It was one of the distilleries where experimentation on the technique of drying distillery effluent for use as cattle feed was pioneered.

WATER The Ballintomb Burn.

Distillation 1979 **Strength** 40% abv

Sweetness 6 Peatiness 7 Availability 4

Colour Amber with yellow/gold highlights **Nose** Quite full-bodied, medium-dry with a clean green freshness and a good peatiness **Flavour** Medium-sweet with a green edge, quite rich dark chocolatey and a firm peatiness **Finish** Clean, long, medium-sweet and delicately smokey**Notes** Gordon & MacPhail bottling

Distillation 1970 **Strength** 40% abv

Sweetness 6 Peatiness 7 Availability 4

Colour Bright amber with good gold highlights **Nose** Medium-peaty, medium-sweet, oaky, lightly mashy with green fruit at the back **Flavour** Almost medium-dry, quite full-bodied, peaty, smooth and oily-creamy **Finish** Smooth, quite long, a touch smoky and with a peanut character **Notes** Gordon & MacPhail bottling

HOGMANAY DRAM

Age 16 years **Distillation** 1976 **Strength** 43% abv

Sweetness 5 Peatiness 7 Availability 0

Colour Very pale straw with a green tinge **Nose** Quite full, smoky, aromatic and medium-dry with a green fruitiness **Flavour** Slightly off-dry, smoky and full-bodied **Finish** Long, smoky and smooth **Notes** Master of Malt "Hogmanay Dram 1992" - cask no 7559

Age 12 years **Strength** 65% abv

Sweetness 7 Peatiness 6 Availability 4

Colour Slightly hazy, pale straw/yellow **Nose** Full, sweetish, malty and spirity **Flavour** Quite sweet, smooth, almost creamy, lightly smoky **Finish** Long, quite spicy, strong and quite scented, strangely chocolatey **Notes** James MacArthur bottling

Age 14 years **Distillation** 1979 **Strength** 64.9% abv

Sweetness 6 Peatiness 5 Availability 4

Colour Very pale straw with yellow/lemon highlights **Nose** Warm, with an unusual spiritiness, very fruity and medium-sweet **Flavour** Warm, soft, smooth, woody and tangy, medium-sweet and gently smoky **Finish** Quite long, fresh and gently smoky **Notes** Wm Cadenhead bottling

SPEYSIDE
SINGLE MALT
SCOTCH WHISKY

The *Oyster Catcher* is a common *sight*
around the

INCHGOWER

distillery, which stands *close* to the *sea*
on the mouth of the *RIVER SPEY*
near *BUCKIE. Inchgower,*
established in 1824, produces *one* of the
most *distinctive single* malt whiskies
in *SPEYSIDE.* It is a malt for the
discerning drinker ~ a *complex* aroma
precedes a *fruity, spicy*
taste *with* a hint of *salt.*

A G E D **14** Y E A R S

43% vol   Distilled & Bottled in SCOTLAND. INCHGOWER DISTILLERY, Buckie, Banffshire, Scotland   70 cl

BUCKIE, BANFFSHIRE EST. 1871

Built by Alexander Wilson and Company as "The great distillery of Inchgower" to replace Tochineal, which had become outdated and cramped. The company celebrated its centenary on 12 July 1922. It was purchased by Buckie Town Council for £1,000 in 1936 and sold on to Arthur Bell and Sons in 1938, reputedly for £4,000. Doubled to four stills in 1966. Now part of United Distillers plc.

L O C A T I O N   On the north side of the A98 between Fochabers and Buckie.

N O T E S   A farm on the hill above the distillery was once the home of a noted local smuggler by the name of Macpherson. His still, well hidden at the back of the hill, was only discovered when some stray Highland cattle dislodged a large piece of turf, thus exposing the still to the farmer driving his cattle home. Sad to say for Macpherson, the farmer was quick to tip off the Excisemen and claim his reward.

W A T E R   Springs in the Menduff Hills.

Age 14 years   **Strength** 43% abv

Sweetness 7   Peatiness 3   Availability 6

Colour Straw with lemon yellow highlights **Nose** Medium-sweet, good richness with vanilla and a greenness at the back **Flavour** Smooth, creamy vanilla, medium-sweet with a fresh greenness **Finish** Long, clean and fresh with a hint of coffee on the tail **Notes** United Distillers bottling

Age 12 years   **Strength** 40% abv

Sweetness 8   Peatiness 6   Availability 0

Colour Pale golden/straw **Nose** Slightly sweet and peaty **Flavour** Rich, sweet and full-bodied with a delicate peatiness **Finish** Distinguished, long and delicately sweet **Notes** Arthur Bell (pre-Guinness) bottling

Age 13 years   **Strength** 43% abv

Sweetness 7   Peatiness 3   Availability 1

Colour Pale amber/straw with lemon highlights **Nose** Quite good body, fresh, quite sweet, gently peated and gently nutty **Flavour** Clean, quite zingy, medium-sweet, fruity and rich with good body **Finish** Quite long, fresh and clean **Notes** Master of Malt bottling

Distillation 1966   **Strength** 61.6% abv

Sweetness 7   Peatiness 4   Availability 2

Colour Mid amber with old gold highlights **Nose** Sweet with an aroma of unctuous oily oak, almost buttery and quite a fresh, ripe green fruitiness **Flavour** Medium-sweet with good body, chewy oaky tannins and a smooth, slight toffee note **Finish** Rich toffee, good length with a touch of menthol **Notes** Scotch Malt Whisky Society bottling; Cask no. 16.5; bottled May, 1994

INCHMURRIN

INCHMURRIN
SINGLE HIGHLAND MALT

SCOTCH WHISKY

Distilled by
THE LOCH LOMOND DISTILLERY
DUNBARTONSHIRE SCOTLAND

70cl ℮   40%vol
PRODUCT OF SCOTLAND

ALEXANDRIA, DUNBARTONSHIRE EST. 1965

One of two styles of malt produced by the Loch Lomond distillery, built in 1965/66 by the Littlemill Distillery Company Ltd. Closed 1984 and re-opened in 1987 after being purchased by Glen Catrine Bonded Warehouse Ltd. Two stills.

LOCATION Alexandria is at the southern end of Loch Lomond on the A82 Glasgow to Fort William road.

NOTES An earlier distillery of the same name existed at Arrochar, at the other end of Loch Lomond from 1814 to 1817. The stills are of an unusual design, allowing them to produce two very different styles of malt whisky, the other style being called Rhosdhu.

WATER Loch Lomond

Age No age statement **Strength** 40% abv
Sweetness 4 Peatiness 5 Availability 4

Colour Quite pale, with good yellow highlights and slight hints of green **Nose** Malty, spirity, quite dry and with a rubbery character **Flavour** Spirity, quite dry but with a sweet edge, slightly spicy **Finish** The spirit follows through with an almost medicinal finish **Notes** Glen Catrine bottling

Age 9 years **Distillation** 1985 **Strength** 64% abv
Sweetness 4 Peatiness 3 Availability 2

Colour Pale watery straw with lemon highlights **Nose** Young, mashy, vegetal and dry with just a hint of sweetness at the back **Flavour** Medium-sweet, vegetal and mashy with a citrus note, slightly harsh and austere **Finish** Earthy, quite short and spirity **Notes** Wm Cadenhead bottling, distilled March, 1985

L

GLASGOW ROAD, DUMBARTON EST. 1938

Inverleven was built in 1938 by Hiram Walker & Sons, Scotland, within the site of the Dumbarton grain distillery complex. Licensed to George Ballantine & Son Ltd. Now part of Allied Domecq, but closed in 1991.

LOCATION Next to the River Clyde in the centre of Dumbarton.

NOTES Two stills for malt whisky production at Dumbarton. There was also a third Lomond-type still which produced a heavier style of spirit known as Lomond.

WATER Loch Lomond

INVERLEVEN
Distillation 1979 **Strength** 40% abv

Sweetness 6	Peatiness 1	Availability 4

Colour Mid-amber with gold highlights **Nose** Quite light and cerealy with a touch of apple fruit, medium-dry with an edge of richness **Flavour** Medium-sweet with good richness and a smooth, creamy character **Finish** Long, spicy, quite sweet and tangy **Notes** Gordon & MacPhail bottling

LOMOND
Age 30 years **Strength** 60% approx. abv

Sweetness 2	Peatiness 3	Availability 0

Colour Pale straw/amber with yellowy green highlights **Nose** Quite full-bodied, good richness and still with a touch of greenness **Flavour** Full, spirity, dry, but with a richness at the back, the greenness of the aroma is still present **Finish** Long, quite light and spicy **Notes** A "Lomond" cask sample supplied by Whyte & Mackay for a tasting tutored by Richard Paterson held at Christie's, Glasgow

CRAIGHOUSE, ISLE OF JURA, ARGYLL   EST. 1810

After passing through several different owners in its early years, Jura blossomed in the late 1800s when it came into the hands of Messrs James Ferguson & Sons in 1875, being rebuilt at a cost of £25,000. However, it closed in the early 1900s because, it is said, of an argument over the rent, after which the distiller upped and went, taking his still and equipment with him. Jura was abandoned until the late 1950s when a rebuilding programme was begun. The first spirit for more than 50 years flowed in 1963. Enlarged from two to four stills in 1978. Now owned by Invergordon Distillers plc, which was in turn taken over by Whyte & Mackay in 1994.

LOCATION   Across from Islay on the leeward east coast of Jura, on a bay where a string of islands forms a natural breakwater.

NOTES   Records are said to trace distilling on Jura as far back as 1502. After the distillery had been rebuilt in the 1870s it gained a reputation for being one of the most efficient in Scotland. However it was once discovered that the spent wash from the stills was finding its way into a local cattle trough. The effect on the animals, it is said, was most interesting.

WATER   Loch a' Bhaile Mhargaidh (Market Loch)

Age 10 years   **Strength** 40% abv

Sweetness 3   Peatiness 7   Availability 10

Colour Pale straw with very slight green tinges **Nose** Full, pleasantly dry **Flavour** Very delicate, lightly smoky with a pleasant oily nuttiness **Finish** Very smooth and lingers well **Notes** Invergordon Distillers bottling

TOWERS ROAD, AIRDRIE, LANARKSHIRE EST. 1965

Killyloch was a second still at Moffat Distillery which produced a malt for blending purposes only (see Glen Flagler). The whisky was supposed to be named "Lillyloch", from the water source on the outskirts of Airdrie, but at the time of filling, it was discovered that the cask stencil had been mis-spelt. As the whisky was intended for blending purposes only, it was decided to leave the name as Killyloch.

LOCATION Within the Glen Flagler complex at Moffat Distillery.

NOTES Prior to June, 1994, its make had never been bottled as a single malt.

WATER Lillyloch.

Age 22 years **Distillation** 1972 **Strength** 52.6% abv
Sweetness 4 Peatiness 2 Availability 0

Colour Pale mid-amber with lemon/gold highlights **Nose** Medium-bodied, cerealy, a fairly harsh spirit character and a slightly green, almost leafy, dry and with a creamy oiliness **Flavour** Medium-dry, soft with good richness, a touch of spice and medium-bodied with gentle tannins **Finish** Medium-length with good sweetness, a light smokiness and a fresh green note **Notes** Signatory bottling, distilled 21 March 1972 and bottled June 1994

CONNOISSEURS
CHOICE

Connoisseurs Choice, a
range of single malts from
various districts of
Scotland.

The lowlands
traditionally produce
smooth soft and mellow
whiskies.

SINGLE LOWLAND
MALT SCOTCH WHISKY

DISTILLED AT

KINCLAITH
DISTILLERY

Trade Mark of Proprietors: Long John Distillers Ltd

DISTILLED **1967** DISTILLED

Specially selected, produced and bottled by and under the responsibility of

70cl   GORDON & MACPHAIL   40%vol
REGD. BOTTLER · ELGIN · SCOTLAND
PRODUCT OF SCOTLAND

MOFFAT STREET, GLASGOW EST. 1957

Built 1957/58 by Strathclyde & Long John Distilleries Ltd, at that time a subsidiary of the American company Seager Evans & Co. Ltd. Sold to Whitbread & Co. Ltd in 1975 and dismantled in 1976 to make way for an enlarged Strathclyde grain distillery. Two stills.

LOCATION   In the centre of Glasgow within the Strathclyde Grain Distilling complex.

NOTES   The last of Glasgow's once numerous malt whisky distilleries.

WATER   The local Glasgow water supply, which comes from Loch Katrine.

Age 20 years   **Strength** 46% abv

Sweetness 6   Peatiness 3   Availability 1

Colour Very pale straw with yellow/green highlights **Nose** Quite sweet oak, rich and full-bodied **Flavour** Creamy, smooth and medium-sweet **Finish** Peppery and spicy with a dry, clean tail **Notes** Wm Cadenhead bottling

Distillation 1966   **Strength** 40% abv

Sweetness 6   Peatiness 3   Availability 4

Colour Amber with old gold highlights **Nose** Medium-bodied, lightly peated and medium-sweet with a leather and shoe wax aroma **Flavour** Medium-sweet and quite full-bodied with gentle oaky tannins and a leathery smokiness **Finish** Long, rich and creamy with dry tannins and almost chewy **Notes** Gordon & MacPhail bottling

KNOCKANDO, MORAY EST. 1898

Built by the Knockando-Glenlivet Distillery Co. Owned by J Thomson & Co from 1900-3. Acquired by W & A Gilbey in 1904. Now managed by Justerini & Brooks, a subsidiary of IDV.

LOCATION South of the B9102 between Knockando and Archiestown, sited on the banks of the River Spey.

NOTES Much of the make is used in the J & B blend. An individual feature of the malt is that its bottle states both its year of distillation and date of bottling. If you believe that whisky, like wine, has vintage years, then Knockando is worthy of close study. Knockando is "cnoc an dhu" in Gaelic which means "little black hillock".

WATER The Cardnach Spring.

Distillation 1980 **Strength** 43% abv

Sweetness 6 Peatiness 3 Availability 7

Colour Mid straw with pale lemon highlights **Nose** Round, soft rich and leafy, quite full-bodied and medium-sweet with a toffee/coffee character, delicately peated and with a slight lanolin oakiness **Flavour** Soft, smooth, medium-dry, quite rich and fresh with a touch of spiciness **Finish** Long, rich, slightly tangy with a hint of coffee **Notes** J&B bottling at export strength

KNOCKANDO EXTRA RESERVE

Age 21 years **Strength** 43% abv

Sweetness 7 Peatiness 3 Availability 1

Colour Straw, lightly peaty with pale greeny-gold highlights **Nose** Lightly peated, medium-dry, rich and leafy with pleasantly oaky vanilla **Flavour** Medium weight, slightly green, medium-sweet and round **Finish** Smooth, not quite medium-sweet, delicately spicy and quite long **Notes** J&B bottling in 1995

PURE MALT SCOTCH WHISKY
from

LADYBURN
Distillery

Proprietors: William Grant & Sons Ltd.

75 cl

Bottled by Wm. Cadenhead,
18 Golden Square, Aberdeen
Scotland

46% vol

GIRVAN, AYRSHIRE EST. 1966

Opened in 1966 by William Grant & Sons Ltd, Ladyburn has not produced any spirit since 1976. Four stills.

LOCATION   Ladyburn is part of the complex which includes the Girvan grain distillery.

NOTES   William Grant & Sons are also the proud owners of the Speyside malts Glenfiddich and The Balvenie, but Ladyburn is much harder to come by, as it is only occasionally released through the independent bottlers none being available from the owners although there is a rumour that William Grant & Sons have 30 casks laid down for future bottling.

WATER   Penwapple reservoir

Age 20 years   **Strength** 46% abv

Sweetness 4   Peatiness 4   Availability 1

Colour Pale straw with lemon/gold highlights **Nose** Malty, lightly peated, leafy and slightly rich with an oily character **Flavour** Almost dry, smooth, round, soft and peaty; quite simple, but with good body **Finish** Slightly smoky, a touch of spice and of reasonable length **Notes** Wm Cadenhead bottling

NEAR PORT ELLEN, ISLAY, ARGYLL EST. 1816

Originally two legal distilleries were set up on the site, the first in 1816 was Lagavulin, founded by John Johnson. The second, the following year, was established by Archibald Campbell and is believed to have been known as Kildalton. In Alfred Barnard's report on his visit of 1887, he stated that the make was "principally sold in Glasgow, England and the Colonies." Lagavulin has long been important to White Horse blended whisky, becoming part of DCL in 1927 and managed by SMD from 1930. Rebuilt in 1962 when the stills from Malt Mill (see below) were incorporated. Four stills. Now part of United Distillers plc.

LOCATION Occupying a site of six acres, Lagavulin stands at the head of a small bay. The ruins of Dunyvaig Castle are next door.

NOTES Lagganmhouillin, or Lagavulin, means "mill in the valley". Distilling on the site is thought to date from as early as 1742 when there were ten small bothies there. One of United Distillers' Classic Malts portfolio. Mackie & Co, owners at the turn of the century, were also the agents for Laphroaig next door. When they lost the agency in 1907, they built a new distillery within the Lagavulin complex to produce a similar style of whisky. Called Malt Mill, it had its own maltings which had a haircloth-floored kiln fired only with open peat fires. The Lagavulin mash tun was utilised, but there were two independent wash backs and two pear-shaped stills. Malt Mill closed in 1960 and the stills incorporated in Lagavulin.

WATER The Solan Lochs

Age 16 years   **Strength** 43% abv

Sweetness 3   Peatiness 10   Availability 10

Colour Deep amber with rich gold highlights **Nose** Distinctive, pungent, burnt heather, very peaty and full-bodied **Flavour** Big, peaty, dry, very smooth and powerfully complex **Finish** Long and smoky with an almost burnt character, very persistent **Notes** United Distillers bottling

Age 12 years   **Strength** 40% abv

Sweetness 3   Peatiness 10   Availability 0

Colour Golden brown, like a peat-stained burn **Nose** Big, powerful, burnt mahogany, lots of peat **Flavour** Full, heavy and smokily powerful with a strangely sweet edge **Finish** Explosive, spicy and smokily pungent **Notes** DCL (pre-Guinness) bottling

Age 15 years   **Distillation** 1978   **Strength** 64.4% abv

Sweetness 5   Peatiness 9   Availability 3

Colour Pale amber with a greenish tinge and yellow highlights **Nose** Full and pungent with ozone, burnt heather and a rich, slightly creamily unctuous character **Flavour** Seaweed with great richness and quite big tannins, quite sweet, powerful and pungent **Finish** Long, lingering, smoky and rich **Notes** Wm Cadenhead bottling

LAPHROAIG®

SINGLE ISLAY MALT
SCOTCH WHISKY

10
Years Old

The most richly flavoured of
all Scotch whiskies

ESTABLISHED
1815

DISTILLED AND BOTTLED IN SCOTLAND BY

D. JOHNSTON & CO., (LAPHROAIG), LAPHROAIG DISTILLERY, ISLE OF ISLAY.

40%vol IMPORTADOR WENCESLAO PAZ MARTINEZ **70cl**
DOMICILIO C HADDU S/N R.S. NUM 40.1.125 ML.

L00205

NEAR PORT ELLEN, ISLAY, ARGYLL EST. 1815

Said to have been founded by Donald and Alex Johnston. Originally a farm distillery, records show distilling took place on the site in 1812. By 1815, when the forerunner of today's distillery opened, distilling had overtaken farming in importance to the Johnston family. Laphroaig remained in the Johnston family until 1954, when the then proprietor, Ian Hunter, bequeathed it to Bessie Williamson. At this time she was company secretary, having worked in the business for many years, and went on to become a most important and respected figure in the Scotch whisky industry before she retired as managing director in 1972. Miss Williamson sold Laphroaig to Long John Distillers Ltd between 1962 and 1967 and the business is now part of Allied Domecq and operated by Allied Distillers Ltd. Enlarged from two to four stills in 1923, to six in 1968-9 and to seven in 1974.

LOCATION Situated on a small bay, frequented by otters, swans and a heron, it has been greatly influenced by the sea throughout its history.

NOTES Generally accepted as being the most individually flavoured of all single malts. Although Laphroaig, like all the distilleries on the island, is built on the coast, it has always been maintained that it is not only the sea air, but also the peat which accounts for the distinctiveness of the make. The peat used by the distillery has a high proportion of moss in its content and this is said to give Laphroaig its particular flavour. Laphroaig has its own floor maltings. Part of the site occupied by the modern Laphroaig distillery includes that of the old Ardenistle Distillery (1837- c. 1848).

WATER The Kilbride Dam.

Age 10 years **Strength** 40% abv

Sweetness 2   Peatiness 10   Availability 10

Colour Palish amber with slightly greenish tones **Nose** Dry, heavy and peaty with a heathery smokiness **Flavour** Full of character, very peaty and smoky with iodine/medicinal notes **Finish** Lingering, smoky, smooth and unique **Notes** Caledonian Distillers bottling

Age 15 years **Strength** 43% abv

Sweetness 2   Peatiness 10   Availability 6

Colour Amber/peaty with good gold highlights **Nose** Peaty, full and medicinal with a slightly fruity edge **Flavour** Soft, smoky, round and smooth with a slightly sweet middle to the palate **Finish** Long, smoky and refined **Notes** Caledonian Distillers bottling

SPEYSIDE
SINGLE MALT
SCOTCH WHISKY

LINKWOOD

distillery stands on the *River Lossie*,
close to *ELGIN* in *Speyside*. The *distillery*
has retained its *traditional atmosphere*
since its *establishment* in 1821.
Great care has always
been taken to *safeguard* the
character of the *whisky* which has
remained the same through the
years. Linkwood is one of the
FINEST Single Malt Scotch Whiskies
available - *full bodied* with a *hint* of
sweetness and a *slightly smoky aroma*.

YEARS **12** OLD

43% vol
Distilled & Bottled in *SCOTLAND*
LINKWOOD DISTILLERY
Elgin, Moray, *Scotland.*
70 cl

ELGIN, MORAY EST. 1821

Built by Peter Brown in 1835 and named after the estate on which it was built. The Elgin Courant of 10 April 1874 reported that the old buildings of Linkwood distillery were being pulled down and that new, more extensive buildings were being erected. By 1887 Linkwood had a 2,000 gallon wash still and a 1,850 gallon spirit still and was producing 50,000 gallons a year. It was bought by SMD in 1933 and rebuilt twice more: in 1962 and again in 1971, when a second distillery unit was built alongside the original extending it from two to six stills. Now part of United Distillers plc.

LOCATION On the A941 south of Elgin and on the River Lossie.

NOTES A very picturesque distillery with a reservoir of water for cooling purposes, which is inhabited by swans, alongside the buildings. It is surrounded by woodlands, hence the name. Roderick Mackenzie, who was manager from 1945 to 1963, believed that the character of the spirit depended not just on the vessels in which it was made, but also on everything in their immediate environment. He is even reputed not to have permitted the removal even of spiders' webs in case the character of the whisky were to alter as a result.

WATER Springs near Millbuies Loch.

LINKWOOD

Age 12 years   **Strength** 43% abv

Sweetness 7   Peatiness 5   Availability 6

Colour Straw/amber with lemon highlights **Nose** Medium to full-bodied, medium-sweet with an appley character and a soft smokiness at the back **Flavour** Good weight, medium-sweet, fruity and lightly smoky **Finish** Long and spicy with a nice edge of sweetness **Notes** United Distillers bottling

Age 12 years   **Strength** 40% abv

Sweetness 8   Peatiness 4   Availability 0

Colour Clear golden, like sunlit peat-stained loch water over a sandy bottom **Nose** Fruity, with a sweetness reminiscent of apples **Flavour** Pleasantly light, round, sweet and slightly spicy **Finish** Long and elegant **Notes** DCL (pre-Guinness) bottling

Age 15 years   **Strength** 40% abv

Sweetness 7   Peatiness 5   Availability 4

Colour Quite full mid-amber with a tinge of green and gold highlights **Nose** Quite full-bodied, musty apples and oak with a fresh smokiness **Flavour** Medium-sweet and full-bodied with a touch of spice and oaky vanilla **Finish** Smooth and appley with a dry smoky finish **Notes** Gordon & MacPhail bottling

Age 21 years   **Strength** 40% abv

Sweetness 8   Peatiness 6   Availability 4

Colour Quite deep amber with bronze highlights **Nose** Smooth, dark and nutty with a touch of demerara sugar, medium-sweet and rich with a musty apple aroma **Flavour** Sweet, quite full-bodied and smooth with a delicate, but firm, peatiness **Finish** Long and sweet with just a hint of smokiness on the tail **Notes** Gordon & MacPhail bottling

Distillation 1979   **Age** 14 years   **Strength** 58.5% abv

Sweetness 3   Peatiness 6   Availability 2

Colour Deep, treacly amber with deep bronze/ruby highlights **Nose** Big-bodied, burnt wood peatiness, a dark nuttiness, medium-dry with the soft aroma of one of Leith's old tea warehouses **Flavour** Big, burnt and almost dry with chewy tannins **Finish** Soft, rich, long, chewy and off-dry **Notes** Wm Cadenhead bottling

PRODUCT OF SCOTLAND

LITTLEMILL

Established 1772

SINGLE LOWLAND MALT
SCOTCH WHISKY

DISTILLED AND BOTTLED IN SCOTLAND BY
LITTLEMILL DISTILLERY CO.,LTD.
BOWLING, DUNBARTONSHIRE, SCOTLAND

70cl ℮ 40%vol

BOWLING, DUMBARTONSHIRE EST. 1772

The distillery has had numerous owners over its two centuries of operation, although its origins are somewhat obscure. Littlemill could be Scotland's oldest distillery. It is possible that whisky was distilled on the site as long ago as the fourteenth century, when the Colquhouns built Dunglas Castle to guard crossing the Clyde. About 1750, George Buchanan, a wealthy maltster from Glasgow bought Littlemill when he purchased the Auchterlonie estate and in 1772 he had to build houses for the Excise officers. Annual production in 1821 is recorded as 20,000 gallons. Rebuilt in 1875, Littlemill used triple distillation until the 1930s. The distillery closed in 1984 and was re-opened by Gibson International in 1989. Following that company's failure late in 1994, Littlemill is now owned by Glen Catrine Bonded Warehouse Ltd but is again closed. It has two stills.

LOCATION Between the main road, the A82 and the River Clyde at the foot of the Kilpatrick Hills, 12 miles from Glasgow city centre towards Dumbarton.

NOTES Although strictly speaking a Lowland distillery, this is another which takes its water supply from north of the Highland Line. The present stills are of a most unusual design.

WATER A spring in the Kilpatrick Hills.

Age 8 years **Strength** 40% abv

Sweetness 6 Peatiness 1 Availability 3

Colour Straw with yellow/gold highlights **Nose** Quite young, slightly mashy with an unpeated green, new-mown grassiness, medium-dry and with quite good body **Flavour** Fresh, quite mashy, medium-sweet and clean with good body **Finish** Quite rich and clean, of good length with just a suggestion of darkness at the end **Notes** Glen Catrine bottling

Age 8 years **Strength** 43% abv

Sweetness **2** Peatiness **6** Availability **3**

Colour Pale straw with greeny-gold highlights **Nose** Light, spirity, medium-dry, malty and fruity with vanilla notes **Flavour** Lightish, spicy, quite soft, oatmeal-mashy, peppery and slightly oily **Finish** Almost dry, of average length and spicy **Notes** Gibson International bottling

Age 18 years **Distillation** 1975 **Strength** 55.8% abv

Sweetness **4** Peatiness **5** Availability **0**

Colour Pale straw with lemon highlights **Nose** Quite full-bodied, fresh, clean and quite lightly smoky with just a touch of richness **Flavour** Medium-sweet, fresh and rich with a slightly green peatiness and good body **Finish** Gently smoky with good richness and a slight chewiness **Notes** Master of Malt bottling - cask no 2144 distilled 8 May 1975

MONTROSE, ANGUS EST. 1957

Established on the site of Deuchar's brewery in 1957 by Joseph Hobbs, formerly of Associated Scottish Distillers, as a grain and malt distillery and blending and bottling plant. It was to be run by Hobbs under the operational company, MacNab Distilleries Ltd. It was sold to Destilerias y Crianza de Whisky S.A. of Madrid in November, 1973. Originally four pot stills and one Coffey (grain) still, the latter was closed in 1970.

LOCATION At the north end of Montrose, at the junction of the coastal Aberdeen to Dundee road (the A92) and the A935 from Montrose to Brechin.

NOTES All of the make used to be bottled at the distillery by MacNab Distilleries. A small loch once existed opposite the distillery, hence the name. Most of the malt went to export, in bulk as well as bottle, with Spain being the main market because of the company's Spanish owners. Some of the whisky was available in bottle locally. The stills ceased production in the mid-1980s and the plant is now closed.

WATER A bore well beneath the distillery.

Age 10 years **Strength** 40% abv

Sweetness 3 Peatiness 5 Availability 1

Colour Light straw with gold highlights **Nose** Quite light, floral, leafy and slightly sweet **Flavour** Medium-dry, round and spicy, of medium weight **Finish** Leafy with hints of coffee, quite smooth **Notes** MacNab Distilleries bottling

DISTILLED AND BOTTLED IN SCOTLAND

LONGMORN

Highland Single Malt

SCOTCH WHISKY

This outstanding single malt whisky is produced only at the
Longmorn distillery, which stands on the site of an ancient abbey,
in the heart of the Scottish Highlands.

70 cl e

MATURED IN OAK CASKS
15 YEARS

45%vol

NEAR ELGIN, MORAY   EST. 1894

Built by the Longmorn Distillery Company, which was amalgamated with The Glenlivet and Glen Grant Distilleries and Hill, Thomson & Co Ltd to form The Glenlivet Distilleries Limited. Owned by the Seagram Company of Canada since 1977. Extended from four to six stills in 1972 and eight in 1974.

LOCATION   On the A941 Elgin to Rothes and Craigellachie road.

NOTES   Professor R J S McDowall considered Longmorn to be one of the four finest malts. The name Longmorn comes from the Gaelic Lhanmorgund meaning "place of the holy man", the distillery reputedly being on the site of an ancient chapel. The distillery houses an old steam engine which is occasionally used and it also has a disused water wheel. This malt is much favoured by blenders as a "top dressing" for their blends.

WATER   Local springs.

Age 15 years   **Strength** 43% abv

Sweetness 6   Peatiness 4   Availability 6

Colour Mid-amber with gold highlights **Nose** Rich, full-bodied with soft oak and a cooked apples/grapey fruitiness, slightly peppery **Flavour** Quite full-bodied, round, soft and smooth, medium-sweet with a delicate edge of smokiness and gentle tannins **Finish** Rich, smooth and elegant with just a touch of smokiness **Notes** Seagram bottling

Age 12 years **Strength** 40% abv

Sweetness 6 Peatiness 5 Availability 4

Colour Amber with old gold highlights **Nose** Medium-bodied, a light sweet smokiness, a touch of creamy toffee and an almost menthol character **Flavour** Medium-dry, round, slightly creamy and smooth with a dark nuttiness **Finish** Long and nutty with a slight fragrant smokiness and a floral tail **Notes** Gordon & MacPhail bottling

Age 12 years **Strength** 58.6% abv

Sweetness 8 Peatiness 3 Availability 1

Colour Pale/mid-amber with pale yellow/gold highlights **Nose** Sweet, unctuous banana fruitiness with quite good body and delicately peated **Flavour** Sweet, round, soft and full-flavoured, gently tannic with a good, clean chocolatey peatiness **Finish** Long, sweet, rich and lingering with a smooth oaky vanilla background **Notes** Blackadder International Limited Editions bottling

CAMPBELTOWN, ARGYLL EST. 1973

L ongrow is a particular type of malt produced occasionally from one of the stills within Springbank distillery.

LOCATION In the centre of Campbeltown.

NOTES Although the current brand was only introduced in 1973, the name was originally given to a distillery that once stood next door to Springbank, said to have been founded in 1824. It had closed by 1896. The old Longrow distillery site is now Springbank's car park. Very little Longrow has ever been released, and we understand from the brand's owners that it will be at least a couple of years before any more malt of this style is ready for release.

WATER Crosshill Loch and a spring on the premises.

Distillation 1973 **Strength** 43% abv

Sweetness 4 Peatiness 7 Availability 0

Colour Pale gold with green edges **Nose** Peaty and quite full with an edge of sweetness **Flavour** Smoky and dry with a touch of sweetness, slightly woody **Finish** Long and round with the smokiness to the end **Notes** J & A Mitchell & Co. Ltd bottling

Distillation 1974 **Strength** 46% abv

Sweetness 3 Peatiness 6 Availability 1

Colour Pale straw with a green tinge and lemon yellow high-lights **Nose** Dry and of medium weight with a smoky peatiness and a salty/seaweed character **Flavour** Smooth, round, of medium weight with an edge of sweetness, an earthy peatiness and a salty tang **Finish** Long and lightly smoky with a nice sweetness on the tail **Notes** J & A Mitchell & Co. Ltd bottling

CRAIGELLACHIE, MORAY EST. 1824

Until the bridge at Craigellachie was built by Thomas Telford in 1814, the ford across the Spey at Easter Elchies was one of the few on the river. It was much used by cattle drovers, and whisky distilled at the old farm distillery which preceded the licensed distillery was a popular feature of the river crossing for them. The licensed distillery was founded by Alexander Reid in 1824. Macallan, although now a public limited company, was until recently, controlled by the successors of Roderick Kemp who purchased it in 1892. Even today they are much involved in the business. The distillery was extended in the early 1950s and again in 1959, but the demand for Macallan fillings was such that it was doubled from six to twelve stills in 1965, increased to eighteen in 1974 and to twenty-one in 1975. The stills are small.

LOCATION On a hillside overlooking the Spey with the old Easter Elchies manor now magnificently refurbished as corporate offices.

NOTES The makers of The Macallan have championed the use of sherry casks for maturing whisky and have helped to reverse the trend away from their use. All The Macallan's make is now aged in various types of sherry wood. Old vintages of The Macallan are very valuable, with a 60 year old being bought by the owner of a bar in Osaka, Japan, for £6,400 in 1993.

WATER From bore holes.

Age 7 years   **Strength** 40% abv

Sweetness 8   Peatiness 2   Availability 1

Colour Pale amber with yellow/lemon highlights **Nose** Young, cerealy, rich and medium-sweet, a slight unctuous-oily character and medium-bodied with a slightly green touch **Flavour** Quite light and sweet with a caramelly-tablet flavour **Finish** Quite short and sweet **Notes** Macallan bottling for Giovanetti in the Italian market

Age 10 years   **Strength** 40% abv

Sweetness 7   Peatiness 4   Availability 10

Colour Fairly full amber with old gold highlights **Nose** Quite full-bodied with a slight green touch, good peatiness, a slightly rich sweet, sherried nutty vanilla character **Flavour** A chewy nuttiness with a vanilla overlay, quite full-bodied, smooth, quite rich and medium-sweet **Finish** Quite clean and long with a slight burnt nutty character **Notes** Macallan bottling

Age 18 years   **Distillation** 1967   **Strength** 43% abv

Sweetness 6   Peatiness 3   Availability 1

Colour Rich and deeply golden **Nose** Rich, sherry-sweet with oaky-vanilla **Flavour** Sweet and round, rich, velvety smooth and less spirity than the 10 years old **Finish** Long, sweet and very distinguished **Notes** Macallan bottling

Age 18 years   **Distillation** 1971   **Strength** 43% abv

Sweetness 8   **Peatiness** 3   **Availability** 2

Colour Rich amber with good gold highlights **Nose** Medium-sweet , quite full-bodied and with a slight oily nuttiness **Flavour** Medium-dry, nutty, round and medium-bodied **Finish** Clean and fresh with a nice touch of richness and slightly smoky **Notes** Macallan bottling

Age 18 years   **Distillation** 1976   **Strength** 43% abv

Sweetness 7   **Peatiness** 3   **Availability** 6

Colour Full amber with old gold highlights **Nose** Quite full-bodied, rich and medium-sweet, nutty and honeyed with a beeswax character **Flavour** Full-bodied, round with gently chewy tannins, rich and medium-sweet with the beeswax unctuous texture **Finish** Long and rich with a touch of spice and pleasantly chewy **Notes** 1995 Macallan bottling

Age 20 years   **Distillation** 1974   **Strength** 53.9% abv

Sweetness 5   **Peatiness** 6   **Availability** 2

Colour Deep amber with old gold highlights **Nose** Full-bodied, dark and nutty, medium-sweet with an edge of richness and a sooty, burnt peat character **Flavour** Medium-sweet, rich, soft and very smooth with gentle tannins **Finish** Nutty and peaty with a touch of spiciness **Notes** Wm Cadenhead bottling

Age 25 years   **Distillation** 1963   **Strength** 43% abv

Sweetness 7   **Peatiness** 3   **Availability** 2

Colour Deep oaky amber with lovely gold highlights **Nose** Full, rich and nutty with a sherry-sweetness **Flavour** Big, rich, medium-sweet, creamy ,oaky and velvety smooth **Finish** Long, lightly spicy and nutty, finishes dry **Notes** Macallan bottling

MANNOCHMORE

SPEYSIDE
SINGLE MALT *SCOTCH WHISKY*

MANNOCHMORE

distillery stands a few miles *south* of Elgin in *Morayshire*. The nearby
Millbuies Woods are rich in birdlife, including the Great *Spotted* Woodpecker.
The *distillery* draws process *water* from the Bardon Burn,
which has its *source* in the MANNOCH HILLS, and *cooling water* from
the Gedloch Burn and the *Burn of Foths*. Mannochmore *single*
MALT WHISKY has a *light, fruity* aroma and a *smooth*, mellow *taste*.

AGED **12** YEARS

43% vol   Distilled & Bottled in *SCOTLAND*. MANNOCHMORE DISTILLERY, Elgin, Moray, *Scotland*.   70 cl

ELGIN, MORAY EST. 1971

Established by SMD in 1971 and licensed to John Haig & Co.,
Mannochmore was built on the same 25 acre (10 hectare) site as
the older Glenlossie (1876). Mannochmore does not utilise a purifier
between the lyne arm and condenser as does Glenlossie. Part of
United Distillers plc. Mothballed in 1985, but re-opened in 1989.

LOCATION Sited next to Glenlossie at Thomshill on an unclassified road to the west of the A941, two miles south of Elgin.

NOTES Not often available as a single, Mannochmore is important
to a number of blends, including Haig.

WATER The Bardon Burn.

Age 12 years   **Strength** 43% abv

Sweetness 5 Peatiness 3 Availability 5

Colour Very pale, almost watery with lemon highlights **Nose**
Quite full, cerealy and yeasty with green fruit, medium-dry and
quite lightly peated **Flavour** Medium-dry, mashy, quite fresh,
clean and aromatic **Finish** Light and clean with a hint of coffee, lasts well **Notes** United Distillers bottling

Age 16 years   **Distillation** 1977   **Strength** 61% abv

Sweetness 7 Peatiness 6 Availability 3

Colour Straw with yellow-gold highlights **Nose** Fresh, good
body and medium-sweet with green apple character, quite light
peat and soft oak **Flavour** Soft, round, smooth and medium-
sweet with gentle tannins **Finish** Long and chewy with a dry
edge, spicy with a soft smokiness **notes** United Distillers bottling

MILLBURN ROAD, INVERNESS   EST. 1807

Said to have been founded by a Mr Welsh. The earliest recorded reference held by United Distillers dates from 1825, when James Rose and Alexander Macdonald were named as the licence holders. Used as a flour mill in 1853, it was rebuilt and re-opened on 28 September 1876. It was then remodelled internally in late 1898. Owned from 1921 to 1937 by gin distillers, Booth's, who were themselves taken over by DCL in that year. Management was transferred to SMD in 1943. Two stills.

LOCATION   Millburn was located about one mile east of the centre of Inverness, on the banks of the Mill Burn from which the distillery and the district take their name.

NOTES   Fire broke out on 26 April 1922, but the local fire brigade, "greatly assisted" by the Cameron Highlanders, saved the stillhouse and storage warehouses. The commander of the 3rd Battalion, Lt-Col. David Price Haig, had owned the distillery until 1921. The site was sold for property development in 1988 and the buildings remain as the "Beefeater Distillery Restaurant".

WATER   Loch Duntelchaig.

Age 18 years   **Strength** 58.9% abv

Sweetness 5   Peatiness 7   Availability 2

Colour Very pale amber with pale lemon highlights **Nose** Medium to full-bodied with a dark, deep smoky character, quite pungent and medium-dry **Flavour** Quite round with good peaty smokiness and a touch of bitter chocolate **Finish** Long and clean with an edge of richness, quite smoky with quite gentle oaky tannins **Notes** United Distillers bottling

Distillation 1966 **Strength** 40% abv

Sweetness 6 Peatiness 6 Availability 2

Colour Deep, syrupy golden **Nose** Woody, spirity and dryish **Flavour** Round and medium-sweet, slightly woody with a touch of fruit **Finish** A little flat spot, then finishes well and dry **Notes** Gordon & MacPhail bottling

Distillation 1971 **Strength** 40% abv

Sweetness 6 Peatiness 5 Availability 3

Colour Mid-amber/straw with gold/yellow highlights **Nose** Rich, medium-sweet, delicately peated with touches of oily nuttiness **Flavour** Medium-dry, gently smoky, medium to full-bodied, smooth and round **Finish** Soft with a touch of spiciness, quite long and gently smoky **Notes** Gordon & MacPhail bottling

Age 11 years **Distillation** 1983 **Strength** 59.7% abv

Sweetness 7 Peatiness 4 Availability 3

Colour Mid-amber with yellow/gold highlights **Nose** Medium-bodied with a slight richness, medium-sweet with a green smokiness **Flavour** Medium-sweet, rich and round with gentle peatiness and a slight nuttiness **Finish** Sweet and rich, quite full and smooth **Notes** Wm Cadenhead bottling

MILTONDUFF

NEAR ELGIN, MORAY EST. 1824

Said to have been founded by Pearey & Bain, Miltonduff came into the ownership of Hiram Walker in 1936 and is now a part of the Allied Domecq group. The distillery was extended in the mid-1890s and was largely rebuilt 1974-75. Licensed to George Ballantine & Son Ltd and operated by Allied Distillers Ltd. Six Miltonduff stills and two Lomond stills, which were installed in 1964 and dismantled in 1981. The Lomond stills produced a different style of malt known as "Mosstowie".

LOCATION West of the B9010 to the south of Elgin. A short distance away across the River Lossie are the ruins of Pluscarden Priory.

NOTES In the eighteenth and nineteenth centuries, the waters of the Black Burn supplied scores of illicit stills in the Glen of Pluscarden, the fertile barley-rich plain being ideal for their situation. Milton Duff is the principal malt associated with Ballantine's Scotch Whisky.

WATER Reputedly the Black Burn.

Age 12 years **Strength** 40% abv

Sweetness 9 Peatiness 3 Availability 5

Colour Straw/golden with greenish edges **Nose** Medium to full-bodied, fragrant, slightly floral and sweet **Flavour** Sweet, fruity, full and round **Finish** Almost delicate, refined and long **Notes** Allied Distillers bottling

MOSSTOWIE
Distillation 1970 **Strength** 40% abv

Sweetness 7 Peatiness 3 Availability 1

Colour Mid-amber with gold highlights **Nose** Of medium weight, rich and nutty, medium-sweet with dark, oaky vanilla and quite lightly peated **Flavour** Medium-sweet and nutty with oaky tannins, spicy, round and smooth **Finish** Long, creamy, nutty and spicy **Notes** Gordon & MacPhail bottling

MORTLACH

SPEYSIDE
SINGLE MALT
SCOTCH WHISKY

MORTLACH

was the first of seven
distilleries in *Dufftown*. In the
(19*th* *farm animals* kept in
adjoining byres were fed on
barley left over from processing
Today *water* from springs in
the *CONVAL HILLS* is used to
produce this delightful
smooth, fruity single
MALT SCOTCH WHISKY.

A G E D **16** Y E A R S

Distilled & Bottled in SCOTLAND
MORTLACH DISTILLERY
Dufftown, Keith, Banffshire, Scotland

43% vol   70 cl

DUFFTOWN, BANFFSHIRE EST. 1823

The first of Dufftown's "seven stills". Founded by James Findlater. For a time it was owned by J & J Grant of Glen Grant who removed the distilling utensils. It lay unoccupied for some years, the barley granary serving as a Free Church during the Disruption until a Free Church building could be erected. Extended from three to six stills in 1897. Acquired by John Walker & Son in 1923, by which time it was the largest distillery in the area. Walker's joined DCL in 1925 and management of Mortlach passed to SMD in 1936. The old Mortlach was demolished and rebuilt in the early 1960s, re-opening in 1964. Now part of United Distillers plc.

LOCATION   Sited at the junction of the A941 and B9014 on the eastern outskirts of Dufftown.

NOTES   In the hollow in which the distillery lies (Mortlach means bowl-shaped valley) was fought the battle, in 1010, at which the Scots' king Malcolm II defeated the Danes. Tradition has it that the distillery is on the site of an illicit still which drew its water from a spring called Highland John's Well. Except in 1944, Mortlach had permission to stay open during the Second World War.

WATER   Springs in the Conval Hills.

Age 16 years   **Strength** 43% abv

Sweetness 7   Peatiness 5   Availability 5

Colour Deep amber with old gold highlights **Nose** Full-bodied, deep, dark and nutty, gently peated **Flavour** Full, rich, dark and nutty, big-bodied, smooth and round with soft oaky vanilla notes **Finish** Long, full-flavoured, smooth and darkly sherry cask-nutty **Notes** United Distillers bottling

Distillation 1984 **Strength** 40% abv

Sweetness 6 Peatiness 6 Availability 4

Colour Straw with yellow/pale lemon highlights **Nose** Medium-bodied and medium-sweet with a good dollop of dark peatiness and a slight green apple character **Flavour** Quite big-bodied and medium-sweet with a dark peatiness and gentle tannins **Finish** Long and elegant with a touch of spice and a good balance between sweetness and peatiness **Notes** 1995 Gordon & MacPhail Centenary Reserve bottling

Age 21 years **Strength** 40% abv

Sweetness 8 Peatiness 5 Availability 4

Colour Deep, syrupy amber with dark gold highlights **Nose** Quite dry, woody, slightly astringent and fairly pungent **Flavour** Medium-sweet, slightly woody, but very smooth and round, full and thick in consistency **Finish** Long and velvety with touches of "sticky" sweetness **Notes** Gordon & MacPhail bottling

Age 15 years **Strength** 40% abv

Sweetness 6 Peatiness 6 Availability 4

Colour Light to mid-amber with gold highlights **Nose** Medium-sweet, rich, toffee with a fresh peat character **Flavour** Medium-dry, rich, quite smoky and nutty **Finish** Quite fresh, tangy, nutty and long **Notes** Gordon & MacPhail bottling

Age 22 years **Strength** 46% abv

Sweetness 8 Peatiness 5 Availability 1

Colour Gold/amber with good yellow highlights **Nose** Sweet, creamy oak with a coconut fruitiness **Flavour** Sweet, woody, possibly a little old **Finish** Cold, slightly spicy and oaky **Notes** Wm Cadenhead bottling

Age 50 years **Distillation** 1942 **Strength** 40% abv

Sweetness 5 Peatiness 5 Availability 1

Colour Full amber with old gold highlights **Nose** Full, rich and dark, medium-sweet, oaky vanilla with a lightly charred smoky character **Flavour** Full-bodied, round and rich with an edge of dryness, medium-dry with oaky tannins **Finish** Long, spicy and delicately smoky with firm tannins **Notes** Gordon & MacPhail bottling

CONNOISSEURS CHOICE

Connoisseurs Choice, a range of single malts from various districts of Scotland

In the Highlands are situated the greatest number of malt whisky distilleries.

SINGLE HIGHLAND
MALT SCOTCH WHISKY
DISTILLED AT
NORTH PORT-BRECHIN
DISTILLERY
Proprietors: Mitchel Bros. Ltd

DISTILLED **1974** DISTILLED

SPECIALLY SELECTED, PRODUCED AND BOTTLED BY

70cl   GORDON & MACPHAIL   40%vol
ELGIN · SCOTLAND
PRODUCT OF SCOTLAND

BRECHIN, ANGUS EST. 1820

Founded by David Guthrie, a local farmer, Alfred Barnard referred to it as Brechin Distillery. It originally traded as Townhead Distillery Co., the company name changing to Brechin Distillery Co. in 1823. Barnard wrote "The district around Brechin being highly cultivated, barley of the highest quality is grown and carted" to the distillery, "where nothing but the best barley is malted." Run by SMD since 1922 and licensed to John Hopkins & Co. Ltd, the distillery had two stills. It was closed in 1983 and since demolished

LOCATION   Sited north west of the town centre of Brechin.

NOTES   North Port took its name from the north gate in the ancient city walls, now long since vanished. It was very much a "family" employer, with sons following fathers into the business.

WATER   Loch Lee, which is also the town's supply.

Distillation 1970   **Strength** 40% abv

Sweetness 7   Peatiness 6   Availability 1

Colour Gold with yellow highlights **Nose** Sweet with heather honey aromas and rich **Flavour** Medium-sweet, full and round **Finish** Strangely slightly astringent, but lasts well **Notes** Gordon & MacPhail bottling

Age 17 years   **Distillation** 1976   **Strength** 64.1% abv

Sweetness 4   Peatiness 6   Availability 4

Colour Pale amber with yellow highlights **Nose** Quite light with a burnt oak tang and a touch of perfume, a slight earthy peatiness and medium-dry **Flavour** Quite big and medium-dry with slightly bitter oaky tannins **Finish** Long with a tail of richness and toffee **Notes** Wm Cadenhead bottling

OBAN
'Little Bay of Caves'

ALONG THE SHORES OF LORN LIES A RECORD OF
MAN FAR MORE ANCIENT THAN THAT OF ANY CITY
IN THE LAND. THE FIRST SETTLERS ARRIVED ON
THE MAINLAND IN 5,000 BC AND SHELTERED IN
THE NATURAL CAVES OF THE LAND THEN KNOWN
AS 'AN OB'. THE 'DISTILLERY CAVE' WAS ONE
SUCH SHELTER HIDDEN IN THE CRAG. A MISERAIN
CLIFFS WHICH RISE DRAMATICALLY ABOVE THE
'OBAN DISTILLERY'

Produce of a Delicate

SINGLE MALT

WEST Highland MALT
SCOTCH WHISKY

43% vol   OBAN DISTILLERY OBAN ARGYLL SCOTLAND   70 cl e

STAFFORD STREET, OBAN, ARGYLL EST. 1794

Oban distillery was built, fortress-like, jammed between the cliff, on which sits McCaig's Folly, and the main street, by the Stevenson family, founders also of the town of Oban. It was rebuilt between 1883 and 1887 by Walter Higgin. It became part of DCL in 1925 and has been operated by SMD since 1930. The stillhouse was rebuilt 1969-72 and has two stills. Now part of United Distillers plc.

LOCATION In the centre of Oban overlooking the harbour.

NOTES During enlargement in August, 1890, a cave was discovered which contained bones from the Mesolithic era (4500-3000 BC). These remains are now to be found at the National Museum of Antiquities in Edinburgh. Oban's nose and flavour are reminiscent of Bowmore. One of United Distillers' Classic Malts portfolio.

WATER Two lochs in Ardconnel, one mile inland from the town.

Age 14 years	**Strength** 43% abv	
Sweetness 5	**Peatiness** 7	**Availability** 7

Colour Very pale straw with gold highlights **Nose** Medium-sweet and lightly peated, quite rich with a slight burnt heather character **Flavour** Smooth, lightly sweet and creamy with a very delicate peatiness **Finish** Smoky, dry and delicate **Notes** United Distillers bottling

Age 12 years	**Strength** 40% abv	
Sweetness 4	**Peatiness** 7	**Availability** 0

Colour Dark amber with a syrupy texture **Nose** Clean, slightly spirity with a delicate peaty/heather aroma **Flavour** Very smooth, slightly peppery with hints of heather **Finish** Good length with a smoky aftertaste **Notes** DCL (pre-Guinness)

OLD FETTERCAIRN

ESTABLISHED 1824

10 YEARS OLD
SINGLE HIGHLAND MALT
SCOTCH WHISKY

Distilled, aged and bottled
in Scotland by
FETTERCAIRN DISTILLERS COMPANY
70cl   PRODUCT OF SCOTLAND   43%Vol

FETTERCAIRN, KINCARDINESHIRE EST. 1824

The distillery originally stood two miles further up the mountain in the heart of a smuggling district, but this was abandoned in 1824 when the present building, converted from a former cornmill, was opened. It was rebuilt in 1887-90 after a fire. Silent 1926-39, when acquired by a subsidiary of National Distillers of America. Extended from two to four stills in 1966. Now owned by Whyte & Mackay.

LOCATION Situated just off the B974 close to the River Esk on the outskirts of Fettercairn, the distillery rests at the foot of the Cairngorm mountains.

NOTES According to one contemporary account at the turn of the nineteenth century, the village of Fettercairn was home to 50 weavers, 10 millers, seven shopkeepers, five flaxdressers and one sur-geon. There were also numerous distillers who practiced their illicit trade on the remote slopes of the nearby Cairngorm Mountains, but these, not surprisingly, did not admit to their trade. In 1829, one John Gladstone bought the nearby Fasque estate. He was the father of William Ewart Gladstone, one of Britain's most illustrious prime ministers and probably the best friend the whisky industry ever had amongst their number. He introduced several reforms crucial to the industry, the most important of which was in 1853 when he abol-ished the crippling Malt Tax. Another was to permit the selling of bottled whisky to the public. Extensive warehouses contain some 25,000 casks of whisky in differing stages of maturity, some dating back to 1939.

WATER Springs in the nearby Cairngorm Mountains.

Age No age statement **Strength** 40% abv

Sweetness 4 Peatiness 4 Availability 0

Colour Palish straw/golden with yellow edges **Nose** Light and fresh, delicately peated **Flavour** Slightly dry, leafy and smooth with good body **Finish** Clean with a subtle smokiness **Notes** Whyte & Mackay bottling

Age 10 years **Strength** 40% abv

Sweetness 4 Peatiness 4 Availability 6

Colour Straw with good gold highlights **Nose** Quite full, dryish with notes of oaky vanilla and malty **Flavour** Dry, spicy, of medium weight, creamy and smooth **Finish** Dry, long and chewy **Notes** Whyte & Mackay bottling

Distillation 1980 **Strength** 43% abv

Sweetness 3 Peatiness 6 Availability 2

Colour Quite deep amber with ruby-bronze highlights **Nose** Quite big and nutty with a dark, deep burnt character, a hint of rubber and quite gently peated **Flavour** Good body, round and well-peated with a slight burnt character medium-dry with oaky tannins **Finish** Long and smoky with a touch of richness and spicy with an almost salty tail **Notes** Signatory bottling

Vintage 1980
Single Malt Scotch Whisky

SIGNATORY VINTAGE
S
SCOTCH WHISKY CO. LTD.

Matured in sherry casks for 14 years
Distilled at the Fettercairn Distillery
on 11.9.80 *Bottled 10.94*
Cask nos. 2003-04 *Bottle no.* *of 680*
This whisky has been selected, produced and bottled in
Scotland for and under the sole responsibility of
Signatory Vintage Scotch Whisky Co. Ltd.
70cl *Edinburgh EH6 Scotland* 43%vol

WICK, CAITHNESS EST. 1826

Established by James Henderson. Became part of DCL in 1925, having been purchased by John Dewar & Sons a couple of years earlier. Closed between 1930 and 1951, then revived. In 1955 it was bought by Hiram Walker, now part of Allied Domecq, who rebuilt the distillery in 1959. Pulteney distillery was sold to Inver House Distillers in June, 1995. It has two stills.

LOCATION The most northerly distillery on the U.K. mainland, it is sited on the southern side of Wick, close to the North Sea coast.

NOTES Only available from the independent bottlers. One of the malts associated with Ballantine's blended Scotch Whisky.

WATER The Loch of Hempriggs.

Age 8 years **Strength** 40% abv

Sweetness 3 Peatiness 8 Availability 4

Colour Palish gold with tinges of green **Nose** Delicately pungent with faint tangs of ozone **Flavour** Quite pungent, smoky and clean **Finish** Smoky, dry and refreshing **Notes** Gordon & MacPhail bottling

Age 18 years **Distillation** 1974 **Strength** 59.1% abv

Sweetness 6 Peatiness 8 Availability 1

Colour Straw/pale amber with yellow/gold highlights **Nose** Full-bodied and fresh, medium-dry, peppery with slight smoky apple vanilla **Flavour** Medium-sweet and rich with quite bitter tannins and a smoky/peaty character **Finish** Long and rich with a bitter smokiness and chewy tannins **Notes** Master of Malt bottling - cask no 8492 distilled 26 December 1974

DUFFTOWN, BANFFSHIRE EST. 1975

Built by Arthur Bell & Sons Ltd as a sister to Dufftown and oper-ated in conjunction with it. Four stills. Now part of United Distillers plc. Closed in 1993.

LOCATION Situated in the Dullan Glen on the outskirts of Dufftown near the sixth century Mortlach Parish Church.

NOTES The make uses the same water source as Dufftown and gives a similar whisky.

WATER The distillery draws its process water from two springs, Convalleys and Balliemore.

Age 12 years **Strength** 43% abv

Sweetness 4 Peatiness 6 Availability 6

Colour Amber with old gold highlights **Nose** Round, quite full and malty, spicy, peppery and almost meaty with a coffee tang at the back **Flavour** Medium-dry, quite full-bodied and dark flavoured with a touch of tannin **Finish** Long, chewy and quite big **Notes** United Distillers bottling

Age 12 years **Strength** 56.6% abv

Sweetness 4 Peatiness 7 Availability 4

Colour Straw/amber with pale gold highlights **Nose** Quite peaty and soft with a damp oak character and a touch of green, unripe coffee **Flavour** Medium-dry, a coffee/chocolate character and smoky peatiness with a touch of spice **Finish** Long, lingering, spicy, smooth and nutty **Notes** Wm Cadenhead bottling

Age 12 years **Strength** 54% abv

Sweetness 5 Peatiness 7 Availability 3

Colour Medium to pale amber with lemon highlights **Nose** Medium-bodied, spirity and a hint of toffee/coffee with a greenness at the back, medium peated **Flavour** Medium-dry with a coffee flavour, quite full-flavoured, round and smooth **Finish** Creamy, quite sweet tangy and long with a soft touch of smokiness on the tail **Notes** James MacArthur bottling from cask number 15096

Age 13 years **Strength** 58% abv

Sweetness 4 Peatiness 7 Availability 4

Colour Deep, cough linctus-amber with bronze highlights **Nose** Big-bodied, dark, rich, malty, cerealy and a touch of rubber with a smoky burnt character **Flavour** Big, dark, rich, cerealy and smoky with a little spice **Finish** Quite spirity, long and smoky with a rich centre **Notes** Wm Cadenhead bottling

Age 18 years **Distillation** 1976 **Strength** 53.3% abv

Sweetness 8 Peatiness 2 Availability 2

Colour Pale straw/amber with pale gold highlights **Nose** Fresh and sweet with an almost grapey richness, a slightly unctuous lanolin aroma, a ripe apple character and lightly smoky **Flavour** Quite sweet, full and smooth with a green ripeness **Finish** Long, sweet and clean with a light smokiness on the tail **Notes** Blackadder International bottling

DISTILLED

≋ *1978* ≋

CASK

≋ 63.3% ≋
VOL·

NATURAL HIGH STRENGTH

NATURAL CASK STRENGTH

1978

63.3% VOL

70cl

SINGLE MALT
SCOTCH WHISKY
FROM
PORT ELLEN
DISTILLERY

LOW ROBERTSON & CO LIMITED

SPECIALLY SELECTED, PRODUCED AND BOTTLED BY
GORDON & MACPHAIL
ELGIN·SCOTLAND

PRODUCT OF SCOTLAND

CASK No.
2698

DISTILLED
21/4/78

BOTTLED
September 1994

PORT ELLEN, ISLAY, ARGYLL EST. 1825

Founded by Alexander Ker Mackay, with the support of landowner Walter Campbell, shortly after the Excise Act of 1824. Acquired by John Ramsay and run by him, and his heirs, until 1920, when sold to John Dewar & Sons Ltd & James Buchanan & Co., both of which companies merged with DCL in 1925. Port Ellen's management was transferred to SMD in 1930. Although silent 1929 to 1966, the maltings continued in use. The distillery was extensively rebuilt in 1967, when it was increased from two to four stills. A large new maltings was erected in 1973. The distiller's licence was held by Low, Robertson & Co. Ltd. Although the distillery ceased production permanently in May, 1983, the maltings now serves all the Islay distilleries, and also nearby Jura, following an historic concordat between the producing companies in 1987.

LOCATION   Situated about half a mile from the centre of Port Ellen, the maltings building now dominates the shoreline.

NOTES   The Excise Act of 1824 enforced the introduction of the spirit safe in distilleries. Tests had to be made to ensure that it had no harmful effects on the make. The official experiments were carried out in Port Ellen. The maltings were visited by Her Majesty Queen Elizabeth on 11 August 1980 and a commemorative bottling was produced.

WATER   The Leorin Lochs

Age 13 years **Strength** 43% abv

Sweetness 2 Peatiness 9 Availability 1

Colour Very pale, almost exceptionally so, with hints of lemon-yellow **Nose** Medium to full-bodied, a burnt, peaty character and a greenness at the back with a rich lanolin-oily character **Flavour** Smoky, quite rich, pungent and full with good sweet oak **Finish** Long and smooth with smoky oaky vanilla **Notes** Master of Malt bottling from cask nos. 1832-1836

Distillation 1970 **Strength** 40% abv

Sweetness 2 Peatiness 9 Availability 4

Colour Peaty/gold with bright highlights **Nose** Big-bodied, pungent and peaty with a slight rubbery character and dry **Flavour** Big, powerful, burnt peat with an edge of sweetness, very distinctive **Finish** Long, pungent and smoky **Notes** Gordon & MacPhail bottling

Distillation 1971 **Strength** 40% abv

Sweetness 1 Peatiness 9 Availability 4

Colour Bright gold/amber with golden/yellow highlights **Nose** Smoky peat, ozone, burnt heather roots with a very slight hint of sweetness **Flavour** Quite full, round, smoky, quite smooth and almost medicinal **Finish** Dry and smoky with the burnt heather roots lingering **Notes** Gordon & MacPhail bottling

Age 14 years **Distillation** 1977 **Strength** 59.7% abv

Sweetness 0 Peatiness 9 Availability 4

Colour Mid-amber with old gold highlights **Nose** Big, pungently smoky and dry with an earthy burnt peat character **Flavour** Big, powerful dark peatiness, a real "peat reek", and dry with a slight richness **Finish** Long and very peaty **Notes** Gordon & MacPhail bottling; cask no 2017 distilled 14 April 1977

OLD RHOSDHU

Single Highland Malt

40% vol   SCOTCH WHISKY   70 cl e

PRODUCE OF SCOTLAND

DISTILLED AND MATURED AT
LOCH LOMOND DISTILLERY·ALEXANDRIA·SCOTLAND

ALEXANDRIA, DUNBARTONSHIRE EST. 1965

One of two styles of malt produced by the Loch Lomond distillery, built in 1965/66 by the Littlemill Distillery Company Ltd. Closed 1984 and re-opened in 1987 after being purchased by Glen Catrine Bonded Warehouse Ltd. Two stills.

LOCATION Alexandria is at the southern end of Loch Lomond on the A82 Glasgow to Fort William road.

NOTES An earlier distillery of the same name existed at Arrochar, at the other end of Loch Lomond from 1814 to 1817. The stills are of an unusual design, allowing them to produce two very different styles of malt whisky, the other style being called Inchmurrin

WATER Loch Lomond

Age 9 years **Distillation** 1985 **Strength** 60.5% abv

Sweetness 6 Peatiness 4 Availability 2

Colour Straw with lemon yellow highlights **Nose** Quite full, young, spirity and mashy, a dry earthy smokiness with just an edge of sweetness **Flavour** Medium-sweet, mashy and vegetal, medium-bodied **Finish** Sweet, cerealy, of medium length and with a burnt toffee tail **Notes** Wm Cadenhead bottling

LOWLAND
SINGLE MALT
SCOTCH WHISKY

Established on its present
site at *CAMELON* in 1840

ROSEBANK

distillery stands on the
banks of the *FORTH*
and *CLYDE CANAL*.
This was once
a busy thoroughfare with
boats and steamers
continually passing by;
it is still the source
of water for cooling.
This single *MALT*
SCOTCH WHISKY is
triple distilled which
accounts for its *light*
distinctive nose and *well*
balanced flavour.

A G E D **12** Y E A R S

Distilled & Bottled in *SCOTLAND*.
ROSEBANK DISTILLERY
Falkirk, Stirlingshire, *Scotland*

43% vol 70 cl

FALKIRK, STIRLINGSHIRE EST. 1840

The distillery, established by James Rankine, was converted from the maltings of the earlier Camelon distillery. It was rebuilt by his son in 1864. It was Rankine's objective to distil a whisky which would stand comparison with his competitors' finest makes. By the 1890s, there was an extraordinary demand for Rosebank and customers were put on allocation. In 1914 the Rosebank Distillery Ltd, as it was then called, was one of the original founders of Scottish Malt Distillers Ltd. Now part of United Distillers plc, Rosebank was closed in May, 1993.

LOCATION Sited on the banks of the Forth and Clyde canal where the A803 intersects with the canal to the west of Falkirk.

NOTES The make was triple distilled with one wash still and two spirit stills. The licensees were The Distillers Agency Ltd.

WATER Carron Valley Reservoir.

Age 12 years **Strength** 43% abv
Sweetness 2 Peatiness 4 Availability 4

Colour Straw/light amber with gold and lemon highlights **Nose** Medium-bodied and spirity with a touch of greenness, lightly oily, medium-dry with a good edge of richness **Flavour** Light and smooth, dryish with a mashy character **Finish** Smooth, dry and oaky with a pleasant lightness **Notes** United Distillers bottling

Age 12 years **Strength** 43% abv

Sweetness 2 Peatiness 5 Availability 0

Colour Palish gold/amber with green tinges **Nose** Light and spirity, a little astringent **Flavour** Dry, a little spirity with a touch of spice **Finish** Quite good length, if somewhat fiery **Notes** DCL (pre-Guinness) bottling

Age 17 years **Strength** 43% abv

Sweetness 2 Peatiness 4 Availability 0

Colour Mid-amber with a touch of green **Nose** Medium-bodied and dryish, but with a richness at the back, a green nuttiness and malty with an almost honeyed touch **Flavour** Dry, spicy, quite full-bodied, round, soft and smooth **Finish** Long and quite rich with a toffee-like tail **Notes** Master of Malt bottling - cask no 5064

Age 19 years **Distillation** 1974 **Strength** 43% abv

Sweetness 1 Peatiness 4 Availability 2

Colour Mid-amber with pale gold highlights **Nose** Medium-bodied, quite fresh and slightly perfumed, medium-dry with a sweet oak note and a malty fruitiness **Flavour** Dry, fresh and quite lightly peated with an underpinning of vanilla **Finish** Fresh, quite clean and smoky **Notes** Master of Malt bottling from cask no. 5049 distilled 30 November 1974

Distillation 1969 **Strength** 51.7% abv

Sweetness 5 Peatiness 3 Availability 2

Colour Pale straw/amber with pale gold highlights **Nose** Malty, cerealy and soft with a slight oily oakiness and quite full with an edge of richness **Flavour** Quite full-bodied, sweet and rich, lightly peated with a green, fresh edge **Finish** Long, sweet and rich with a touch of chocolate **Notes** Signatory bottling

HIGHLAND

SINGLE MALT *SCOTCH WHISKY*

ROYAL BRACKLA

distillery, established in 1812, *&* lies on the
southern shore of the MORAY FIRTH at *Cawdor* near *Nairn*.
Woods around the *distillery* are home to the *SISKIN*;
although a *shy bird*, it can often be seen *feeding* on *conifer* seeds.

In 1835 a *Royal Warrant* was granted to the *distillery* by King William IV,
who enjoyed the *fresh, grassy, fruity* aroma of this *single malt whisky*.

AGED **10** YEARS

43% vol   Distilled & Bottled in *SCOTLAND*. ROYAL BRACKLA DISTILLERY, Cawdor, Nairn, Scotland.   70 cl

CAWDOR, NEAR NAIRN   EST. 1812

Founded by Captain William Fraser of Brackla House. A map of the Cawdor Estate dated 1773 shows a "malt brewhouse" on the site. The distillery was sold to John Bisset & Co. Ltd, who became part of DCL in 1943, when management was transferred to SMD. It was rebuilt between 1964 and 1965 and the number of stills was increased from two to four in 1970. Closed in 1985, Royal Brackla re-opened in 1991.

LOCATION   Sited to the north west of the B9090, one mile south of Nairn.

NOTES   Despite being regularly fined by HM Customs & Excise for irregularities, Brackla was the first distillery to be granted a Royal Warrant in 1835. It was referred to at that time as "Brackla" or "The King's Own Whisky". Some of the older buildings were converted to a visitor centre in 1982/83, the distillery being three quarters of a mile from Cawdor Castle. During demolition in November 1994 of Number 4 Warehouse, which had not been used for some years, a hive of wild bees was discovered in one of the warehouse walls. The hive was between 10 and 15 feet across and it was estimated that the bees had inhabited this site for approximately 70 years. Demolition of that wall was postponed until the Spring of 1995, when the queens were removed to another site temporarily. Ultimately, the bees are to be returned to beehives in the shape of pagoda roofs which will be built close to the original site of Number 4 Warehouse.

WATER   The Cawdor Burn

Age No age statement **Strength** 40% abv

Sweetness 6 Peatiness 7 Availability 8

Colour Pale straw with pale yellow highlights **Nose** Medium-bodied, quite peaty and round with a slight liquorice character **Flavour** Medium-sweet, rich and slightly spicy with a good smoky peatiness and good body **Finish** Quite clean and fresh with almost a hint of bitter chocolate on the end **Notes** United Distillers bottling •

Age 10 years **Strength** 43% abv

Sweetness 7 Peatiness 5 Availability 6

Colour Quite pale straw with yellow highlights **Nose** Fresh, clean and medium-sweet with a fruitiness and a floral note, with gentle peat in the background **Flavour** Round, medium-sweet and quite full-bodied with a green fruity character **Finish** Long, fresh and clean **Notes** United Distillers bottling

Age 18 years **Strength** 46% abv

Sweetness 8 Peatiness 5 Availability 4

Colour Pale straw with good yellow highlights and a definite green tinge **Nose** Round, sweet and fruity **Flavour** Sweet, smooth, round and rich **Finish** Velvety smooth, long and distinguished **Notes** Wm Cadenhead bottling

Age 14 years **Distillation** 1978 **Strength** 43% abv

Sweetness 5 Peatiness 5 Availability 2

Colour Very pale watery straw with pale lemon/gold highlights **Nose** Medium bodied with a vegetal touch, medium-sweet, firm and meaty with a ripe character; the peat is held at the back **Flavour** Medium-dry, rich, firm and round with good body and a dark, nutty character **Finish** Long and nutty with firm tannins and a good edge of sweetness **Notes** Master of Malt bottling from cask no. 11081 distilled 14 December 1978

Distillation 1970 **Strength** 40% abv

Sweetness 6 Peatiness 6 Availability 4

Colour Pale mid-amber with yellow gold highlights **Nose** Good body with oak, cold apples and a peaty smokiness **Flavour** Medium-dry, oaky, quite mellow and smooth with a slight oiliness and a medium peatiness **Finish** Reasonable oaky finish with a touch of richness **Notes** Gordon & MacPhail bottling

ROYAL LOCHNAGAR
Single Highland Malt
SCOTCH WHISKY
Produced in Scotland
BY
Royal Lochnagar Distillery

CRATHIE, DEESIDE
ABERDEENSHIRE
SCOTLAND

70 cl   40 % vol

ESTᴰ 1845

BY APPOINTMENT TO THEIR LATE MAJESTIES
QUEEN VICTORIA, KING EDWARD VII & KING GEORGE V

CRATHIE, BALLATER, ABERDEENSHIRE EST. 1845

Originally known as "New Lochnagar", as another Lochnagar distillery had been built nearby in 1826. This had closed by 1860. Lochnagar obtained the Royal Warrant after its owner, John Begg, had invited Queen Victoria and Prince Albert to view the distillery in 1848. The distillery was rebuilt in 1906 and acquired by John Dewar & Sons Ltd in 1916, passing to the DCL in 1925 and operated by SMD from 1930. Now part of United Distillers plc.

LOCATION   On Royal Deeside overlooking Balmoral Castle and about one mile from the Queen's Bedroom, from which the young Queen Victoria is said to have looked out at the distillery.

NOTES   The story the locals tell is of John Begg looking out of the window one evening and seeing a few figures making their way towards the distillery through the gathering dusk. The figures turned out to be Queen Victoria, her husband, children and lady-in-waiting. The Royal party had just arrived for their first stay at Balmoral, and Begg had delivered the Queen a note inviting her on a not to be missed tour round his new distillery. Prince Albert was particularly interested, being enthusiastic about all new technology. Royal Lochnagar is now the only remaining distillery of the several that used to operate on Deeside. There is a very popular visitor centre, converted from the old distillery farm steading. Scottish children try to trick one another by asking how deep Lochnagar is. The catch is that Lochnagar is not a loch, but a mountain. At 3789 feet (1155m) its bulk dominates the countryside around Balmoral.

WATER   Springs in the foothills of Lochnagar.

Age 12 years   **Strength** 40% abv

Sweetness 7   Peatiness 4   Availability 4

Colour Mid-amber with old gold highlights **Nose** Medium-bodied, soft and round with creamy sweet vanilla oak notes **Flavour** Soft, gently peated and round with creamy sweet vanilla oak notes **Finish** Fresh, lingering and medium-sweet with a slightly smoky tang **Notes** United distillers bottling

Age 12 years   **Strength** 40% abv

Sweetness 8   Peatiness 4   Availability 0

Colour Pale straw with bright gold highlights **Nose** Pleasantly sweet, slightly peppery and fruity **Flavour** Sweet, clean, creamy and slightly peppery **Finish** Smooth and with good length **Notes** DCL (pre-Guinness) bottling

ROYAL LOCHNAGAR SELECTED RESERVE
Age No statement   **Strength** 43% abv

Sweetness 8   Peatiness 3   Availability 3

Colour Deep peaty amber with good gold highlights **Nose** Rich, wet oak, vanilla, sweet and lightly sherried **Flavour** Full, round and rich, mellow, nutty and creamy **Finish** Long, slightly spicy and very smooth **Notes** As "Royal Lochnagar Selected Reserve", it has no age statement because it is produced from selected casks and the age could vary from bottling to bottling

RARE MALTS
S E L E C T I O N

Each individual vintage has been specially selected from Scotland's finest single malt stocks of rare or now silent distilleries. The limited bottlings of these scarce and unique whiskies are at natural cask strength for the enjoyment of the true connoisseur.

NATURAL
CASK STRENGTH
SINGLE MALT
SCOTCH WHISKY

AGED **23** YEARS

DISTILLED IN 1970 AT THE
ST MAGDALENE
DISTILLERY
ESTABLISHED 1765
LINLITHGOW

58.43%vol 70cle
PRODUCE OF SCOTLAND
LIMITED BOTTLING

LINLITHGOW, WEST LOTHIAN EST. PRE-1797

Said to have been founded in the eighteenth century on the lands of St Magdalene's Cross, the former site of an annual fair and of St Magdalene's Hospital. The earliest record is of Adam Dawson as distiller in 1797. It was taken over by DCL on 16 November 1912, prior to which the owning company was A & J Dawson Ltd. St Magdalene was one of the five founding distilleries of SMD in July 1914.

LOCATION Sited at the eastern end of Linlithgow, where the railway line, running alongside the Union Canal, intersects with the A706 to Edinburgh.

NOTES Linlithgow was a centre of milling and malting in the seventeenth century and brewing and distilling in the eighteenth century. The distillery closed in 1983 and its buildings have been converted into housing.

WATER The town's domestic supply, which comes from Loch Lomond.

Age 23 years **Strength** 58.1% abv

Sweetness 2 Peatiness 3 Availability 2

Colour Amber with gold highlights and a tinge of green **Nose** Gentle, soft and medium-dry with a bread yeasty aroma and a slightly oaky acetone character **Flavour** Big-bodied, quite dry, but with an edge of richness, tannic and yeasty **Finish** Long, quite powerful and quite tannic **Notes** United Distillers bottling

Distillation 1965 **Strength** 40% abv

Sweetness 1 Peatiness 4 Availability 4

Colour Light to mid-amber with gold highlights and just a tinge of green **Nose** Quite fresh with a light oak character, quite lightweight and dry, a little spirity **Flavour** Dry with oaky tannins, of medium weight and lightly smoky **Finish** Dry, oaky and chewy with dry tannins **Notes** Gordon & MacPhail bottling

Age 10 years **Distillation** 1982 **Strength** 62.3% abv

Sweetness 2 Peatiness 2 Availability 2

Colour Pale straw with lemon/yellow highlights **Nose** Fresh, clean, fruity and spirity, medium-dry with a slight touch of oak and a light mashy character **Flavour** Medium-dry with good richness and round with quite good body **Finish** Good length, rich and smooth **Notes** Wm Cadenhead bottling

Distillation 1980 **Strength** 40% abv

Sweetness 3 Peatiness 3 Availability 4

Colour Straw with pale lemon/pale gold highlights **Nose** Quite good body with a fresh, almost fruity richness, off-dry, lightly peated and green with a slight edge of sweetness **Flavour** Smooth, mashy, malty, clean, medium-dry and quite rich **Finish** Quite long and rich with a slightly green freshness **Notes** 1995 Gordon & Macphail Centenary Reserve bottling

SCAPA

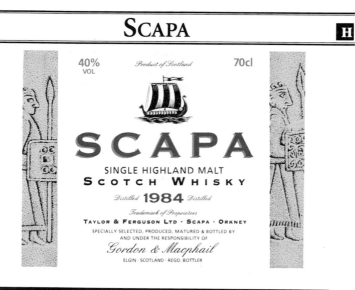

40% VOL — *Product of Scotland* — 70cl

SCAPA
SINGLE HIGHLAND MALT
SCOTCH WHISKY
Distilled **1984** *Distilled*
Trademark of Proprietors
TAYLOR & FERGUSON LTD · SCAPA · ORKNEY
SPECIALLY SELECTED, PRODUCED, MATURED & BOTTLED BY
AND UNDER THE RESPONSIBILITY OF
Gordon & Macphail
ELGIN · SCOTLAND · REGD. BOTTLER

KIRKWALL, ORKNEY EST. 1885

Built by Macfarlane & Townsend. Owned by Hiram Walker (now part of Allied Domecq) since 1954. Two stills. The wash still was replaced by a "Lomond" still in 1959, this producing a heavier spirit than the more traditional long-necked stills. Operated by Allied Distillers Ltd.

LOCATION Sited on the Lingro Burn two miles south west of Kirkwall on the A964 at the head of Scapa Bay.

NOTES Scapa Flow was where the German Fleet was scuttled at the end of World War I. When whisky chronicler Alfred Barnard visited the distillery in 1886, it had been open for just a year. He wrote about it as being "one of the most complete little Distilleries in the Kingdom". The stills were described as being of "the newest type and heated by steam instead of fire, and are both fitted with "collapse" valves, which allow air to enter in the event of a vacuum being formed". For a malt with such a pronounced astringent nose in its youth, the palate is unusually surprisingly sweet. Scapa is one of the main malts associated with Ballantine's blended Scotch Whisky.

WATER The Lingro Burn and nearby springs.

Distillation 1983 **Strength** 40% abv
Sweetness 2 **Peatiness** 4 **Availability** 4

Colour Mid-amber with old gold highlights **Nose** Fresh, clean, malty and slightly green with a slight nuttiness and medium-dry **Flavour** Almost dry, quite full-bodied, slightly spicy and tangy, and gently smoky **Finish** Long and clean with a touch of richness **Notes** Gordon & MacPhail bottling

Age 14 years **Distillation** 1979 **Strength** 43% abv

Sweetness 6 Peatiness 5 Availability 2

Colour Pale straw with yellow/lemon highlights **Nose** Round, smooth and medium-sweet, slightly unctuous with a fresh floral character and rich with a maltiness at the back **Flavour** Medium-dry, quite full and round, quite smooth with tannic oak **Finish** Long and full, quite rich with a toffee tail **Notes** Master of Malt bottling from cask no. 3851/2 distilled 9 May 1979

Age 24 years **Distillation** 1965 **Strength** 50.1% abv

Sweetness 8 Peatiness 6 Availability 1

Colour Straw with lemony gold highlights **Nose** Sweet, quite fresh and rich with a creamy peatiness and an underpinning of oak **Flavour** Quite sweet, softly peated, light and quite delicate **Finish** Smooth and smoky with a lanolin character **Notes** Wm Cadenhead bottling, September 1990

Age 8 years **Strength** 57% abv

Sweetness 8 Peatiness 7 Availability 3

Colour Peaty/amber with good gold highlights and a greenish tinge **Nose** Spirity, somewhat astringent, young and peaty **Flavour** Sweet, rich, full-bodied, lightly oaky and malty **Finish** Good, spicy and long lasting **Notes** Gordon & MacPhail bottling

Distillation 1979 **Strength** 56.3% abv

Sweetness 8 Peatiness 6 Availability 2

Colour Straw with yellow/lemon highlights **Nose** Full-bodied, fruity (strawberries), bubble-gummy, medium sweet and finely peated **Flavour** Sweet, round, quite spicy, smooth, almost grapey **Finish** Long, sweet and clean **Notes** Scotch Malt Whisky Society bottling; Cask no. 17.13; bottled May, 1994

The Singleton of Auchroisk, to give the whisky its full name is produced at the Auchroisk distillery. That name being rather a mouthful, the company's own bottlings are marketed as "The Singleton". The distillery is managed by Justerini & Brooks (Scotland) Ltd, a subsidiary of IDV, which is itself part of Grand Metropolitan. Eight stills.

LOCATION On the north side of the A95 between Keith and Aberlour.

NOTES A new distillery producing its first make in 1975. Despite being a modern complex, the buildings are in the Scots vernacular style and the distillery received a Saltire Award (for outstanding architectural achievement in a traditional Scottish style). Sherry casks are used predominantly. Auchroisk is a showpiece distillery and has an old steam engine from Strathmill preserved in its entrance hall.

WATER Dorie's Well.

Distillation 1981 **Strength** 43% abv
Sweetness 7 Peatiness 5 Availability 4

Colour Amber with gold highlights **Nose** Full-bodied, clean, medium-sweet and fresh with a slightly green unripe peachy fruitiness and a delicately perfumed smokiness at the back **Flavour** Medium-sweet, quite smoky, creamily smooth with an almost chocolatey flavour **Finish** Long and round with a hint of coffee **Notes** IDV bottling

Distillation 1983 **Strength** 40% abv

Sweetness 4 Peatiness 3 Availability 10

Colour Full amber with old gold highlights **Nose** Quite rich and medium-sweet with a dark nuttiness and reasonable weight **Flavour** Medium-bodied, round, dark, nutty and medium-dry **Finish** Almost dry, slightly bitter and with a toffee-like tail **Notes** IDV bottling

Distillation 1976 **Strength** 40% abv

Sweetness 7 Peatiness 4 Availability 2

Colour Amber with gold highlights **Nose** Rich, quite full-bodied and minty with a peachy sweetness and good weight **Flavour** Quite full-bodied and smooth with a sherried nuttiness, a vanilla oaky-oiliness and quite delicately peated **Finish** Quite long, nutty and dark with a smokiness on the tail **Notes** IDV bottling

AUCHROISK

Age 12 years **Distillation** 1978 **Strength** 59.3% abv

Sweetness 8 Peatiness 3 Availability 3

Colour Pale straw with lemon/yellow highlights **Nose** Fresh, fruity-citrus and cherries, quite full-bodied with a touch of raisins at the back **Flavour** Sweet, fruity, smooth and round with good oaky tannins and quite spirity **Finish** Smooth and spirity with a hint of cloves and quite long **Notes** Wm Cadenhead bottling as Auchroisk

ROTHES, MORAY EST. 1897

Built by John Hopkins & Co. for the Speyburn-Glenlivet Distillery Company Ltd. Local tradition has it that the walls were built of stones "extracted by man and beast" from the bed of the River Spey. DCL bought John Hopkins & Co. in 1916, but The Speyburn-Glenlivet Distillery Co. Ltd was not wound up until 1962, when Speyburn's management was transferred to SMD. It was the first distillery to install a drum maltings, this unit being closed in 1968. The distillery has two stills and is now owned by Inver House Distillers, who purchased it in 1991.

LOCATION Situated a quarter of a mile north west of the B9105 on the northern outskirts of Rothes.

NOTES Speyburn started up in the last week of December 1897. Doors and windows still had not been fitted to the stillhouse and, as a severe snowstorm was sweeping the district, employees had to work in overcoats. Just one butt of spirit was bonded with 1897 on its head.

WATER The Granty (or Birchfield) Burn.

Age 10 years **Strength** 40% abv

Sweetness 8 Peatiness 2 Availability 7

Colour Very pale straw with lemon highlights **Nose** Fresh, clean and aromatic with a rich lemony fruitiness, medium-bodied and quite lightly peated **Flavour** Fresh, clean, rich and medium-sweet; quite full-bodied **Finish** Long and sweet with a touch of spice **Notes** Inver House bottling

SPEYBURN

Distillation 1971 **Strength** 40% abv

Sweetness 8 Peatiness 5 Availability 4

Colour Rich peaty, amber with good gold highlights **Nose** Sweet, fruity and slightly spirity **Flavour** Medium-sweet, quite light and smooth **Finish** Mellow, of reasonable length with oak on the end **Notes** Gordon & MacPhail bottling

Age 15 years **Distillation** 1975 **Strength** 60.1% abv

Sweetness 7 Peatiness 5 Availability 4

Colour Straw with pale gold highlights **Nose** Medium-sweet and fresh with a touch of greenness, light, nutty and biscuity **Flavour** Medium-sweet with a good dollop of creamy freshness, fresh, clean, smooth and round **Finish** Sweet, fresh and creamy with an edge of greenness and good length **Notes** Wm Cadenhead bottling

CAMPBELTOWN, ARGYLL EST. 1828

Said to have been originally licensed to the Reid family. It was acquired by John and William Mitchell in 1837 and run by various members of the family until 1897 when the present owning company, J & A Mitchell & Company was incorporated. The fact that Springbank has three stills has encouraged debate as to whether the whisky is triple distilled. In fact, only a proportion of the spirit is distilled three times.

LOCATION The distillery is in the centre of the town.

NOTES The family owners of Springbank are direct descendants of the illicit distillers who established the once numerous Campbeltown distilleries, and the present managing director is the great-great-great-grandson of its founder. The Campbeltown area once boasted around 30 legal distilleries, but the years of Depression after World War I and prohibition in America almost brought about the total demise of Campbeltown whisky. Springbank is now one of only two survivors and the only one open at the time of writing (Spring, 1995). Fortunately Springbank now continues to go from strength to strength, its reputation and renown being second to none. It is the only distillery where everything from malting through to bottling is carried out on the premises for all of the distillery's own production.

WATER Crosshill Loch.

Age 9 years   **Strength** 61.2% abv

Colour Very pale watery straw with pale mint green highlights **Nose** Young, spirity, mashy, quite full-bodied with a dark peatiness and almost dry **Flavour** Almost dry, but with a developing richness and a dark smokiness, good body, a lanolin smoothness and mashy **Finish** Spicy, elegantly smoky with a salty tail and a sweetness to the edge **Notes** Wm Cadenhead botlling

Age 10 years   **Strength** 46% abv

Colour Pale straw with yellow highlights **Nose** Quite light and sweet with hints of coconut oil **Flavour** Sweet, smooth and creamy with a slight hint of coconut **Finish** Good, smooth and distinctive **Notes** J & A Mitchell botlling

Age 15 years   **Strength** 46% abv

Colour Light mid-amber (honey-coloured) with lemony highlights **Nose** Medium weight, rich, oily oak with a touch of greenness, quite lightly peated **Flavour** Clean, smooth, medium-dry with good creamy oak and a touch of sweetness and greenness **Finish** Long and smooth with a touch of tannin and hints of richness and saltiness on the tail **Notes** J & A Mitchell botlling

Age 21 years   **Strength** 46% abv

Colour Deep amber **Nose** Definite fruity notes, stickily sweet in their richness, also floral notes and a suggestion of coconut and medicinal cloves **Flavour** Silkily smooth, full-bodied and creamy with a salty tang **Finish** Very fine, long, dark and oaky **Notes** J & A Mitchell botlling

Age 25 years   **Strength** 46% abv

Colour Full, peaty amber with bronze highlights **Nose** Rich, ripe, sweet and full-bodied, smoky with a touch of ozone and oak **Flavour** Full, round, smoky and medium-sweet with oaky tannins and a salty tang **Finish** Long, smoky-oak and tangy with a touch of spiciness **Notes** J & A Mitchell botlling

SPRINGBANK

S

Age 30 years **Strength** 46% abv

Sweetness 8 Peatiness 6 Availability 3

Colour Full amber with old gold highlights **Nose** Full and rich, almost raisiny with a touch of liquorice, almost tarry and medium-dry **Flavour** Sweet, and rich with a good peaty character, flavour of bitter chocolate and a salty tang **Finish** Long and tangy with good sweetness **Notes** J & A Mitchell botlling

Age 18 years **Distillation** 1975 **Strength** 43% abv

Sweetness 7 Peatiness 4 Availability 1

Colour Pale amber with pale yellow highlights **Nose** Quite full-bodied, rich and medium-sweet underpinned by peat and with a hint of green coffee **Flavour** Fresh, green, rich, round and medium-sweet, almost grapey with a vanilla note **Finish** Long, salty, lingering and gently smoky **Notes** "The Ultimate Collection" bottled for Van Wees of Holland from cask no 3596 distilled 17 December 1975

Age 17 years **Distillation** 1975 **Strength** 55.8% abv

Sweetness 7 Peatiness 4 Availability 2

Colour Mid-amber with gold highlights **Nose** Dry, fresh, smoky and rich, quite full-bodied with a good richness at the back **Flavour** Big-bodied, medium-sweet and rich with gentle tannins and delicately peated **Finish** Tangy and rich with good length and a touch of spice **Notes** Signatory bottling from cask nos. 3592/3 distilled 17 December 1975

Age 28 years **Distillation** 1965 **Strength** 53.2% abv

Sweetness 7 Peatiness 5 Availability 2

Colour Full amber with old gold highlights **Nose** Full, warm, nutty (hazelnuts), medium-sweet with a fruitcake richness and a green peatiness at the back, a lanolin oaky unctuousness and a slight medicinal touch **Flavour** Medium-dry, very rich, quite big-bodied with chewy tannins, good body and quite delicately peated **Finish** Powerful with good richness - even a sweetness at the end - and a salty tang on the tail **Notes** Adelphi Distillery bottling; bottled 1993

"STRATHISLA"
PURE HIGHLAND MALT
SCOTCH WHISKY
THE OLDEST DISTILLERY IN THE HIGHLANDS

AGED **12** YEARS

70cl ℮   DISTILLED AND BOTTLED BY CHIVAS BROTHERS LTD
STRATHISLA DISTILLERY, KEITH, AB55 3BS, SCOTLAND   43%vol

KEITH, BANFFSHIRE EST. 1786

Built in 1786 as Milltown (Keith was the centre of the Scottish linen industry) and later known as Milton, Strathisla was originally the name of the make and subsequently also became that of the distillery. It was converted into a flour mill in 1838. After reconversion to distilling, the distillery was twice badly damaged in the 1870s: first by fire in 1876 and three years later by an explosion. Extensive modernisation took place after these events and again in 1965, when the distillery was enlarged from two to four stills. It is today owned by Chivas Brothers Ltd, a subsidiary of The Seagram Company of Canada.

LOCATION Half a mile from the centre of Keith.

NOTES On 15 June 1993 Strathisla received an unexpected visitor from Louisville, Kentucky; a young black and white cat fell asleep among some bourbon barrels in a container awaiting shipment to Scotland. On opening the container some four weeks later, the cat staggered out, weak from hunger and drunk from the bourbon fumes in the enclosed space. After six months' quarantine, the cat, for obvious reasons called Dizzy, is now employed by Chivas Bros. as a "mouser".

WATER The Broomhill Spring. The reservoir which holds the distillery's water supply is said to be visited nightly by the "water kelpies" which could account for its special flavour.

Age 8 years **Strength** 40% abv

Sweetness 8 **Peatiness** 3 **Availability** 4

Colour Amber with good gold highlights **Nose** Fruity, spirity and sweet with a lanolin oiliness **Flavour** Spicy, quite smooth and medium-sweet with a touch of oak **Finish** Good body, although perhaps a little short because of its youth **Notes** Gordon & MacPhail bottling

Age 12 years **Strength** 40% abv

Sweetness 8 **Peatiness** 3 **Availability** 4

Colour Bright gold/straw **Nose** Full-bodied, sweet, fruity, appley, very pronounced and rich **Flavour** Rich, warm, quite full and sweet **Finish** Long, fine and mellow **Notes** Gordon & MacPhail bottling

Age 12 years **Strength** 43% abv

Sweetness 5 **Peatiness** 5 **Availability** 6

Colour Mid-amber with yellow/gold highlights **Nose** Quite big and round, a dark hazelnut character with good richness at the back, just a hint of sweetness and a delicate burnt peaty character **Flavour** Medium-dry with a smoky nuttiness and a touch of dark, oaky tannins with a nice green edge **Finish** Quite long, hazelnut and smoky **Notes** Seagram bottling

Age 18 years **Distillation** 1974 **Strength** 57.8% abv

Sweetness 6 **Peatiness** 7 **Availability** 4

Colour Amber with old gold highlights **Nose** Full-bodied with a dark nuttiness and medium-dry oaky vanilla **Flavour** Smoky with a dark nuttiness, medium-sweet with gentle oaky tannins and a slight astringency **Finish** Long, creamy & smoky with a background of sweetness **Notes** Gordon & MacPhail bottling Distilled 23 March 1974

Age 21 years **Strength** 40% abv

Sweetness 8 **Peatiness** 4 **Availability** 4

Colour Amber with bright copper highlights **Nose** Medium-sweet and malty, lightly peated and oaky **Flavour** Medium-dry, oaky and spicy and creamy **Finish** Long and spicy with hints of bitter chocolate **Notes** Gordon & MacPhail bottling

KEITH, BANFFSHIRE EST. 1891

Originally a corn and flour mill, it was converted in 1891 as Glenisla-Glenlivet. Acquired by W & A Gilbey in 1895, when it was renamed Strathmill. Became part of IDV in 1962 and now absorbed into Grand Metropolitan. Four stills.

LOCATION Just off the B9014 from Keith to Dufftown.

NOTES Very rare as a single malt, most of the make goes into the J&B blend. The above label has not been used for over thirty years.

WATER A spring at the distillery.

Age 12 years   **Strength** 55.5% abv

Sweetness 6 Peatiness 3 Availability 0

Colour Very pale watery with watery green highlights **Nose** Light and cerealy, lightly smoky with a touch of perfume and a delicate nuttiness **Flavour** Medium-sweet, smooth and quite round with good body **Finish** Long and spicy with a pleasant leafy greenness **Notes** A cask sample kindly supplied by J&B Scotland Ltd, who also supplied the above label from their archives. The whisky is not now available bottled by J&B.

Age 11 years **Distillation** 1980 **Strength** 60.6% abv

Sweetness 7 Peatiness 3 Availability 4

Colour Pale straw with lemon highlights **Nose** Fresh, young, mashy vegetal greenness with an edge of richness, medium-sweet and lightly peated **Flavour** Cerealy, corn flake-like, medium-sweet with soft tannins, smooth and quite round **Finish** Good sweetness, quite good length, clean with a mashy vegetal character and a green edge to the tail **Notes** Wm Cadenhead bottling

ISLE OF SKYE

TALISKER
SINGLE MALT SCOTCH WHISKY

Beyond Carbost Village close to the Shore is a gentle haven sheltered from the bleak ravines which sweep down to the coast. Here in the shadow of the distant Cuillin Hills lies the island's only distillery Talisker. The Golden Spirit of Skye has more than a hint of local seaweed peppered with sour & sweet notes and a memorable warm peaty finish.

45.8% VOL TALISKER DISTILLERY CARBOST SKYE 70 cl e

CARBOST, ISLE OF SKYE EST. 1830

The distillery was originally sited at Snizort, to the north of the island, but was closed and mysteriously moved. The current buildings were founded by Hugh and Kenneth MacAskill in 1830. Rebuilt 1880-1887 and further extended in 1900. Merged into Dailuaine-Talisker Distilleries Ltd in 1898, under which name it still trades although absorbed fully into DCL in 1925. Operated by SMD. Rebuilt again 1960-62 after the stillhouse was destroyed by fire on 22 November 1960. Five stills.

LOCATION Situated in a gentle bowl which forms a lonely, very sheltered glen on the west coast of Skye.

NOTES The only distillery on the island of Skye, it took its name from a farm about six miles distant. The make was triple distilled until 1928. One of United Distillers' Classic Malts portfolio.

WATER A burn on the slopes of Cnoc nan Speireag (Hawk Hill), cooling water comes from the Carbost Burn.

Age 10 years **Strength** 45.8% abv

Sweetness 1 Peatiness 10 Availability 8

Colour Straw with gold highlights **Nose** Pungent, peaty with a burnt heather character and hints of ozone **Flavour** Peaty, dry, spicy and quite creamy **Finish** Smoky, spicy, smooth, almost salty at the end **Notes** United Distillers bottling

Age 8 years   **Strength** 45.8% abv

Sweetness 3   **Peatiness** 10   **Availability** 0

Colour Full amber with green highlights **Nose** Pungent, full and peaty, but soft **Flavour** Pungent, dry, spicy and full-bodied with a lot of smokiness **Finish** Long with a burst of flavour on swallowing **Notes** DCL (pre-Guinness) bottling

Age 14 years   **Distillation** 1979   **Strength** 64.3% abv

Sweetness 2   **Peatiness** 9   **Availability** 3

Colour Straw with gold/yellow highlights and just a tinge of green **Nose** Quite big and pungently smoky with a medicinal burnt oak character and a slight touch of richness **Flavour** Big, powerful with quite gentle pungency, earthily oaky and quite soft richness **Finish** Long, smoky with a touch of fresh greenness and pungent with a salty tang **Notes** Wm Cadenhead bottling

Age 38 years   **Distillation** 1955   **Strength** 53.6% abv

Sweetness 2   **Peatiness** 9   **Availability** 1

Colour Deep amber with bronze highlights **Nose** Deep, dark, nutty and woody with a medicinal character and just an edge of richness **Flavour** Big, dark and tannic, quite pungent with an almost burnt peaty character and a touch of richness **Finish** Long, tannic, chewy and pungent. **Notes** Gordon & MacPhail bottling; cask nos. 1257, 1310 & 1311 distilled 12 and 28 May 1955

KNOCKANDO, MORAY EST. 1897

Built by the Tamdhu Distillery Company Ltd which was owned by a consortium of blenders. Owned by Highland Distilleries Company since 1898. Closed from 1927-47, but extended in 1972 from two to four stills and again to six stills in 1975. A feature is Tamdhu's Saladin Maltings which have been largely rebuilt.

LOCATION Sited on the banks of the River Spey south of the B9102 between Knockando and Archiestown.

NOTES The old railway station at Knockando has been converted into a visitor centre for Tamdhu. Tamdhu does not have the traditional pagoda heads atop its kilns, having instead a short, square concrete chimney. The Visitor's Centre was closed at the time of writing, but it may open again for the 1996 season.

WATER A spring under the distillery

Age 10 years **Strength** 40% abv

Sweetness 8 Peatiness 4 Availability 4

Colour Pale golden with amber highlights **Nose** Lightish with a sweetness akin to apples **Flavour** Round, mellow, slightly spicy and lightly peated **Finish** Soft, creamily smooth and lightly smoky **Notes** Highland Distillers bottling

Age No age statement **Strength** 40% abv

Sweetness 7 Peatiness 4 Availability 8

Colour Straw/amber with yellow highlights **Nose** Medium-bodied, fruity and a touch floral, medium-sweet with a greenness **Flavour** Medium-sweet, quite light, mashy, biscuity and quite smooth **Finish** Quite short; spirity and sweet **Notes** Highland Distillers bottling

TOMNAVOULIN, BANFFSHIRE EST. 1966

Built by the Tamnavulin-Glenlivet Distillery Company, a subsidiary of Invergordon Distillers and now owned by Whyte & Mackay. A very modern distillery, it can be operated by just a handful of technicians. Mothballed early in 1995.

LOCATION On the B9008 at the village of Tomnavoulin.

NOTES The only distillery actually positioned on the River Livet, from which the cooling waters are drawn. Tomnavoulin from the Gaelic means "mill on the hill" and an old carding mill which stands at the riverside just below the distillery has been converted into a very attractive visitor centre. The mill machinery has been preserved inside. Equally pleasant are the grassy banks of the river which have been turned into a picnic area.

WATER Subterranean springs at Easterton in the local hills.

Age 10 years **Strength** 40% abv

Sweetness 9 Peatiness 3 Availability 7

Colour Very pale straw with golden highlights **Nose** Light and sweet with a slightly floral edge **Flavour** Mature, sweet, light and gently oaky **Finish** Long, easy and slightly spicy **Notes** Invergordon bottling

Age 18 years **Strength** 46% abv

Sweetness 8 Peatiness 3 Availability 2

Colour Very dark, teak coloured **Nose** Nutty, quite spirity, light and medium-sweet **Flavour** Smooth, oaky, quite velvety and nutty **Finish** Smooth and spirity, quite long with a dry end **Notes** Wm Cadenhead bottling

HIGHLAND
SINGLE MALT
SCOTCH WHISKY

The *Cromarty Firth* is one of the few places in
the British Isles inhabited by *PORPOISE*. They
can be seen quite regularly, *swimming*
close to the shore *& less* than a *mile* from

TEANINICH

distillery. Founded in 1817 in the *Ross-shire*
town of ALNESS, the *distillery* is now one
of the largest in *Scotland*. TEANINICH
is an assertive *single MALT WHISKY*
with a *spicy*, smoky, *satisfying* taste.

AGED **10** YEARS

43% vol

Distilled & Bottled in *SCOTLAND*
TEANINICH DISTILLERY.
Alness, Ross-shire, *Scotland*

70 cl

ALNESS, ROSS-SHIRE EST. 1817

Founded by Captain Hugh Munro. Sold to SMD in 1933. When SMD took over, there were four stills, two of which were described as being very small. When production restarted after World War II, the two smaller stills were removed. Capacity was increased from two to four larger stills in 1962 and to ten when an entirely new distillation unit named "A side" began production in 1970. The milling, mashing and fermentation part of the old distillery, "B side", was rebuilt 1973. Now owned by United Distillers.

LOCATION Sited to the south of the A9 on the western outskirts of Alness and on the west bank of the River Alness, threequarters of a mile from its outflow into the Cromarty Firth.

NOTES Alfred Barnard recorded in 1887 that Teaninich was the only distillery north of Inverness to be "lighted by electricity". In 1925 both malting floors were of solid clay. "A side" is in production, but "B side" was mothballed in the mid-1980s.

WATER The Dairywell Spring.

Age 10 years   **Strength** 43% abv
Sweetness 7 Peatiness 5 Availability 6

Colour Pale straw with yellow highlights and a tinge of lemon **Nose** Fresh and quite light with a good green peatiness, medium-sweet with an appley character **Flavour** Medium-dry, gently smoky, smooth and round **Finish** Clean and fresh with a sweet tail **Notes** United Distillers bottling

Age 18 years   **Distillation** 1975   **Strength** 43% abv

Sweetness **7**   Peatiness **5**   Availability **1**

Colour Straw/pale amber with pale lemon highlights **Nose** Fresh, green, quite cerealy and clean, medium-sweet and quite full-bodied **Flavour** Fresh and clean with an earthy smokiness, medium to full-bodied and medium-sweet with a touch of richness **Finish** Clean, quite long with an almost perfumed smokiness **Notes** Master of Malt bottling; cask no 13988 distilled 12 November 1975

Age 17 years   **Distillation** 1975   **Strength** 43% abv

Sweetness **9**   Peatiness **3**   Availability **1**

Colour Quite pale straw with lemon highlights **Nose** Quite full-bodied, spirity and fresh, almost salty with fruity and floral notes **Flavour** Quite sweet, round, spicy, full-bodied, rich and delicately peated with a nutty character **Finish** Long, sweet and slightly smoky **Notes** Master of Malt bottling from cask no. 13984

The mash tun

TOBERMORY, ISLE OF MULL EST. 1798

Established by local merchant John Sinclair. Owned from 1890-1916 by John Hopkins & Son & Co., when taken over by the DCL. Silent from 1930 to 1972 when revived as the Ledaig Distillery (Tobermory) Ltd. This company went into receivership in 1975 and the business was acquired in 1978 by the Kirkleavington Property Co. of Cleckheaton. Tobermory was in production between 1979 and 1981, before closing again until 1989. It was purchased in 1993 by Burn Stewart Distillers for £600,000 plus £200,000 for stock. Four stills.

LOCATION Situated at the head of Tobermory Bay.

NOTES The only distillery on Mull. Because the distillery was closed for several years, very little Tobermory single malt has been produced until recently, all distilled between 1972 and 1975 and 1979 and 1981. Tobermory is now becoming more readily available, however. The older bottlings of Tobermory that are available have been bottled as Ledaig. Owner Burn Stewart has decided to use only unpeated barley in the production of Tobermory, although a few mashes will be produced each year using peated barley. These will be reserved for whiskies marketed under the name Ledaig.

WATER A small private loch close by the Mishnish Lochs.

TOBERMORY
Age No age statement   **Strength** 40% abv
Sweetness 4 Peatiness 6 Availability 5

Colour Straw/amber with bright gold highlights **Nose** Quite full-bodied, medium-dry with an edge of richness, a touch of liquorice to the smokiness, a fresh, green hedgerow note and a mashy character **Flavour** Quite rich, clean and round with a slight coffee tang **Finish** Fresh, clean, quite long and rich with a slight tangy touch and liquorice on the tail **Notes** Burn Stewart bottling

LEDAIG

SINGLE MALT
FROM
THE ISLE OF MULL

1974
Vintage

This rare old single malt whisky was distilled at the Ledaig Distillery on the Isle of Mull by Ledaig Distillers (Tobermory) Ltd.

PRODUCE OF SCOTLAND

70cl   43%Vol

LEDAIG
Age 18 years   **Distillation** 1974   **Strength** 43% abv
Sweetness 2 Peatiness 8 Availability 1

Colour Medium-pale straw with lemony/gold highlights **Nose** Medium-bodied, woody with a slight greenness and smokiness at the back and an almost Christmas cake yeasty character **Flavour** Medium-bodied, oaky with a slight greenness and good richness at the back **Finish** Of good length with a green smoky tail **Notes** Ledaig Distillers (Tobermory) bottling

LEDAIG
Age 21 years   **Distillation** 1974   **Strength** 60% abv
Sweetness 3 Peatiness 6 Availability 1

Colour Very pale straw with pale yellow highlights **Nose** Fresh, clean, quite delicately peated, a slight flowral note and a touch of citrus/sherbet **Flavour** Clean, medium-dry, quite rich, fresh with a citrus character **Finish** Fresh, of quite good length with a slight coffee tang **Notes** Blackadder international bottling

TOMATIN, INVERNESS-SHIRE EST. 1897

Founded by the Tomatin Spey District Distillery Co. Ltd. Extended from two to four stills in 1956, to six in 1958, to ten in 1961, to 11 in 1964 and finally to 23 in 1974.

LOCATION   Sited on the west of the A9 at the village of Tomatin, 12 miles south of Inverness. At 1,028 above sea level, it is one of Scotland's highest distilleries.

NOTES   The first Scottish distillery to be owned by a Japanese company, when purchased by the Takara and Okura Consortium following its then owner's liquidation in 1985. It has the potential for the greatest output (more than 12 million litres of alcohol) of all the malt distilleries. From the Gaelic, Tomatin means "the hill of the bushes".

WATER   Allt-na-Frithe (a local burn).

Age 10 years   **Strength** 43% abv

Sweetness 6 Peatiness 5 Availability 5

Colour Honey with straw/gold highlights **Nose** Light, slightly sweet, a little spirity, malty and leafy **Flavour** Light, sweet, malty and peaty with a hint of pepperiness **Finish** Smooth, slightly spicy and grapey **Notes** Tomatin Distillers bottling

Age 13 years   **Distillation** 1976   **Strength** 60.5% abv

Sweetness 6 Peatiness 5 Availability 4

Colour Pale amber with gold highlights **Nose** Medium weight with a hint of green hedgerows, fresh, light oak notes, medium-sweet with a light smokiness at the back **Flavour** Medium-sweet, clean, tangy and lightly smoky **Finish** Quite sweet and spicy with good length **Notes** Wm Cadenhead bottling

TOMINTOUL

NEAR TOMINTOUL, BANFFSHIRE EST. 1964

A modern distillery, production only began in 1965 and it was not until 1972 that the make began to appear in bottle. Built by Tomintoul Distillery Ltd and bought by Scottish Universal Investment Trust (part of Lonrho) in 1973. Managed by Whyte & Mackay, which was itself bought from Lonrho by Brent Walker in February, 1989 and subsequently sold to American Brands Inc. the following year. Doubled from two to four stills in 1974.

LOCATION Situated in the valley of the River Avon on the B9136 off the A939 Grantown-on-Spey to Tomintoul road.

NOTES Tomintoul is the highest village in the Scottish Highlands, although the distillery itself, being outside the village, is not quite as high above sea level as Dalwhinnie. Tomintoul is regularly cut off by snow in winter.

WATER The Ballantruan Spring.

Age 12 years **Strength** 43% abv

Sweetness 7 Peatiness 3 Availability 6

Colour Peaty straw with good gold highlights **Nose** Medium-sweet, rich and slightly spirity with vanilla and fruity, almost orangey, notes **Flavour** Medium-sweet, lightish, slightly peppery and with an oaky touch **Finish** A little spirity, although quite smooth and the oaky vanilla lingers **Notes** Whyte & Mackay bottling

Age 17 years **Strength** 43% abv

Sweetness 9 Peatiness 4 Availability 1

Colour Pale amber/straw with yellow highlights **Nose** Rich, sweet and nutty and delicately peated **Flavour** Sweet and rich with quite good body and a gentle peatiness **Finish** Clean, quite long and rich with a delicately smoky tail **Notes** Blackadder International bottling

ADVIE, GRANTOWN-ON-SPEY, MORAY   EST. 1958

Built 1958-60 by Long John Distillers Ltd. Now part of Allied Domecq and operated by Allied Distillers Ltd. Doubled from four to eight stills in 1972.

LOCATION   South of the A95 between Grantown-on-Spey and the Bridge of Avon.

NOTES   The first new Highland malt distillery buildings to be constructed in the twentieth century. Glen Keith, established the previous year, used the buildings of a former mill. Tormore distillery and associated buildings are of a most striking design, the work of Sir Arthur Richardson, a past president of the Royal Academy.

WATER   The Achvochkie Burn.

Age 10 years   **Strength** 40% abv

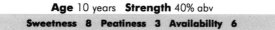

Sweetness 8 Peatiness 3 Availability 6

Colour Pale golden **Nose** Light and quite delicate with a strange dryness which is sometimes described as flintiness **Flavour** Slightly sweet, of medium weight and slightly spirity **Finish** Fine, distinguished and long **Notes** Caledonian Distillers bottling

PRODUCT OF SCOTLAND

Tullibardine

SINGLE HIGHLAND MALT
SCOTCH WHISKY

A Single Malt Scotch Whisky of quality
and distinction distilled and bottled by
TULLIBARDINE DISTILLERY LIMITED
BLACKFORD   PERTHSHIRE   SCOTLAND

40%vol   70cl

BLACKFORD, PERTHSHIRE   EST. 1949

There was a previous distillery of the same name near Blackford which was established in 1798, although its exact location is not known. The new distillery was the work of Delme Evans, who also designed Jura and Glenallachie. Owned by Invergordon Distillers since 1971, and Whyte & Mackay since 1993. Rebuilt 1973-74 and enlarged from two to four stills. Mothballed January, 1995.

LOCATION   Situated north of the new A9 on the south-western outskirts of the village of Blackford, four miles south of Auchterarder.

NOTES   On the site of an ancient brewery, the distillery takes its name from the nearby Tullibardine Moor, home of Gleneagles Hotel and golf courses. This area has always been famed for its water: Highland Spring and Gleneagles mineral waters are both from Blackford. Tradition has it that the fair Queen Helen of Scotland was drowned at a ford on the Allan Water (the local river), hence the name Blackford.

WATER   The Danny Burn.

Age 10 years   **Strength** 40% abv

Sweetness 3   Peatiness 6   Availability 6

Colour Straw with golden-green highlights **Nose** Quite full, soft, malty and earthy **Flavour** Quite dry and spicy with a rich-ness and roundness, quite smooth **Finish** Peppery, warm and quite long with a slight bitterness at the end **Notes** Invergordon bottling

VATTED MALTS

BLACK RIBBON
Age No age statement   **Strength** 40% abv

Sweetness 7   Peatiness 7   Availability 0

Colour Mid-Amber with yellow and gold/green highlights **Nose** Medium-bodied, gently smoky with hints of apple and coffee and an edge of sweetness **Flavour** Quite full-bodied and round, smoky, oily smooth and medium-sweet, quite rich with hints of coffee and toffee and with a slight greenness at the end **Finish** Full with a hint of spice, a gentle greenness and a dark smokiness **Notes** A vatted malt, vatted in Scotland and bottled in Sweden by Vin & Sprit. Only available in Sweden

GLENCOE
Age 8 years   **Strength** 57% abv

Sweetness 8   Peatiness 4   Availability 6

Colour Bright mid-amber with lemony gold highlights **Nose** Malty, spirity with an apple character, quite full-bodied, medium-dry with a touch of peat **Flavour** Medium-dry, round and smooth, appley with good body **Finish** Sweet and of good length **Notes** R N Macdonald bottling

OLD ELGIN
Age 8 years   **Strength** 40% abv

Sweetness 7   Peatiness 6   Availability 4

Colour Mid-amber with gold highlights **Nose** Medium to full-bodied, medium-dry and smoky with a touch of greenness and dark, appley fruit **Flavour** Rich, medium-sweet, quite full-bodied and peppery, fresh, round and smooth **Finish** Fresh, medium-sweet and clean **Notes** Bottled by Gordon & MacPhail

POIT DHUBH

Age 12 years   **Strength** 40% abv

Sweetness 6 Peatiness 4 Availability 4

Colour Amber with good yellow highlights **Nose** Medium-sweet, slightly green and quite rich **Flavour** Smooth with a touch of dryness, lightly peated and quite elegant, although light **Finish** Long, smoky and slightly perfumed **Notes** Bottled by Praban na Linne

POIT DUBH GREEN LABEL

Age 12 years   **Strength** 46% abv

Sweetness 7 Peatiness 7 Availability 3

Colour Light amber with gold highlights **Nose** Medium-bodied with good body, firm dark smokiness, a touch of liquorice, a slight rich green touch of citrus **Flavour** Quite full-bodied, medium-sweet and rich with a good backbone of peatiness **Finish** Long, smooth and smoky **Notes** Bottled by Praban na Linne

PRIDE OF ISLAY

Age 12 years   **Strength** 40% abv

Sweetness 1 Peatiness 10 Availability 4

Colour Mid-amber with yellowy gold highlights **Nose** Full-bodied and smoky with a rich, chocolatey nuttiness **Flavour** Big and smoky, quite pungent and bone dry with a slight edge of richness **Finish** Full, long and smoky with a slight tang of bitter chocolate **Notes** Bottled by Gordon & MacPhail

VATTED MALTS

YEARS **12** OLD

PRIDE of the LOWLANDS

Malt

SCOTCH WHISKY

DISTILLED IN THE LOWLANDS

PRODUCED & BOTTLED IN SCOTLAND

70 cl **GORDON & MACPHAIL**
ELGIN, SCOTLAND 40%vol

PRIDE OF THE LOWLANDS
Age 12 years **Strength** 40% abv

Sweetness 3 Peatiness 2 Availability 4

Colour Amber with yellowy gold highlights **Nose** Medium weight, fresh, oily-rich and medium-dry with a slight unripe grapey character **Flavour** Smooth and medium-dry with a touch of coffee and good richness; medium weight **Finish** Quite long and fresh with the tang of coffee on the tail **Notes** Bottled by Gordon & MacPhail

PRIDE OF ORKNEY
Age 12 years **Strength** 40% abv

Sweetness 2 Peatiness 5 Availability 4

Colour Light to mid-amber with gold highlights **Nose** Quite light and rich with dried fruit characters and hints of honey **Flavour** Off-dry, smooth, lightly smoky and malty **Finish** Clean with a refreshing greenness **Notes** Bottled by Gordon & MacPhail

PRIDE OF STRATHSPEY
Age 12 years **Strength** 40% abv

Sweetness 8 Peatiness 3 Availability 4

Colour Amber with gold highlights **Nose** Medium-sweet with a touch of creamy oiliness, rich oak and a hint of nuttiness **Flavour** Medium-sweet, quite full-bodied, smooth and round with a hazelnut character **Finish** Long and nutty with a dry edge and nice oaky tannins **Notes** Bottled by Gordon & MacPhail

The Original Oldbury

SHEEP DIP

Whisky is the traditional drink of British farmers, and in certain parts of the country it is affectionately known as "Sheep Dip". From that custom comes the name of our Malt Whisky.

This whisky, distilled traditionally by pot still in the Highlands of Scotland, is an eight-year-old malt of the very highest quality and excellence.

70 cl

5 011311 091033

DISTILLED AND BOTTLED IN SCOTLAND

SHEEP DIP
Age 8 years **Strength** 40% abv

Sweetness 3 Peatiness 6 Availability 5

Colour Pale amber with good yellow highlights **Nose** Dry, softly peated and slightly green **Flavour** Dry, but with a nice richness, spicy, a good peatiness, round and medium-bodied **Finish** Of medium length and with a gentle smokiness **Notes** Sheep Dip is said to have become popular with farmers because invoices for "Sheep Dip" could easily be lost in their accounts if they kept a few sheep!

SPEYSIDE
Age 8 years **Strength** 40% abv

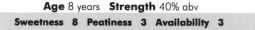

Sweetness 8 Peatiness 3 Availability 3

Colour Straw with good yellowy green highlights **Nose** Fresh, spirity, mealy and malty **Flavour** Sweet, smooth, round and soft **Finish** Malty, spicy and quite long **Notes** Bottled by the Speyside Distillery Company

FINLAGGAN
Distillation 1979 **Strength** 43% abv

Sweetness 1 Peatiness 9 Availability 3

Colour Very pale straw with lemony-yellow highlights **Nose** Full and pungent with an earthy smokiness and fresh hints of ozone **Flavour** Dry, smoky and fresh, clean and big-bodied **Finish** Long and smooth with a smoky-burnt oakiness and a very slight edge of richness **Notes** A single Islay malt from the Vintage Malt Whisky Co.

MACPHAIL'S MALT
Age 10 years **Strength** 40% abv

Sweetness 6 Peatiness 6 Availability 4

Colour Mid-amber with old gold highlights **Nose** Quite light, fresh, dark and smoky, medium-dry **Flavour** Medium-dry with good body, an earthy peatiness and a touch of spiciness **Finish** Fresh, quite smoky and long-lasting with a touch of oak **Notes** Single malt bottling under Gordon & MacPhail's own label

BLAIRFINDY
Age 16 years **Strength** 43% abv

Sweetness 9 Peatiness 3 Availability 2

Colour Pale mid-amber with yellow/gold highlights **Nose** Quite full-bodied, sweet and rich with an unctuous oily oaky vanilla and a light nuttiness with a quite fresh appley character **Flavour** Sweet, rich and round , quite full-bodied and lazily smooth **Finish** Rich, long and elegant with a creamy butteriness **Notes** A single Speyside malt bottled by Blackadder International

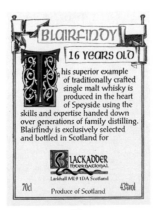

SPECIALIST WHISKY SHOPS

Although some of the major retail chains offer good selections of single malt whiskies at competitive prices, they cannot hope to compete with the specialist for depth of choice and knowledge. Also, if there is a whisky you particularly want, then the specialist will usually try to get it for you.

SCOTLAND

The Cadenhead Whisky Shop, 172 Canongate, Edinburgh EH8 8BN
Cairngorm Whisky Centre, Inverdruie, Aviemore, PH22 1QH
The Cheese and Wine Shop, George Street, Oban PA34 5NT
Clifton Coffee Shop, Tyndrum, Crianlarich, Perthshire FK20 8RY
Eaglesome Ltd, Reform Square, Campbeltown, Argyll PA28 6JA
Loch Fyne Whiskies, Inverary, Argyll PA32 8UD
Luvian's Bottle Shop, 93 Bonnygate, Cupar, Fife KY15 4LG
Mitchell's of Erskine, 2, Bridgewater Shopping Centre, Erskine PA8 7AA
Peter Green & Co., 37 Warrender Park Road, Edinburgh EH9 1HJ
Robertsons, 46 Atholl Road, Pitlochry, Perthshire PH16 5BX
Royal Mile Whiskies, 379/381 High Street, Edinburgh EH1 1PW
Sexton's, 72, Stirling Street, Airdrie ML6 0AS
Strachan of Aboyne, Balmoral Terrace, Aboyne, Aberdeenshire AB34 5HL
T B Watson Ltd, 11-17 English Street, Dumfries DG1 2BU
T B Watson Ltd, 85 High Street, Lockerbie DG11 2JH
The Ubiquitous Chip, 12 Ashton Lane, Glasgow G12 8SJ
The Whisky Castle, Main Street, Tomintoul AB37 9EX
The Whisky Shop, Waverley Market, Princess Street, Edinburgh EH1 1BQ
The Whisky Shop of, Princes Square, Buchanan St, Glasgow G1 3JX
The Whisky Shop of Inverness, 17 Bridge Street, Inverness IV3 5PR
The Whisky Shop of Fort William, 93 High Street, Fort William, PH33 6GH

ENGLAND AND WALES

Bentalls, Dolphin St, Kingston-Upon-Thames KT1 1TX
Bloomsbury Wine & Spirit Co., 3 Bloomsbury St, London WC1B 3QE
The Brighton Malt House, One North Road, Brighton BN1 1YA
Carley & Webb, 29 Market Hill, Ipswich, Suffolk IP13 9AN
Constantine Stores Ltd, 30 Fore St, Falmouth, Cornwall TR11 5AB
The County Stores, 52 North Street, Taunton, Somerset TA1 1ND
The Covent Garden Whisky Shop, 3 Russell St, London, WC2B 5JD
Dartmouth Vintners, The Butterwalk, 6 Duke Street, Dartmouth TQ6 9EB
Donnington Wines, The Hollow, Castle Donnington DE7 42PN
Fortnum & Mason, 181 Piccadilly, London W1A 1ER
Harrod's, 87-135 Brompton Rd, Knightsbridge, London SW1X 7XL
The Master of Malt, The Pantiles, Tunbridge Wells TN2 5TE
Milroys, 3 Greek St, Soho, London W1A 1ER
Selfridges, 400 Oxford St, London W1A 1AB
Simpkin and James, 5 Cank St, Leicester LE1 5GX
Smiths of Bourne, 25 North St, Bourne, Lincolnshire PE10 9AE
Stephan's Cellar, Lewis Lane, Abergavenney, NP7 5BA
The Vintage House, 42 Old Compton St, Soho, London W1V 6LR
The Whisky Shop, 87 Bailgate, Lincoln LN1 3AR
The Wright Wine Co., Skipton, North Yorkshire BD23 1NT

ACKNOWLEDGEMENTS

Our grateful thanks are due to a great many people for their assistance in completing this book:

James Walker of Adelphi Distillery
Jeremy Weatherhead, Caroline Dewar & Sylvia Corrieri
of Allied Distillers
Colin Ross of Ben Nevis
Zoe Mizen of Berry Bros & Rudd
Ian Macmillan, Fergus Hartley & Robin Dods of Burn Stewart
Neil Clapperton, Alan Murray & Mairi Sih of Cadenheads
Heidi Cohu of Campbell Distillers
Ross Gunn, Anne Millar & J. Preston of Chivas and Glenlivet
Graham Taylor of Glen Catrine
John Grant & Malcolm Greenwood of Glenfarclas
Peter Fairlie of Glenturret
Steven Sleigh of Matthew Gloag
David Urquhart, Sarah Watson and Ian Whitecross of
Gordon & MacPhail
Nick Tilt, Pip Hall, Katrina Joyce and Carl Hasselbach of
William Grant
Yannis Terpitsas of IDV
Nick Wright of Invergordon Distillers
Jacqui Stacey and Alistair Douglas of Inver House Distillers
Michael Borre and John Ryan of Irish Distillers
Jim Turle of Lang Brothers
Robin Lambie of Macallan-Glenelivet
Lesley Young & Alex Nicol of Macdonald & Muir
Gordon Wright of J & A Mitchell
George Hocknull & Jim MacEwan of Morrison Bowmore
Ian Phillips of William Lawson
Andrew Nicoll of J R Phillips
Antony MacCallum of Praban na Linne
David Dean of Seagram
Andrew & Brian Symington of Signatory
Rick Christie of Speyside
Tara Lloyd & Kelvin Shantry of United Distillers
Richard Paterson of Whyte & Mackay

and
Lennie & Celia Maguire of the Cellar Bar, Airdrie

Our sincere apologies to anyone who has been omitted from the above list, as space is limited. You know who you are - we thank you.

Picture credits: Pages 36 and 102 William Grant & Sons.
Page 181 United Distillers.

MALT WHISKY SPECIAL OFFER

This exclusive offer will help you to discover more of the delights of single malt whisky.

Order one of the following sets from us and we will include lists and information for an extensive selection of single malt whiskies, a **free** rare **Blackadder** or **Limited Editions** miniature and a **free** miniature of one of the six **Classic Malts**

(miniatures worth £10 if purchased separately)

ALSO INCLUDED WILL BE

£20 worth of money-saving offers

POSTATGE AND PACKING MUST BE ADDED TO ALL ORDERS AS FOLLOWS: UK £4.95 EUROPE: SET A: £7.50 SET B £12.50 SET C £17.50 SET D £22.50 SET E £27.50 SET F £30 ALL OTHER COUNTRIES ADD £5 TO EUROPE RATE EXCEPT FOR SET A

Set A	Malt whisky information pack plus TWO FREE MINIS	FREE
	(there is no charge for Set A but you must pay postage as above)	
Set B	10 Different miniatures plus TWO FREE MINIS	**£27.95**
Set C	20 Different miniatures plus TWO FREE MINIS	**£59.95**
Set D	30 Different miniatures plus TWO FREE MINIS	**£99**
Set E	40 Different miniatures plus TWO FREE MINIS	**£145**
Set F	50 Different miniatures plus TWO FREE MINIS	**£195**

NOTE: Set prices increase for larger sets because the bigger the set the more rare and expensive the miniatures contained in that set.

This offer is open only to those aged 21 and over. Payment may be made by cheque, Eurocheque, Access, Eurocard, Mastercard, Visa or JCB card. Please give expiry date if paying by card and add carriage as appropriate.

ORDERS SHOULD BE POSTED TO:

Blackadder International (Miniature Offer)
BOX 56, Heathfield, East Sussex TN21 8ZW
Or you can fax orders to: (0) 1435 882 825
E-mail order address: blackadderint@dial.pipex.com

REGISTER TODAY

As soon as we receive your application, you will be registered as a member of the *Friends of the Classic Malts of Scotland Society*.

Membership will have several benefits. These include *The Spirit of the Classics* journal, the opportunity for VIP visits to the Classic Malts of Scotland distilleries and a range of exclusive Classic Malts gift items not generally obtainable elsewhere.

In this way, we hope that being a member will help you gain the maximum pleasure and enjoyment from the Classic Malts of Scotland.

SEE OVERLEAF FOR AN APPLICATION FORM

GLENKINCHIE ◆ TALISKER ◆ LAGAVULIN

MEMBERSHIP APPLICATION

I would like to be registered as a member of the
Friends of The Classic Malts of Scotland Society
(PLEASE PRINT CLEARLY USING CAPITALS)

Name..

Address..

....

....

Postcode...

Country...

Age.................... Sex: M or F (please circle)

Post to:
The Friends of the Classic Malts of Scotland Society
c/o Blackadder International
Logie Green
Larkhall
ML9 1DA
SCOTLAND

*Please photocopy page or write application on a piece
of paper if you do not want to remove this page from
your book.*